T0160759

THE CURIOUS CASE OF
H.P. LOVECRAFT

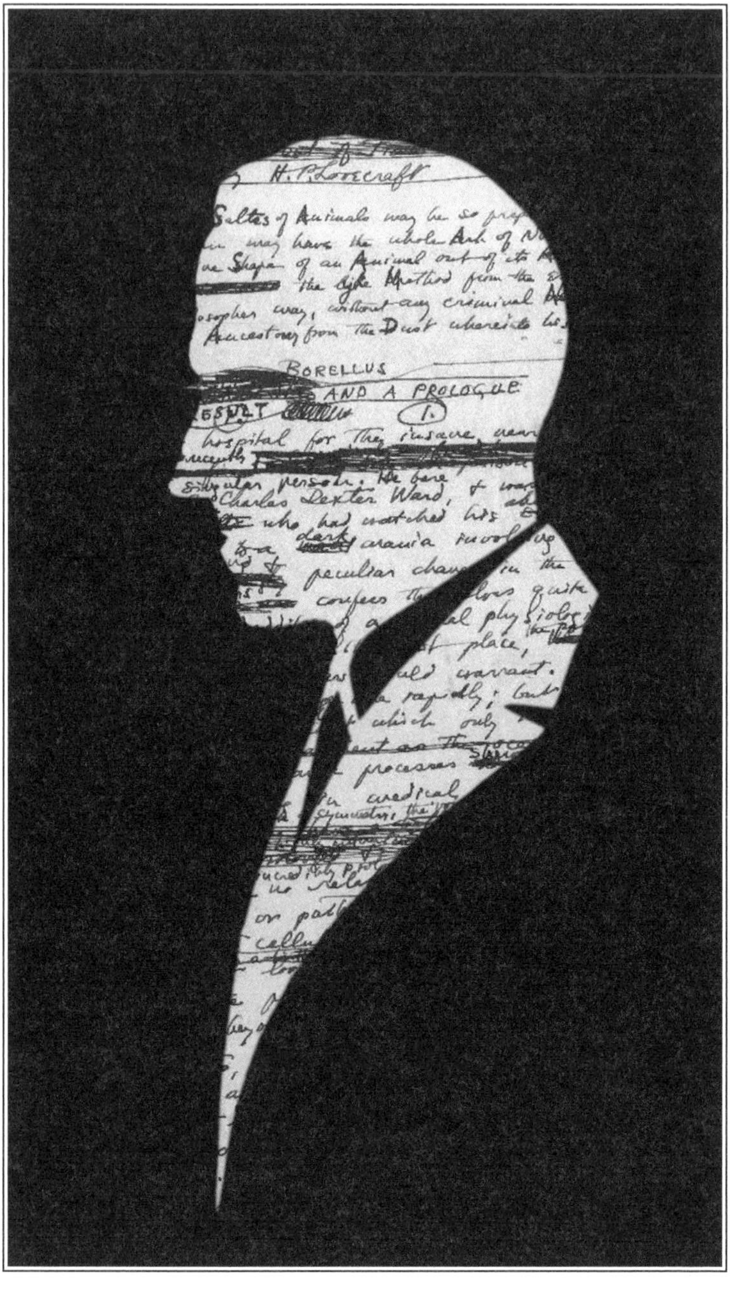
H. P. Lovecraft
BORELLUS
AND A PROLOGUE
Charles Dexter Ward

THE CURIOUS CASE OF
H.P. LOVECRAFT

PAUL ROLAND

Plexus, London

All rights reserved including the right of
reproduction in whole or in part in any form
Copyright © 2014 by Paul Roland
Published by Plexus Publishing Limited
The Studio, Hillgate Place
18-20 Balham Hill
London SW12 9ER

British Library Cataloguing in Publication Data
A catalogue record for this book is available
from the British Library

ISBN-13: 978-0-85965-517-0

Cover Painting of H.P. Lovecraft by Sean Phillips
Cover and book design by Coco Balderrama
Cover background taken from page 1 of
'The Case of Charles Dexter Ward' by H.P. Lovecraft
supplied by the John Hay Library, Brown University
Printed in Great Britain by Bell & Bain Ltd, Glasgow

CONTENTS

To my beloved son Michael.
Dare to dream, but don't forget to come back

The Case of Charles Dexter Ward

By H. P. Lovecraft

"The essential Saltes of Animals may be so prepared & preserved, that an ingenious Man may have the whole Ark of Noah in his owne Studdye, & raise the fine Shape of an Animal out of its Ashes at his Pleasure; and by the lyke Method from the essential Saltes of humane Dust, a Philosopher may, without any criminal Necromancy, call up the Shape of any dead Ancestour from the Dust whereinto his Bodie has been incinerated."

BORELLUS

I. A RESULT AND A PROLOGUE

1.

From a private hospital for the insane near Providence, Rhode Island, there recently disappeared an exceedingly singular person. He bore the name of Charles Dexter Ward, & was placed most reluctantly under restraint by the grieving father who had watched his aberration grow from a mere eccentricity to a dark mania involving both possibility of murderous tendencies & a profound & peculiar change in the apparent contents of his mind. Doctors confess themselves quite baffled by his case, since it presented oddities of a general physiological as well as psychological character. In the first place, he seemed oddly older than his twenty-six years would warrant. Mental disturbance, it is true, will age one rapidly; but the face of this young man had taken on a subtle cast which only the very aged usually acquire. In the second place, his organic processes shewed a certain queerness of proportion which nothing in medical experience can parallel. Respiration & heart action had a baffling lack of symmetry; the loss, so that no sound the voice was lost, so that no sound above a whisper was possible; digestion was incredibly prolonged & minimised, & neural reactions to standard stimuli had no relation at all to anything hitherto recorded, either normal or pathological. The skin had a morbid chill & dryness, & the cellular structure of the tissue seemed exaggeratedly coarse & loosely knit. Even a large olive birthmark on the right hip had vanished, whilst there had formed on the chest a very peculiar mole or blackish spot which had not existed before. In general, all physicians agree that in Ward the processes of metabolism had become retarded to a degree beyond precedent.

Psychologically, too, Charles Ward was unique. His madness held no affinity to any sort recorded in even the latest & most exhaustive treatises, & was conjoined to a mental force which would have made him a genius or a leader had it not been twisted into strange & grotesque forms. Dr. Willett, who was Ward's family physician, affirms that the patient's gross mental capacity, as gauged by his response to matters outside the sphere of his

AUTHOR'S NOTE: I began planning a biography of H.P. Lovecraft in the mid-nineties. At this time, I could find only a handful of American academic titles devoted to his life, in addition to Lin Carter's *A Look Behind the Cthulhu Mythos* (1972), L. Sprague de Camp's *Lovecraft: A Biography* (1975), S.T. Joshi's *H.P. Lovecraft: The Decline of the West* (1990) and an anthology of essays edited by Joshi and Schultz entitled *An Epicure in the Terrible* (1991). Little else was in print and available outside the States – with no internet sources. I persisted periodically over the next twenty years, believing that there was a need for a popular but comprehensive biography, assessing every one of Lovecraft's published stories. I hope that *The Curious Case of H.P. Lovecraft* fills this niche.

I would like to give special thanks to my editor Laura Coulman for her invaluable contributions and to Sandra Wake at Plexus for having faith in me and in this project. Thanks are also due to Nicky Adamson for her extensive editorial suggestions, April James, Coco Balderrama for creating the look, and Sean Phillips – for allowing us to incorporate his stunning original artwork on the cover of the book.

Dates in parenthesis after story titles indicate the year of completion, not publication.

Paul Roland

EDITOR'S NOTE: We would like to give our thanks to the meticulous Lovecraftian scholar Pietro Guarriello, for his invaluable pictorial contribution. We are also grateful to the following individuals: Ann Morgan Dodge of Brown University, who provided sterling guidance throughout the process of picture research; Sean Branney and Andrew Leman of the H.P. Lovecraft Historical Society; James Van Hise; Frank H. Woodward (producer of the excellent documentary, *Lovecraft: Fear of the Unknown*); Danielle Jacobs at Arkham House; William R. Coker; Jerad Walters at Centipede Press and Donovan Loucks at the H.P. Lovecraft Archive. All of these individuals provided kind and prompt assistance in my endless search for rarer images of H.P. Lovecraft. I would also like to extend my sincere gratitude to Susan Areson at the *Providence Journal*, who kindly gave permission for Sonia Greene's illuminating article, 'Howard Phillips Lovecraft as his Wife Remembers Him' to be reproduced within this book.

Laura Coulman

PREFACE

'You need to read him – he's where the darkness starts.'
– Neil Gaiman

Howard Phillips Lovecraft was haunted by demons. They stalked him in daylight and darkness alike, from childhood until his premature death at the age of 46. They took the form of his earliest memories – of losing his father; of life with his hysterical, emotionally abusive mother.

They leered over his shoulder as he gazed at the distorted reflection in the glass. They taunted him as he struggled to endure blinding migraines, crippling fatigue and periodic breakdowns – debilitating psychosomatic disorders which threatened to suck his vitality and curtail his creativity. He fled from them in his sleep – in dreams so terrifyingly vivid that they left him fearing for his own sanity – and mocked him in the street in the form of 'evil-looking foreigners' who threatened to overrun his picturesque colonial hometown of Providence, New England.

They left him riddled with self-doubt, disappointment and despair, but like a man possessed, he drove them from his mind time and again in bouts of feverish activity. Even as his fortunes declined and various publishing ventures failed to materialise, he worked tirelessly to create an extraordinary and highly influential body of work that has secured him a prominent place in the history of imaginative fiction.

H.P. Lovecraft is widely regarded as the most original writer of modern horror fiction and a pervasive and enduring influence on popular culture. His primordial universe of elder gods and eldritch horrors – existing just on the periphery of the more mundane, ordered world we know as 'reality' – has inspired authors as diverse as Stephen King, Ramsey Campbell, Robert Bloch, Clive Barker, Alan Moore and Neil Gaiman. Lovecraft's most memorable creatures – notably the tentacle-headed god Cthulhu – have been invoked by such giants of rock music as Black Sabbath, Metallica and Iron Maiden, and continue to feature in almost every form of fantasy art: from graphic novels to computer games. His compelling creations have influenced the look of major movies such as *Alien*, *Hellboy* and even *Pirates of the Caribbean* – although the grotesque otherworldliness of Lovecraft's original tales is yet to be captured by any director onscreen in a way that lives up to the author's fantastic vision in the truest sense of the word. Yet this eccentric and reclusive resident of Providence, Rhode Island, did not have a book published by a major commercial house during his lifetime. He died at the age of 46 in comparative obscurity, convinced that he had failed to achieve the recognition he craved.

The Curious Case of H.P. Lovecraft examines the life and work of the man Stephen King called 'the twentieth century's greatest practitioner of the classic horror tale', revealing how Lovecraft's disturbing creations may have been an attempt to exorcise both his inner-demons and the elemental abominations which haunted his recurring nightmares.

There are no happy endings in Lovecraft's world. No light at the end of the dark night of the soul. No hope and no reward for heroic deeds or self-sacrifice. Mankind, according to Lovecraft, exists in an amoral universe at the mercy of destructive forces beyond our comprehension. And yet his vision endures and continues to exert a profound hold on our collective imagination.

Critics have pointed out many shortcomings in Lovecraft's prose, calling it 'stilted', 'overwrought', even 'hysterical', but they overlook the fact that his somewhat overheated style may well have been deliberate. How better to convey the tumultuous inner-state of his characters – many of whom are shown to be struggling to maintain their sanity as ardently as the man who created them. These critics also overlook the fact that Lovecraft's single novel, four novellas and 52 short stories were not written to edify, but to entertain. Their primary purpose is to generate a frisson of electrifying excitement, offering the reader a chance to experience vicariously those things they fear and hope never to face; degeneration, death and madness. And in this endeavour, he succeeds admirably.

A master of his chosen genre, Lovecraft understood better than anyone the arc of an effective horror story. Each of his tales represents a heart-stopping, hair-raising fairground ride – pausing for just a brief interlude of unsettling silence, before picking up speed for the final descent into darkness. Of course, there's a certain degree of panache and carnivalesque showmanship required to carry it off, saving the story from becoming a bloodless exercise in style over substance – but this is an ability that Lovecraft possessed in spades. Playing on instinct rather than intellect, the value of horror fiction cannot be measured by scholarly dissection, but by its ability to crawl under the skin and to linger in the recesses of the mind; to unsettle and to challenge the certainty we seek; to call into question the nature of what we accept as 'reality'. Its grim beauty is in the eye of the beholder and there can be no doubt that Lovecraft's best work exhibits a macabre beauty.

CHAPTER ONE

A STRANGER IN THIS CENTURY

'I know always that I am an outsider; a stranger in this century and among those who are still men.'
– H.P. Lovecraft

Howard Phillips Lovecraft entered the world at 9am on 20 August 1890 in the comparative comfort of the Phillips residence – home of his mother's family – at 194 Angell Street, Providence, Rhode Island. His parents, Winfield Scott Lovecraft, a commercial traveller for the Gorham Silversmiths and Sarah Susan Phillips, the daughter of a wealthy entrepreneur, had been married barely a year and would shortly move into rented accommodation in Dorchester, a suburb south of Boston.

Susan, as she preferred to be known, considered herself a child of the colonial aristocracy and so the realisation that her husband's prospects were not as promising as he'd led her to believe before their wedding (on 12 June 1889) came as a bitter disappointment. Yet, she never lost her penchant for embellishing the truth – a trait she shared with her son Howard, who'd grow up to boast that he was descended from a long line of 'unmixed English gentry'. In fact, little is known of his ancestry, other than that there were respectable New England names on his mother's side; certainly nothing to justify his lifelong claim that he was the last in a line of old-world nobility, or that his birth-right permitted him to live the life of a gentleman of leisure, when he could ill afford to do so. But Howard Phillips Lovecraft was raised on fantasy and extravagant fancies. It was therefore inevitable that he lived out his own, even when a more realistic assessment might have made his existence more tolerable.

According to neighbour Clara Hess, little Howard resembled his mother more than his father, having inherited the 'peculiarly shaped nose which [. . .] gave her a very inquiring expression'. With her porcelain complexion, Susan was considered pretty – despite the fact that her colouring is rumoured to have been caused by habitual doses of arsenic. This substance was used to treat everything from morning sickness to rheumatism and poor circulation. Whether it also contributed to her 'intensely nervous' disposition is not known, but Susan's reputation as a frigid 'touch-me-not' (in the words of Lovecraft's wife Sonia) implies that Winfield's attentions were far from welcome and may well have aggravated her lifelong neuroses.

However, the sole surviving family photograph of the eighteen-month-old Howard and his parents captures a happy child, proudly presented to the camera by his mother – who assumes the manner of a prim schoolmarm – and his father who gives the impression that he might be a congenial companion. Had Winfield lived, there's every chance that Howard could have enjoyed a comparatively happy childhood. With his father's assets valued at $10,000 after his death on 19 July 1898, the family would have wanted for nothing. As it was, Lovecraft lost his father at the tender age of seven. From this point on, he lived a cosseted existence in the 'quiet, shady' suburbs. Indeed, the story of his childhood is not dissimilar to Booth Tarkington's novel, *The Magnificent Ambersons*, with Howard cast as George Minafer – a privileged young man for whom nothing and no one seems quite good enough. But, though Howard was blessed with a 'virtually unlimited' collection of toys, lead soldiers and games, he came perilously close to being suffocated by his mother's acute anxiety. On one occasion, she went so far as to command a friend to stoop when taking her son by the hand for fear that his arm might be pulled from its socket. Indulgence and privilege characterised his childhood in every respect. His grandfather's coachman built him 'an immense summer-house' complete with a staircase leading up to the roof. This served as the centre of operations for the boy's extensive model railway. As Howard grew older, the roof would provide the perfect platform for his telescope, with the house serving as both observatory and private clubhouse – to which only a select few members were invited.

Howard's favourite pastime was the construction of table-top villages using wooden houses, windmills and castles served by a transportation system of streetcars and a landscape littered with railway accessories, toy trees and soil from the garden. These grew into towns inhabited by lead soldiers and, if his mother did not call for them to be dismantled by bedtime, the towns would develop into cities. Such an ambitious enterprise required considerable patience and reverential silence as the architect considered how best to create the desired effect. It was clearly not a project that could be shared with an impatient playmate. It was a solemn and solitary activity, like reading or writing. Besides, it was not a mere game, but a conception. Moreover, the figures were not placed at random, but where their roles required them to be at specific points in the 'plot', as Lovecraft later put it – a plot to which only he was privy. 'Horror-plots were frequent, though (oddly enough) I never attempted to construct fantastic or extra-terrestrial scenes. I was too much of an innate realist to care for fantasy in its purest form.'

Board games were for ordinary children. Howard Phillips Lovecraft was a world builder. He just hadn't got around to deciding who or what the inhabitants might be. 'The children I knew disliked me, and I disliked them . . . Their romping and shouting puzzled me.' His own second cousin Ethel – who once glimpsed him leafing through a large volume with all the earnestness of a schoolmaster studying an essay – found him distant and rather pretentious.

As for Howard, he evidently preferred adult company to playing with children of his own age. In this respect, the precocious child was indulged further – by the poetess Louise Imogen Guiney, with whom his parents lodged in the winter of 1892, whilst waiting to move into their own home. Tragically, due to Winfield's illness, this house was never built and the vacant plot of land was auctioned off.

Lovecraft's earliest memories are of befriending his landlady's St Bernard dogs, one of whom allowed the toddler to put his hand inside its mouth in imitation of a lion tamer, leaving Howard fiercely proud that he had faced his fear and emerged with all his fingers intact. He later claimed that the dog, named Brontë after the author, trotted obediently beside his pram and growled at strangers if any dared to approach it; the idea of being protected by such a magnificent beast evidently added to his self-esteem.

It was at the Guiney house that he learned how words could enthral an audience and elicit approval. Recitals of 'Mother Goose' and other nursery rhymes brought immediate appreciation from his hostess – not for the quality of the performance, Lovecraft later admitted, but for the mere fact that he was able to recite verse from memory at the age of two, long before he could read. He quickly graduated to more adult offerings, most notably 'Sheridan's Ride' by T.B. Read at the behest of his father who favoured military subjects. The child, now an undisputed prodigy – at least in his parents' eyes and that of the indulgent Miss Guiney – delivered the text with such gusto that he drew a roar of applause and experienced the heady rush of 'painful egotism'.

The young Lovecraft enjoyed the patronage of the famous poet, but if he remembered her fondly he did not regard her as someone worth reading for he later wrote that, 'Miss Guiney followed vaguer literary deities, of whom the Miltonic spirit chaos seems to be the leader'.

Lovecraft's sheltered existence was shattered, however, in April 1893 with the news that Winfield had suffered a nervous breakdown whilst on a business trip to Chicago. It was said that he had been raving, accusing a chamber maid of insulting him and crying uncontrollably that his wife had been assaulted in her hotel room. Susan was, of course, not present and Winfield had had to be forcibly restrained. On his return to Boston, he was diagnosed as psychotic and confined in the Butler Hospital, a psychiatric institution where he would die five years later of 'general paresis' or paralysis. Though the true nature of his disorder has never been revealed, there has been speculation it may have been syphilis. The fact that Winfield's cousin, Joshua Elliott Lovecraft, also died of general paresis some months later is suggestive of an inherited disorder, although the official cause of Joshua's death was recorded as 'business anxiety', a euphemism for stress. Susan would die in the same institution twenty-three years later in 1921. Though she died of complications arising from a botched gall bladder operation, it seems she had lost the will to live long before this. Howard, it appears, was destined to learn from the earliest age that happiness was fleeting and that life was as transient as his dreams.

Following his father's committal, mother and son moved back to the Phillips' family home in Providence where Howard came under the care of his maternal grandfather Whipple Van Buren, his grandmother Robie Alzada Place and his doting spinster aunts Lillian, a keen amateur painter, and Annie, a sociable soul who, in her nephew's estimation, brought a 'touch of gayety to a rather conservative household'.

Little was said of Winfield's fate and the boy was encouraged to remember his father as a smartly dressed, hard-working man with 'an extremely precise and cultivated English voice' who had been struck down by an unspecified malady at the age of 45. 'I can just remember my father – an immaculate figure in black coat and vest and grey-striped trousers. I had a childish habit of slapping him on the knees and shouting, "Papa, you look just like a young man!" I don't know where I picked that phrase up; but I was vain and self-conscious, and given to repeating things which I saw tickled my elders.'

Ella Sweeney, a school teacher and family friend, formed a less favourable impression describing Winfield as 'a pompous Englishman' (despite the fact that he was born in Rochester, NY) whose avowed dislike for the nasal whine, dress sense and mannerisms of his neighbours had not made him many friends – but then the Phillips clan considered every American with antecedents in England to be an Englishman and therefore stiff-necked, self-righteous and overbearing. Their antipathy however only encouraged the boy's fierce Anglophilia which took the form of a stubborn refusal to use American spellings.

In his early twenties Lovecraft took to wearing his father's ties and wing collars. Perhaps he acted in the vague hope that by doing so he might forge some form of connection with the man? Either way, his longing to make this faintest memory of his father more real is wholly understandable. After all, how well could a young man know his own character if he had no father against whom he could measure himself? Tellingly, Lovecraft was never able to face up to the true cause of his father's death. Instead, he'd tell friends of how Winfield – weakened by insomnia and perpetual nervous strain – had suffered a stroke. Whether he came to believe this version of events is unclear . . .

As a child he pleaded with his mother to tell him stories about his father, but as she was reluctant to be reminded of a subject which evidently gave her much pain, the boy was forced to entreat his 'beloved' grandfather who soon became 'the centre of my entire universe'.

Whipple Van Buren was a wealthy industrialist who had made and lost several fortunes by the time he became a surrogate father to the three-year-old Howard. But unlike many elderly gentleman of his generation who lived for their work and the accumulation of wealth and status, Whipple welcomed the opportunity to mentor the boy and nurture the young mind that had been entrusted to him. Though he might have adopted a gruff, no-nonsense manner in dealing with his employees, Whipple was said to be demonstrably affectionate towards his grandson and determined to counter what he saw as his daughter's overtly feminine influence, particularly regarding the boy's attire and shoulder-length curls. Susan made no secret of the fact that she had wished for a girl and her son was eager to please her, but by the age of six the novelty had worn off and he insisted his mother take him to the barber.

Dressing young boys in frocks and feminine clothes was common among the middle and upper classes in the Victorian era, but Howard's grandfather frowned on such practices and determined to impress masculine virtues in the child. He promised to tell the boy stories, but only if he behaved himself and changed into trousers. If the old man couldn't play physically taxing games because of his health and age, he would instil a sense of adventure in the boy by relating the dangers he had overcome to acquire the artefacts in his extensive art and antiquities collection, embellishing the tale with each re-telling to reinforce his heroic image as a real-life Allan Quatermain, hero of H. Rider Haggard's *King Solomon's Mines* (1885).

But what made such a profound impression on the child was the realisation that the Roman coins he was given to weigh and examine had been passed from hand to hand by real people twenty centuries ago. In his mind, their monetary value and aesthetic qualities paled in comparison to their psychometric value – the promise of a psychic link to the past. In later life, Lovecraft may have professed a distrust of those who claimed to be able to commune with spirits, or to have experienced supernatural phenomena, but he felt an affinity for those writers who evoked the past so vividly that their words would act as an invocation, transporting him back through the centuries. The more vivid the prose, the stronger would be the psychic link.

Grandfather Whipple also entertained the child with dark gothic stories adapted from traditional fairy tales and regaled him with Greek myths and legends. 'I never heard oral weird tales except from my grandfather who, observing my tastes in reading, used to devise all sorts of impromptu original yarns about black woods, unfathomed caves, winged horrors (like the "night-gaunts" of my dreams, about which I used to tell him), old witches with sinister cauldrons, and "deep, low, moaning sounds". He obviously drew most of his imagery from the early Gothic romances – Radcliffe, Lewis, Maturin etc. – which he seemed to like better than Poe or other later fantasists.'

Then when the boy was old enough to read for himself, the bewhiskered old gentleman threw open the doors to his magnificent library, informing his grandson that the wealth of the world lay not in precious objects and material riches but in the secrets of the stars, of the mysteries of life and death possessed by lost civilisations and in the ideas of its greatest thinkers, inventors, philosophers and writers. No more needed to be said after this to encourage the child to feed his fertile imagination. After devouring a child-friendly edition of *Grimms' Fairy Tales* at the age of four, he tells us that he moved on to a translation of *The Arabian Nights* which offered him 'a gateway of glittering vistas of wonder and freedom'.

Inspired by these, he begged his indulgent mother to furnish his room in the manner befitting a Persian prince with rugs and trinkets purchased from a number of Oriental curio shops. In honour of his new imaginary status, he renamed himself Abdul Alhazred (All

Has Read), though he subsequently admitted that he couldn't remember the origin of the name or when exactly he first adopted it. But of all the texts that impressed him at that tender age, the most significant was Coleridge's 'Rime of the Ancient Mariner' for it was the first to leave him with a feeling of dread that he simply could not shake off, even if he had wanted to.

It was not so much the language that thrilled him, but the illustrations. He came upon the atlas-sized folio in the home of a friend of his aunts. It was leaning against the mantel of a fireplace in a high-ceilinged Victorian library and bore the legend, 'with illustrations by Gustave Doré' in gilt letters on the cover. The name was familiar from his grandfather's handsome leather-bound volume of Milton's *Paradise Lost* and so no invitation was necessary to encourage the boy to reacquaint himself with the 'dark, supernal magic' of the French artist's engravings, the most striking of which depicted the ghastly corpse-ship with tattered sails becalmed under a pallid moon.

'I turn a page . . . God! A spectral, half-transparent ship on whose deck a corpse and a skeleton play at dice!'

A normal, sensitive child of that age would doubtless have run screaming from the room, but not young Lovecraft, who found himself fascinated like a small animal by the cobra's stare. Every illustration offered fresh horrors: 'A sea full of rotting serpents, and death-fires dancing in the black air . . . troops of angels and daemons . . . crazed, dying, distorted forms . . . dead men rising in their putrescence and lifelessly manning the dank rigging of a fate-doomed barque.'

If the child was not possessed of a morbid temperament before his exposure to such macabre imagery, he certainly became so afterward, for the death of his maternal grandmother in January 1896 plunged the household into a fog of gloom that the boy found suffocating. To be fair, it would have taken an uncommonly cheerful disposition to remain impervious to the elaborate bereavement rituals that accompanied Victorian mourning and the now six-year-old Howard Phillips Lovecraft was encumbered in that respect by the presence of his acutely morbidly-minded mother. 'The black attire of my mother and aunts terrified and repelled me.'

It affected him so deeply that he began to suffer from 'hideous' nightmares inhabited by black, faceless winged creatures with barbed tails that he named night-gaunts. Years later he wondered if they might have originated with the demons drawn by Doré which he had seen in his grandfather's deluxe edition of *Paradise Lost* and which he felt compelled to sketch upon waking in an effort to exorcise them from his mind. Alas, they continued to appear, carrying him through space at a sickening speed while goading him with their tridents. He was tormented by them for the better part of five years, so much so that he made a great effort of will to stay awake and to stave off the onset of sleep, but it only left him tired and strained during the day. Fifteen years later – at the age of 25 – he was still haunted by the memory of those restless nights and forced himself to stay awake into the small hours.

One would have imagined that these nightmares would have compelled him to seek the sunlight and companionship of children his own age, but Lovecraft was instead lured to the windowless attic of the Phillips' family home. There, he discovered leather-bound issues of the *Spectator* and *Tatler*, and musty folios by Dryden, Pope and other men of letters that his grandfather had consigned to that 'nighted aerial crypt' in the belief that they would be of no interest to anyone. By candlelight and kerosene lamp he was borne way back through the decades into the late seventeenth, eighteenth and early nineteenth centuries until he could boast that he was 'probably the only living person to whom the ancient eighteenth-century idiom is actually a prose and mother tongue'.

But Whipple was more than a mentor and educator. He brought the boy through the darkness of his childhood fears by coaxing him through unlit rooms in the Phillips family home (now renumbered 454 Angell Street) when Howard was barely five. This did not, however, rid him of the night terrors. It simply left him with a preference for being active and productive in the early hours.

By day these phantoms evaporated and Howard sought companionship in books. His grandfather's library was the treasure house of dreams in which he immersed himself for hours at a time. But he would occasionally venture beyond that panelled chamber to explore the semi-rural surroundings of Providence, the 'primal and open New England countryside' which helped him to cultivate a keen sense of place and period that would later serve as primary locations for his most memorable fiction. The 'rolling meadows, stone walls, cart paths, brooks, deep woods, mystic ravines, lofty river-bluffs, planted fields, white ancient farmhouses, barns, and byres, gnarled hillside orchards, great lone elms, and all the authentic marks of a rural milieu unchanged since the seventeenth and eighteenth centuries'(letter to Frank Belknap Long, 27 February 1931). This was not the pastoral idyll which inspired the romantic poets, but the dark woods and rough-hewn tracks leading to isolated houses where the shutters would be drawn at close of day and a pall of ominous silence would fall with the dying sun. At least, that was the way Lovecraft envisaged his hometown and its historic remnants with the exception, of course, of the Phillips house, the last private nineteenth-century two-storey residence in a paved street behind which spread a broad acreage of ground planted with great elms and cherry trees, a fountain, ivy-covered arch way and cultivated gardens separated from an open field by a stone wall. The land was large enough to accommodate a stable and a two-storey coach house (in which the coachman lived with his wife) and the main house sufficiently spacious for the family and four servants. It was a setting fit for a Booth Tarkington novel (the Pulitzer Prize winning author of *The Magnificent Ambersons* and astute observer of the American class system at the turn of the century), furnished as it was with plush hangings, paintings, statues and a broad staircase, down which the hostess could sweep to greet her guests.

Neighbours doubtless described their town and its environs as quiet and picturesque with an old-world colonial charm. But for Lovecraft, buildings were more than wood, bricks and mortar. They were charged with the residual personal energy of their previous inhabitants, be they human or otherwise.

He later recalled that he felt a 'strange magic and fascination' mixed with a 'vague unease and perhaps a touch of mild fear' for the historic houses with their saltbox roofs, fan lighted doorways and railed flights of steps. One can only presume that such feelings originated with his mother, for an impressionable child assimilates its initial impressions of the world from its parents and Susan Phillips was already bordering on the hysteric. Even the reassuring influence of her father could not alleviate her fears that both she and her son would suffer the fate that befell her husband, for syphilis is a congenital disease.

Nevertheless her son derived a pleasurable frisson from his walks up 'the venerable hill'. The historic part of town was 'a magic, secret world' which felt more real to him than the nineteenth-century houses of his own neighbourhood – all of which suggests that he was unconsciously drawn, even at a tender age, to atmospheric locations which retained the indelible impression of their former inhabitants.

Although Susan Phillips refused to speak of her husband, either for shame or from grief, she could not restrain herself from indulging in periodic outbursts of self-pity, lamenting the 'curse' that had robbed her of her husband and left her dependent on her family. The child witnessed her histrionics and though he didn't fully understand the implications, was profoundly affected by her suffering, noting that her entreaties to God had been in vain.

To avoid further emotional upheaval, he withdrew into himself. The less stable his mother became, the more he resolved to suppress his own feelings for fear of provoking another hysterical outburst. Soon it was not enough to lose himself in books; he began writing to shut out his mother's tirades, substituting her voice for his own. His first attempt – at the age of seven – appears to have been a retelling of *The Odyssey* 'for young people', though he later claimed to have begun writing in earnest a year earlier. However, the handwritten 'Second Edition' of the 88-line 'Poem of Ulysses', dated 8 November 1897, is the earliest surviving example of the precocious poet's pseudo-classical verse, or as he described it on the title page 'An Epick Poem Writ by Howard Lovecraft, Gent'. The word 'Epick' is italicised to emphasize the scale of the endeavour.

One can imagine the pleasure the little book would have given his doting mother, adoring aunts and proud grandfather, and deservedly so; it's a notable feat for someone twice that age to produce 88 lines of iambic heptameter. And though its author knew at the time that it was 'pretty bad', it shows a rudimentary understanding of the form and a commendable facility for condensing a story down to its essential elements, especially in one so young.

> The nighte was darke! O readers, Hark!
> And see Ulysses fleet!
> From trumpets sound back homeward bound
> He hopes his spouse to greet.'

But Lovecraft was no idle dreamer. He may have remained unworldly in certain respects, but he knew there was money to be made from a bestseller and that bibliophiles like his grandfather would pay handsomely for a valued book and cherish it if it was attractively presented. So on the final page the 'publisher', Providence Classics, advertised their current and forthcoming titles in the hope of securing advance orders at between five and twenty-five cents a copy.

Anyone under the impression that Lovecraft was a humourless, intense individual might be surprised at the impish cheek exhibited in his younger self's assertion at the end of the preface. 'The latter works may be much better than this because the author will have more practice.' These included 'The Young Folks Iliad in Verse', 'The Aeneid', 'Ovid's Metamorphoses', 'Mythology For The Young' and 'An Old Egyptian Myth Prepared Specially For Small Children'.

Lovecraft enjoyed playing at publishing, but took his research seriously, pestering his mother and aunts to take him to the Rhode Island School of Design which housed a collection of Greek and Roman plaster casts in its basement, after which he began a modest collection of his own with the profits from sales of his handwritten books – eagerly purchased by his mother, aunts and grandfather.

An appreciation of antiquities and a prodigious imagination led him to build altars to the Greek gods where he'd pray for their appearance to confirm his faith. While his neighbours' children were playing cowboys and Indians in their back gardens, the eight-year-old Lovecraft became 'a genuine pagan', watching in the woods and fields for the nature spirits to materialise. 'Once I firmly thought I beheld some of these sylvan creatures dancing under autumnal oaks . . . I have seen the hoofed Pan and the sisters of the Hesperian

Phaethusa.' This quasi-mystical experience was as real to him as the 'subjective ecstasies of any Christian'.

This sense of being an outsider would permeate the more fanciful passages of his work, arguably revealing more about his inner life than any more direct correspondence – just as the secrets of our subconscious are unwittingly played out in dreams. In this passage taken from 'The Tomb' (June 1917), the line between author and protagonist seems especially blurred:

> I have dwelt ever in realms apart from the visible world; spending my youth and adolescence in ancient and little-known books, and in roaming the fields and groves of the region near my ancestral home. I do not think that what I read in these books or saw in these fields and groves was exactly what other boys read and saw there; but of this I must say little, since detailed speech would but confirm those cruel slanders upon my intellect which I sometimes overhear from the whispers of the stealthy attendants around me.

Had he continued to occupy himself with the myths and legends of the ancient world and perhaps thereafter study classics at university, he might have secured himself a 'respectable' career as a classics scholar and with it a regular income. But a chance encounter with a volume of Edgar Allan Poe's fantastic fiction in 1898 determined the direction his life would take from that moment on.

'It was my downfall, and at the age of eight I saw the blue firmament of Argos and Sicily darkened by the miasmal exhalations of the tomb!'

CHAPTER TWO

DEMONS ON ANGELL STREET

*'There are not many persons who know what
wonders are opened to them in the stories and visions
of their youth; for when as children we learn and dream, we
think but half-formed thoughts, and when as men we try
to remember, we are dulled and prosaic
with the poison of life.'*
– H.P. Lovecraft

The discovery of Poe was nothing short of a revelation, but it did not have an immediate effect on the young author's own work. As a boy, Lovecraft devoured Penny Dreadful and dime novel detective stories. The influence of these can be traced in his earliest lurid little thrillers: 'The Mysterious Ship', 'The Mystery of the Grave-Yard', 'The Haunted House', 'The Little Glass Bottle', 'The Secret Cave', 'John the Detective' and 'The Noble Eavesdropper' (Lovecraft's first surviving story and the first to be typewritten). Telling of a boy who happens upon a gathering of subterranean beings deep within a cave, the latter is believed to date from 1897 – the same year he wrote his first poem. Yet Poe's preoccupation with death, insanity and self-imposed isolation gripped the young author, whose 'kinship with Poe's gloomy heroes with their broken fortunes' would only intensify in years to come, with his own dramatic change in circumstance.

His carefree existence was curtailed that same year with his enrolment in Slater Avenue Primary School. Fortunately, his discomfort in the classroom lasted only as long as it took his teachers to realise that he already had a better education than they were able to offer him. In addition to his uncommonly large vocabulary and grasp of history, he must have been the only eight-year-old in Providence with a basic understanding of Latin and a practical knowledge of science – the former due to his grandfather's tuition and the latter acquired through his reading. While poring over the illustrations in *Webster's Unabridged Dictionary* he had become 'veritably hypnotised' by the images of scientific apparatus. It was not the subject itself which appealed to him so much as the idea of owning a fully equipped laboratory. 'Being a "spoiled child" I had but to ask, and it was mine.' He was also fortunate in having an aunt who was willing to tutor him in his chosen subject, Lillian having studied chemistry herself at boarding school. A copy of Professor Appleton's *The Young Chemist* and a good sized cellar were his without much debate and he was in business. 'The laboratory "work" – or play – seemed delightful, and despite a few mishaps, explosions and broken instruments, I got along splendidly.'

Needless to say, this new hobby inspired a series of self-produced 'in-house' publications including the weekly single sheet *Scientific Gazette* and a short series of chemical articles which could be purchased for the princely sum of five cents.

His passion, restless ambition and intense nature however had a detrimental effect on his somewhat fragile health. He suffered from headaches, nervous irritability, involuntary facial tics and exhaustion all through his childhood, leading to the first of what he claimed were several 'near breakdowns' at the age of eight. His father's death just two months prior to his enrolment at Slater Avenue and his distress at being separated from his family at such a time may have been contributing factors, but by his own admission he had not inherited 'a very good set of nerves' and doubtless his heightened sense of melodrama (acquired from his mother) brought him to crisis point – psychosomatic or otherwise. There is also the possibility that this episode was a case of a young boy acting out – seeking extra attention or perhaps an excuse for discontinuing the violin lessons he'd come to loathe. Lovecraft knew that a tantrum or stubborn refusal would not sway his mother who had visions of her prodigy performing to wild applause, so he appealed to her morbid fear of illness by affecting a nervous collapse. Having already lost her husband to a similar – possibly congenital disorder – this was something she could not afford to ignore. It had the added benefit of necessitating his prolonged absence from school, for which he was grateful.

He did not return to Slater Avenue until 1902 – a full three years later (he'd only attended for one year previously) – having kept himself busy by reading mostly Egyptian, Hindu and Teutonic mythology, writing more fiction, some verse and the first of his juvenile histories of Rhode Island and the Spanish-American war. The catalogue of the 'Providence Press' now offered an impressive range of subjects which must have left his family in no doubt that he would be embarking on a career as either an academic, a journalist or an author.

Impressed as they were by his self-discipline, drive and dedication, they were nevertheless concerned that he should socialise with boys of his own age and lead an active life. At his grandfather's suggestion he received a bicycle for his tenth birthday and derived much enjoyment from it, but an attempt to build stamina and a healthy interest in physical exercise at the local gymnasium resulted in a second 'fainting fit' which curtailed that avenue of activity.

In 1902 the science of astronomy supplanted the twelve-year-old Lovecraft's interest in chemistry. Before long, he'd acquired a small collection of telescopes and a library of books devoted to his new favourite subject. However, he continued to publish the *Scientific Gazette* on an ad-hoc basis until January 1909. Astronomy now became his 'principal scientific study', consuming his every waking hour. When he was not mapping the constellations, observing comets and surveying the 'worlds of infinite space', he was writing about them. The contemplation of the cold, black vastness of space and the awesome power unleashed in the creation and destruction of worlds light years away became lifelong obsessions of his. 'The grandeur of that growing conception of the universe still excites a thrill hardly to be duplicated.'

Lovecraft's devotion and understanding of the subject deserves a chapter in itself, but its true significance lies in what it reveals of his belief in the cosmic forces that existed aeons before life began on Earth. God does not figure in this embryonic universe. For both the adolescent Lovecraft and the man, the planets, suns and stars were the result of random chemical interactions and subatomic processes. It is telling that his early essays are not based on a study of astronomical data or observation, but are highly speculative theories on what, or indeed who, created such features as the lunar canals. Clearly, the teenage Lovecraft's primary interest in astronomy was not strictly scientific but supposition as he searches space for the meaning of life and evidence of other civilisations and intelligences. That said, he made painstaking notes on all manner of astronomical phenomena and applied himself to hours of uninterrupted observation – to the point where it caused him physical pain in his neck muscles. It also gave him a habitual stoop – one reason why Susan began referring to her only son as 'deformed'. His dedication to this new subject was as singular and unstinting as his previous devotion to earlier interests, but with a noteworthy addition; Lovecraft had permission to use the Brown University telescope, situated on campus at the Ladd Observatory, where he duly cycled several times a week. This courtesy had been extended to the thirteen-year-old by Professor Upton, a Phillips' family friend, though it did not prevent the youth from noting the telescope's shortcomings in the 1 November 1903 issue of *The Rhode Island Journal of Astronomy* which appeared weekly, then monthly until April 1907, after which two late issues were released in January and February 1909. His private publications were by this time being reproduced in print runs of four copies an issue on a hectograph, a laborious and time consuming process using gelatine. Lovecraft had by this time become something of a local celebrity whose authority on the subject combined with his unbridled enthusiasm led him to make a rare semi-public appearance – a course of lantern-slide lectures to family and invited guests (fellow young astronomers) free of charge in his home.

According to those who were present, he addressed them in a high piping voice that was not unpleasant and conversed in an undertone with little modulation, suggestive of an even temper. He was a model of self-control, at least in company and rarely betrayed his emotions, except in his work and private correspondence (as he did when launching 'a campaign of invective and satire' against astrology in 1914). He was otherwise serious, intense and composed, meeting every attempt to scrutinise him with a passive expression behind thin-rimmed spectacles. A model scholar to those who saw him striding through the streets of Providence, a cache of books under one arm. Head lowered, he'd ignore all attempts to engage him in conversation – not out of rudeness, but an inability to engage in social interaction. He couldn't make small talk even if he'd cared to. It served no purpose for him. It was of no value. Lovecraft spoke only to those who interested him, those who had something to say, or those to whom he had something to say. He was immersed in his own world, fascinated by his own ideas and it did not permit intruders. Talk of his 'feeble health', inherited nervous disorders and fatigue seems incompatible with the image of the almost six-foot tall, broad-shouldered, solidly built youth who must have cut an imposing figure in the eyes of his slighter peers. An acquaintance described Lovecraft as having a 'magnificent physique', one which would give any man cause to think twice before engaging him in a fist fight. Later in life he was proud and approving of the description given of him by his friend Frank Belknap Long in the latter's 1927 short story 'The Space Eaters', in which Lovecraft played a central role. 'In profile his face was impressive. He had an extremely broad forehead, long nose and a slightly protuberant chin – a strong sensitive face which suggested a wildly imaginative nature held in restraint by a sceptical and truly extraordinary intellect.'

Yet, in his youth, Lovecraft formed a wildly unflattering self-image, one which continued to undermine his self-esteem for as long as he lived. He considered himself 'an invalid' and was dismissive of anyone who dared to suggest the malady was all in his mind.

Had he been born a century later he might have been diagnosed with borderline Asperger Syndrome, clinically termed high-functioning autism. He certainly displayed all the symptoms: a lack of empathy and concern for others, obsessive interests and a work ethic bordering on the compulsive. Asperger sufferers typically demonstrate a degree of emotional immaturity, physical awkwardness and high anxiety which can manifest in a reluctance to leave their familiar environment (Lovecraft lived virtually all his life under the same roof and rarely ate at a café or restaurant until he moved to New York where he lived in a turmoil of mixed emotions – enjoying the company of his young companions and sightseeing, but suffering pangs of homesickness for the comforts of Providence). Asperger children are invariably of above average intelligence and so focussed on a single subject that it has become known as 'the little Professor syndrome'. But their inability to 'read' other people can leave the impression that they are disinterested in others and so appear aloof. All these characteristics describe Lovecraft's mannerisms and behaviour. Add to this the fact that many Asperger people are highly imaginative – so much so that many become writers, artists and musicians – and it seems likely that Lovecraft's 'eccentricities' may be largely due to a condition that was unknown during his lifetime.

Having resumed his studies at Slater Avenue, the awkward teenager found himself forced to mix with the local boys – most of whom found him odd but endearing. His ability to dream up gruesome murder mysteries for them to solve may have had a good deal to do with his growing popularity, as was his leadership of the Providence Detective Agency whose members were armed with copies of *The Detective* magazine in case they spotted a wanted criminal lurking in the neighbourhood.

His classmates have testified to his shyness and air of affected indifference, but also to his generosity and considerable personal charm when they persisted in their attempts to befriend him. Within a term or two he had cultivated a number of genuine friendships with boys with whom he shared a haughty, anti-authoritarian attitude – adopted for the sole purpose of provoking their teachers. Lovecraft's behaviour however was not sufficiently outrageous as to blot his academic record and he graduated in June 1903, marking the occasion with a hastily prepared speech on the life and work of astronomer Sir William Herschel, replete with the longest words in his vocabulary. If he had expected it to be greeted with open-mouthed admiration, he was to be sorely disappointed for the adults were all smiles, recognising a pretentious young man when they heard one.

All good things, however, must come to an end and in the spring of 1904 Lovecraft experienced a dramatic change of fortune, one every bit as traumatic as that suffered by the fictional George Minafer, although unlike Tarkington's character Howard did not deserve his fate. The spoilt, snobbish heir of a wealthy family, Minafer grows to be both condescending and cruel – sabotaging his own mother's chance of happiness out of spite. Everyone in his hometown wishes earnestly for his 'comeuppance', which comes with the death of his grandfather. At the reading of the will, it transpires that George stands to inherit significantly less than he'd always hoped for . . .

On 24 March, Lovecraft lost his beloved grandfather Whipple Van Buren. Due to a string of disastrous ventures (namely two failed dam projects in Idaho) his firm – the Owyhee Land and Irrigation Company – was in financial dire straits. Whipple had saved himself and the family from ruin with the sale of his personal property. Yet, the strain was clearly weighing heavy upon him. While visiting his friend Alderman Gray, he was seized by the 'paralytic shock' (most likely a stroke) that killed him. When the board voted to dissolve the corporation, Susan and Howard were forced to vacate the family home and move into a small cramped house down the street at number 598 – which they shared with one other family. (Lillian and Annie had married and moved out of the Phillips house some years before). For the first time in his life the thirteen-year-old felt so desolate he saw no reason to continue living. 'Oh hell!' he wrote. 'Why not slough off consciousness altogether?'

Though it's clear from his journal (in which he considers the merits and potential problems of various methods of self-destruction) that he was never in earnest, there is an underlying hint of despair in these entries that seems all too real. Lovecraft had already lost faith in religion and could no longer believe that an omnipotent deity would intervene to save him or his loved ones. He might eventually have reconciled himself to his father's death, but the loss of his gentle and benevolent grandfather at such an impressionable age appeared to justify his avowed atheism. The year before, he had petitioned his mother to remove him from Sunday school after an altercation with the 'pious preceptors' there. He'd challenged them to provide proof of the existence of God rather than taking their faith for granted. By his thirteenth birthday, he had already convinced himself of man's 'impermanence and insignificance' and so the seeds were sown for the pessimistic cosmic view that would inform his fiction with 'the futility of existence' as well as a profound scepticism regarding human progress. In 1922, he'd expound on this philosophy in 'A Confession of Unfaith', and in several other essays in which he poured scorn on organised religion as institutionalised superstition.

'All notions of cosmic consciousness and purpose, and of the importance of man in the limitless pattern of the universe, are plainly myths born of the imperfect information of man's early days,' he wrote (*Against Religion: The Atheist Writings of H.P. Lovecraft*, edited by Joshi, 2010).

Above all else, it was his unquenchable thirst for knowledge that drove him to endure when less resilient souls might have succumbed. There was simply too much he did not know about the world. Enlightenment was what he craved and he refused to be deprived of the opportunity to acquire it. If mankind was not destined to evolve, at least Howard Phillips Lovecraft would overcome his own personal limitations and develop into a writer of some renown.

One of the principal attributes of youth is, of course, adaptability. It took just one semester at his new school, the aptly named Hope Street English and Classical High School, to restore his spirits and dispel his antipathy toward authority after he found himself 'a gentleman amongst gentlemen'. Lovecraft responded favourably to the more informal atmosphere and to the predominantly male staff who were able to accommodate his erratic punctuality knowing that he would deliver first-rate work if left to his own devices.

It is all the more surprising therefore that he left full-time state education a year before graduation. But then he saw little merit or value in formal qualifications and had no intention of pursuing a particular profession, despite the precarious financial state in which he and his mother now found themselves. After a childhood in which he had been applauded and indulged, and an adolescence in which he had fared well academically (though not to the standard required to secure a place at university), sordid reality could not be permitted to shatter his fragile self-image. If he was as gifted as he believed himself to be, the world, or at least his small corner of it, would surely recognise and reward it. It was only a matter of time.

For all his intelligence, it appears that he shared one discreditable trait with his late father and with certain members of the Phillips family: an insufferable, conceited belief in his own superiority. This manifested in contempt for non-white races and a professed anti-Semitism. His prejudice against the former was rooted in a spurious pseudoscientific theory prevalent at the time which stated that 'negroes' were biologically inferior and the latter largely, but not entirely, from the suspicion that the Jews were considered intellectually superior and so must be denigrated and excluded to give the anti-Semites a chance to catch up. Like many racists, Lovecraft's affected 'superiority' was dependent on his assumption that it would never be challenged. The more threatened and insecure he felt, the more fervent his attacks became. Lovecraft had acquired much knowledge – so much so that his classmates named him 'professor' – but precious little common sense or compassion for those he considered his inferiors.

In a letter to Rheinhart Kleiner dated 16 November 1916 he wrote: 'Hope Street is near enough to the "North End" to have a considerable Jewish attendance. It was there that I formed my intractable aversion to the Semitic race. The Jews were brilliant in their classes – calculatingly and schemingly brilliant – but their ideals were sordid and their manners coarse. I became rather well known as an anti-Semite before I had been at Hope Street many days.'

He was equally disparaging of those of Asian origin and expressed fear for the future if interracial relationships continued to 'dilute' the purity of the Aryan race. And yet, he subsequently married a Jewess who suffered many of his rants in silence, but was occasionally forced to remind him to tone down his racist outbursts in public. He also counted the Jewish poet Samuel Loveman among his closest friends, going so far as to act as Loveman's secretary to ensure his poems were preserved for posterity, poems which Lovecraft admitted were superior to his own and confessing, 'Jew or not, I am rather proud to be his sponsor'.

While it may be true that racial prejudice was endemic in the nineteenth century, many were immune to such reprehensible beliefs and of these it can be assumed a number were considerably less well educated than Lovecraft. Bigotry, indefensible in any age, is the bastard child of both ignorance and arrogance and as such Howard Phillips Lovecraft was better placed than most to know better.

Time, however, did not rectify his distorted perception nor temper his intolerance as his private correspondence attests. After living in New York for a few years during the 1920s he wrote, 'loathsome Asiatic hordes trail their dirty carcasses over streets where white men once moved, and air their odious presence and twisted visage and stunted forms till we shall be driven either to murder them or emigrate ourselves . . . It is not good for a proud, light-skinned Nordic to be cast away alone amongst squat, squint-eyed jabberers with coarse ways and alien emotions whom his deepest cell tissue hates and loathes as the mammal hates and loathes the reptile, with an instinct as old as history.'

While one might admire his talent, drive and dedication, it is to his discredit that he saw fit to commit his racist views to the printed page, in numerous examples of his private correspondence and even in verse. The deficiencies of the man do not, however, debase the quality of his best work. If anything, they invest it with a twisted passion that is missing from his more fantastic fiction. The most notorious example, 'The Horror At Red Hook', which novelist China Melville calls 'extraordinarily racist' and 'a fever dream of prejudice', gains its nightmarish quality from its narrator's xenophobic paranoia, whereas the reader rightly recoils in disgust from the racist language in 'Herbert West: Reanimator' because it is gratuitous and is clearly not the protagonist's opinion but that of the author.

'He was a loathsome, gorilla-like thing, with abnormally long arms that I could not help calling fore legs, and a face that conjured up thoughts of unspeakable Congo secrets and tom-tom poundings under an eerie moon. The body must have looked even worse in life – but the world holds many ugly things.' Such passages strike a sour note even among Lovecraft's most ardent admirers and must have dissuaded others from reading him at all.

All too frequently great artists are revealed to be fatally flawed human beings – alcoholics, drug addicts, insufferable boors and antisocial eccentrics – but when they are inspired, they channel and ground their creative force like a lightning rod. It is as if some higher self takes over. If in such moments it is true what the esoterics say and the ordinary mind is asleep at the wheel and the subconscious takes control, then it is permissible to detach the man from his muse, as we would with Richard Wagner, H.G. Wells or even Agatha Christie (the world's most popular author after Shakespeare, her fiction is regrettably pitted with anti-Semitic asides) if we are to derive pleasure from his work.

Although it would seem that Lovecraft did not develop emotionally in the years following his grandfather's death, it is beyond question that he did so as a writer, if the evidence of his later juvenile fiction is any indication. 'The Beast in the Cave' and 'The Alchemist' – both dating from Lovecraft's late teens – see the young author finding his voice, though he is far from perfecting it. His laboured attempt to imitate his favourite authors has given way to a more confident command of language, centred on the psychological torture endured by the victim. The first story focuses on a philosophy scholar who becomes separated from a tour party during an expedition to a local cave. He is pursued through the darkness by a beast that he eventually kills. He is then rescued; only to learn that it was a man who had been lost like himself years before.

Lovecraft's love of adjectives is already in evidence – 'my disordered fancy conjured up hideous and fearsome shapes from the sinister darkness that surrounded me, and that actually seemed to press upon my body' – as is his later tendency to contrive effects from a deliberately archaic and ostentatious style. But he creates a sense of claustrophobia and impending danger as the nameless narrator's torch sputters in the darkness and is finally extinguished.

Reflecting on the story in later life, Lovecraft was in two minds about its value, referring to it as both 'ineffably pompous' and the first story of his worth reading. He tended to be his own harshest critic (to the extent that he destroyed all but two stories written between 1903 and '08 in anticipation of concentrating on his scientific journalism). If there is a shortcoming with 'The Beast . . .'

it is that it is too short to maximise tension and the final third is rushed as the narrator flees his pursuer until coming all too conveniently to the protection of his rescuer.

'The Alchemist' reveals further improvement. Although it is highly derivative and its author cannot resist the temptation to populate his setting with huge winged bats and dank, cobwebbed corridors, this revenge tale moves along at an admirably brisk pace and boasts a fine sense of the macabre as the following extract reveals: 'Strangest of all were his eyes, twin caves of abysmal blackness, profound in expression of understanding, yet inhuman in degree of wickedness. These were now fixed upon me, piercing my soul with their hatred, and rooting me to the spot whereon I stood.'

The narrator, the Count Antoine de C–, is the last in a line of noblemen who all died in their thirty-second year as the result of a curse placed upon them in the Middle Ages by the son of a sorcerer. As the Count approaches his thirty-second birthday, he explores his crumbling castle and discovers the sorcerer's son behind a locked door at the end of a nitre-encrusted passage. This last piece of description speaks volumes about the influence of Poe upon Lovecraft's work, since 'nitre' – a mineral form of potassium nitrate which thrives in dark, dank places – is an idiosyncratic term that echoes throughout Poe's fiction (particularly in 'The Cask of Amontillado'). The pair struggle and the sorcerer's son is fatally wounded. With his dying breath, he confesses that he murdered the Count's male ancestors after having discovered the elixir of eternal life.

As Lovecraft scholar S.T. Joshi notes in his exhaustive two-volume biography, *I Am Providence* (Hippocampus Press, 2013), there are thinly veiled references to the writer's personal circumstances in this tale, notably the allusion to a lofty and noble line brought low by poverty, the pride which prevents the protagonist from soiling his hands with work, his solitary existence and the days spent poring over ancient texts while keeping his distance from the 'peasant children' who dwell beyond the castle walls.

In all likelihood Lovecraft's earlier 'near breakdowns' were purely psychosomatic, but the episode he suffered in the summer of 1908 after leaving high school appears to have been a genuine collapse.

Whatever the cause, it gave him the face-saving excuse he needed to abandon his formal education – which he suspected he would fail given his lack of ability in maths. He would have been required to excel at the subject to qualify for an astronomy degree, which was the path he had set his heart on. His decision to abandon this dream dealt another blow to his self-esteem and was a significant contributing factor to his breakdown. However, the fact that he referred to it as 'a sort of breakdown' suggests that it was not formally diagnosed and therefore may not have been sufficiently serious to require admission to a hospital (unless this is another case of Lovecraft glossing over potentially sensational details of his life – regrettably, mental illness carried a certain stigma in the author's lifetime). The 'intense headaches, insomnia and general nervous weakness' that he referred to in a letter to high-school teacher and fellow amateur journalist Maurice W. Moe, (January 1915) and which prevented his 'continuous application to anything' are suggestive of a general malaise and inability to summon up the energy to engage in a long period of formal study. The suspicion is that, industrious though he was, it was not until he was faced with the prospect of enrolling at university that Lovecraft realised enthusiasm and application would not be enough to see him through his exams. The possibility that he would be tested (literally) and found wanting was simply too much to bear and he retreated behind this latest convenient health problem. He appeared to admit as much in a letter to Moe dated April 1931. 'It was clear to me that I hadn't brains enough to be an astronomer – and that was a pill I couldn't swallow with equanimity.'

From 1908 to 1913 – described by Lovecraft as 'my years of feebleness' – he withdrew from the world and wrote nothing of consequence, at least nothing that has survived. He had lived high on nervous energy for so long that he had burnt himself out, or as Poe would have it, 'he was all used up'.

In a letter to R.H. Barlow dated April 1934 Lovecraft admitted, 'in those days I could hardly bear to see or speak to anyone, and liked to shut out the world by pulling down dark shades and using artificial light'. No doubt his already fragile ego – albeit masked by a façade of superiority – had received an almost fatal blow when his own mother, drawing attention to his elongated chin and self-inflicted wounds to his face (made in an attempt to remove ingrowing beard hair), called him 'hideous' and 'deformed'– repeated remarks which led him to restrict his outings to concerts, long solitary trolley car rides and visits to the opera. Neighbour Clara Hess later recounted that, 'Mrs Lovecraft talked continuously of her son who was so hideous that he hid from everyone and did not like to walk upon the streets where people would gaze at him.' This story didn't surface till 1948, however, when it was printed by August Derleth in *The Providence Journal.*

Lovecraft languished in self-pity until 1914, when he caught the attention of Edward F. Daas, president of the United Amateur Press Association, with his erudite ripostes to fellow readers in the *Argosy* regarding the merits, or lack thereof, possessed by its most popular writer of romantic fiction, Fred Jackson. Daas was impressed with both the quality of Lovecraft's well-argued retorts (often in verse form) and his wit – all of which demonstrated that he could engage in an informed and stimulating debate without resorting to personal attacks, as his critics were wont to do. At Daas' invitation Lovecraft entered a prolific though not profitable career as an amateur journalist. Over the next ten years, he wrote on a diverse range of subjects reaching an audience of tens of thousands of readers – more than he could ever have hoped in his wildest imaginings as the publisher of his privately printed scientific periodicals. It was an opportunity for which he was very grateful and to which he devoted his energies. He must have been aware that it had offered him a lifeline at a time when he was in dire need of one.

'Amateur journalism has provided me with the very world in which I live,' he wrote in 1921. 'With the advent of the United [United Amateur official organ of the Association of Amateur Journalists] I obtained a renewed will to live . . . and found a sphere in which I could feel that my efforts were not wholly futile.' ('What Amateurdom and I Have Done For Each Other')

Indeed, the five years he had spent as a virtual recluse were not wasted, even if they were not productive. All the knowledge and material he had ingested during this time was simply gestating within him, awaiting the day when he would emerge reinvigorated and with his passion renewed.

To these influences he added another – contemporary weird fiction – a category of supernatural fantasy that eschewed the conventions and clichés of the traditional ghost story or gothic tale and which is now seen as a precursor of what we broadly define as horror. But there was more to the weird tale than inspiring fear within the reader. Past masters such as Arthur Machen, William Hope Hodgson and Algernon Blackwood had evoked an indefinable strangeness which was unsettling for the reader and invariably fatal for the characters. Eschewing restless spirits, vampires, werewolves and a whole panoply of mythical monsters, exponents of the weird tale from Jean Ray in Belgium and Luigi Ugolini in Italy to Ryunosuke Akutagawa in Japan explored the unsettling impact of the uncanny, blurring the distinction between the material world and imagination in ways that prompted their characters to question the very nature of reality, or their perception of it. Logic and the laws of science were suspended as helpless scientists, explorers and the unwary underwent bizarre physical transformations, or witnessed unholy rituals threatening to unleash forces that would make zombies and mummies look as tame as a pantomime villain. Such tales had begun to appear sporadically in the proto-pulp magazines, *All-Story*, *Argosy* and *Black Cat* at the turn of the century and were becoming increasingly popular – so popular and profitable that each publisher produced several similar titles to meet demand, increasing their frequency from monthly to weekly as circulation soared.

At first Lovecraft found diversion rather than inspiration in these lurid tales. Unlike the highbrow authors he admired, these tales appeared to have little literary merit. Yet he soon became an avid reader and a regular letter writer, offering advice to the editors on which settings and themes would prove more popular and praising his favourite writers – who ranged from A.P. Terhune (author of 'Lassie'), Edgar Rice Burroughs (creator of the *Tarzan* and *John Carter* novels) and Irvin S. Cobb (whose tale 'Fishhead' would be a seminal influence on Lovecraft's own, 'The Shadow Over Innsmouth'). Only a fraction of the tales that appeared in these magazines could be categorised as weird fiction and many of those Lovecraft singled out were exponents of rugged adventure in the style of H. Rider Haggard, but it seems likely that his exposure to contemporary writers of such material offered him a crucial insight into the themes, tone and style that was selling, earning their writers a modest living at least. 'I then gave my prose style the greatest overhauling it has ever had; purging it at once of some vile journalese and some absurd Johnsonianism [after the English essayist, poet and critic, Samuel Johnson]. Little by little I felt that I was forging the instrument I ought to have forged a decade ago – a decent style capable of expressing what I wished to say. But I still wrote verse and persisted in the delusion that I was a poet.'

This is quite a damning statement coming as it does from the author of nearly 300 poems. But Lovecraft was being brutally honest when he admitted that almost all of these had been penned in imitation of his eighteenth-century literary heroes (Pope, Dryden, Milton and Johnson) in the hope that he might evoke the elegance of the period which fate had prohibited him from enjoying. Ironically, perhaps his most appealing – and arguably most charming – poem is one in which he gently mocks his own pretentions as a bard born in the wrong century.

'On The Death of a Rhyming Critic' (July 1917)

A curious fellow in his time,
Fond of old books and prone to rhyme –
A scribbling pedant, of the sort
That scorn the age, and write for sport.
A little wit he sometime had,
But half of what he wrote was bad;
In metre he was very fair;
Of rhetoric he had his share –
But of the past so much he'd prate,
That he was always out of date!

Much of the verse he wrote during this period of enforced hibernation was not published during his lifetime, but not for the reason he imagined. It is true, it was not particularly accomplished, being somewhat laboured, self-conscious and striving too eagerly for effect, but it is also mean spirited and racist. The worst examples are those in which Lovecraft expressed his aversion to the influx of foreign migrants and the threat they posed to his all-white Anglo Saxon world. One suspects that his ire was a projection of his own self-loathing and frustration at having failed to find the courage to make his way in the world, a world that he imagined had rejected him. But it gradually dawned upon him that if journeymen authors like Terhune, Edgar A. Guest and Harold Bell Wright could be published and paid for it, then this dream ought to be within his reach too.

In this belief he was encouraged by a fellow amateur editor and reviewer, W. Paul Cook who saw promise in 'The Beast in the Cave' and 'The Alchemist' and offered to publish them in his paper, *The Vagrant*. After both received a very favourable reader response, Cook requested more of the same. In June 1917 the reluctant author – feeling that he had nothing left to lose – turned his hand back to fiction, producing 'The Tomb' and 'Dagon' within weeks of each other.

CHAPTER THREE

BEYOND THE WALL OF SLEEP

*'They who dream by day are cognizant
of many things which escape those who dream
only by night. In their grey visions they obtain glimpses
of eternity, and thrill, in awaking, to find they have
been upon the verge of the great secret.'*
– Edgar Allan Poe, 'Eleonora'

In 1917 few of America's young men were eager to fight in a war that seemed a world away from home. Lovecraft may have been more politically aware than many of his generation, but he would never know the hardships, horrors and privations experienced by his countrymen when America entered World War One on 8 April that year. Out of a sense of duty and patriotism, he enlisted in May and was accepted into the Coast Artillery. What followed was a source of acute embarrassment to him, for his mother badgered the family physician to intercede on her son's behalf and have him declared unfit for service. Having failed his medical examination, Howard was duly discharged, mortified to have been denied the chance to serve his country and forced to return home under such humiliating circumstances. If he had not harboured any ill-feeling towards his mother before this point, he certainly did so now, although he swallowed his pride and stifled his resentment in the belief that he would have to make his peace with her if they were to continue living together. It is arguable that he felt responsible for her wellbeing and played the role of both surrogate husband and the placatory, dutiful son. Besides, neither he nor his mother was particularly assertive. Both sensitive personalities, they shrank from conflict. Susie – as she was called by those closest to her – would suffer a breakdown the following year, but she was so highly strung that the slightest provocation could have caused her to collapse at any time.

Over the next two years Lovecraft threw himself wholeheartedly into his amateur press activities, a harmless and thoroughly respectable pursuit in the eyes of his mother and an enjoyable, intellectual pastime as far as he was concerned. He wrote numerous papers and articles on every subject that interested him and served as president of the United Amateur Press Association (UAPA) until 1918. That year he offered his services as a ghost writer, revising the work of fellow amateurs which left little time to devote to his own fiction. But that wasn't the only demand on his time and energy.

In the winter of 1918 his mother's health suffered a rapid decline. Bad investments had reduced the Van Buren fortune drastically and the strain of living at subsistence level seemed to sap the last vestiges of Susie's strength. She succumbed to wild fancies of being stalked by 'weird and fantastic creatures', a fear she shared with neighbour Clara Hess one day as they rode on a trolley car with Susie protesting loudly that she didn't know where she was. Such behaviour naturally alarmed her family and friends who had no choice but to seek her committal.

On 13 March 1919, Susie was admitted to Butler Hospital where she would remain until her death from a botched operation two years later. On the day she was admitted her 28-year-old son sank into another black abyss of depression. Unable to work or leave the house, he spent his days moping from room to room, lying in bed or writing letters. He confided to a friend that he felt 'only half alive' – a 'shattered wreck' – and could only potter around the house for four or five hours a day before returning to his bed. He was suffering from acute nervous exhaustion and couldn't summon up either the energy or the inclination to write himself out of it. He had lost any appetite for life. Offers to contribute to amateur periodicals struck him as too arduous to accept. Nothing seemed worth the effort other than to pour out his despair in verse form. Of all his verse, it is the one perhaps in which he distilled his true feelings.

'Despair' (published June 1919)

> O'er the midnight moorlands crying,
> Thro' the cypress forests sighing,
> In the night-wind madly flying,
> Hellish forms with streaming hair;
> In the barren branches creaking,
> By the stagnant swamp-pools speaking,
> Past the shore-cliffs ever shrieking;
> Damn'd daemons of despair.

The third stanza is clearly an allusion to his own plight.

> And the voyager, repining,
> Sees the wicked death-fires shining,
> Hears the wicked petrel's whining
> As he helpless drifts to sea.

And the last to his forlorn hope that all his work might have amounted to something.

> Thus the living, lone and sobbing,
> In the throes of anguish throbbing,
> With the loathsome Furies robbing
> Night and noon of peace and rest.
> But beyond the groans and grating
> Of abhorrent Life, is waiting
> Sweet Oblivion, culminating
> All the years of fruitless quest.

In fact, Lovecraft was overwhelmed by conflicting emotions, on the one hand sorrow and on the other relief. As *Home Brew* editor George Julian Houtain would cryptically observe, 'he was willing to overcome [his professed ailments] and would, but he isn't allowed to do so, because others in his immediate household won't permit him to forget this hereditary nervousness'.

He had a right to resent Susan for all she had done to him with her twisted affections, but he couldn't bring himself to blame her. Instead he visited her whenever he could, walking her through the grounds – but never entering the institution itself as he had a phobia of hospitals – and conversing in his quiet, unhurried way as if they were on a leisurely stroll in the park, with not a care in the world.

The appearance of Lovecraft's first significant tale in the November 1919 issue of *The Vagrant* was announced with uncharacteristic modesty on the part of the author. The magazine's editor and publisher, W. Paul Cook, informed his predominantly young readership that the author of 'Dagon' was 'practically unknown' – partly because few self-produced and self-financed amateur publications had the space to publish lengthy prose, but also because Mr Lovecraft did not consider himself 'a competent storyteller' and had been reluctant to submit any. This may have been an attempt by the 29-year-old writer to elicit praise through his new sponsor, or a genuine lack of confidence in his ability to produce original prose of a sufficiently high standard. Whatever the reason, the reader response was encouraging.

The influence of Poe is particularly apparent in 'The Tomb', the first of his adult tales and the second to be published in *The Vagrant* (in March 1922). As the author himself admitted in a letter to Washington poet Elizabeth Toldridge dated 8 March 1929, 'since Poe affected me most of all horror-writers, I can never feel that a tale starts out right unless it has something of his manner . . . To my mind it is necessary to establish a setting and avenue of approach before the main show can adequately begin.' Indeed, the word 'inspiration' hardly seems sufficient to describe Poe's impact on Lovecraft's evolving style – he provided a model for Lovecraft's tales and effectively served as a virtual tutor to the young writer. 'No aspiring author should content himself with a mere acquisition of technical rules . . . All attempts at gaining literary polish must begin with judicious reading . . . a story of Poe's will impress upon the mind a more vivid notion of powerful and correct description and narration than will ten dry chapters of a bulky textbook,' wrote Lovecraft in his text, *On Literary Composition*, (January 1920).

The debt owed to Poe is evident in what amounts to an homage from the foremost author of twentieth-century horror to his nineteenth-century predecessor, but the opening is inelegant and portentous.

> In relating the circumstances which have led to my confinement within this refuge for the demented, I am aware that my present position will create a natural doubt of the authenticity of my narrative. It is an unfortunate fact that the bulk of humanity is too limited in its mental vision to weigh with patience and intelligence those isolated phenomena, seen and felt only by a psychologically sensitive few, which lie outside its common experience. Men of broader intellect know that there is no sharp distinction betwixt the real and the unreal; that all things appear as they do only by virtue of the delicate individual physical and mental media through which we are made conscious of them; but the prosaic materialism of the majority condemns as madness the flashes of supersight which penetrate the common veil of obvious empiricism.

Lovecraft is clearly trying too hard to impress. But once into the narrative he adopts a leaner style and the pace picks up. The narrator, Jervas Dudley, confesses to being a dreamer and a visionary who has already been confined in an asylum, a fact that should not cast doubt on the veracity of his tale as there is a supernatural element that accounts for his ability to have been in two places at once. Jervas tells of how – as a child of ten – he came upon the ruins of an old mansion near his home and its family crypt which he explored, though it is later said to have been padlocked. It appears the boy had only dreamt of entering the tomb, but on his return home he begins to exhibit strange behaviour more akin to that of an eighteenth-century rake. Convinced that his spirit left his body and entered the crypt, Jervas returns to the scene and there witnesses a costume ball with the guests in full Regency regalia. When a fire breaks out, the guests are consumed in the flames and the mansion is burned to the ground, leaving it in the same state as when he first saw it. Jervas' insistence that he witnessed this tragedy results in his confinement in the asylum, but then comes the twist: a trusted servant breaks into the locked tomb and finds a statuette which is the very likeness of his young master. It bears the initials J.H. In an alcove, the servant sees an empty coffin inscribed with the name 'Jervas'. If the opening of the story is protracted, then the final line is admirably terse and unsettling as Jervas declares, 'In that coffin and in that vault they have promised me I shall be buried.'

If 'The Tomb' is an affectionate pastiche of Poe and a distillation of all the elements assimilated from the gothic tales Lovecraft devoured in his youth, then 'Dagon' aims to establish an authentic twentieth-century language for horror by resisting the temptation to explain the phenomena which overwhelm the characters.

Compare the convoluted and clumsy opening of 'The Tomb' with the first line of 'Dagon': 'I am writing this under an appreciable mental strain, since by tonight I shall be no more.' The first is surely a prime example of strained writing for effect by anybody's standards, poorly constructed and pretentious, while the latter is economical and arresting. In the former we recognise Lovecraft the student of literature shovelling everything into the opening paragraph in a desperate attempt to convince us of his ability, whereas in the latter he secures our interest instantly – with the skill of the journalist who teases with an attention grabbing headline, or the fairground barker beckoning customers into a freak-show. The end too, is suggestive rather than explicit and we are left to imagine something more horrible than the writer could have dreamt up or described in words. 'I hear a noise at the door, as of some immense slippery body lumbering against it. It shall not find me. God, *that hand!* The window! The window!'

In contrast to the protagonists of earlier tales, the morphine-addicted narrator of 'Dagon' has no rational explanation for the events he witnessed (the discovery of a monolith and its apparent worship by a hideous amphibious sea creature.) In visiting unspeakable dread upon his characters for no reason other than the fact that they stumbled upon something beyond their experience, Lovecraft anticipates the visceral terrors of Stephen King, James Herbert and a generation of writers weaned on the garishly coloured and graphic EC Comics of the 1950s (*Tales From The Crypt*, *Vault of Horror*) – all of whom would have been the poorer for not having read Lovecraft.

'Dagon' reveals that at this point Lovecraft was still under the thrall of Poe, his 'god of fiction' from whom Lovecraft adopts the device of having the protagonist serve as narrator and the tone of frenzied insistence that compels the protagonist to unburden himself of the gnawing fear that afflicts him. But the awful vision is Lovecraft's alone. The creature may be a figment of his fevered imagination, but the narrator's distress is real enough and this is what the best horror fiction achieves; generating empathy with the victim. It is not so much the creature we dread, but our own irrational response to the beast; our inability to remain in control when primal instinct takes over.

Despite the positive response he received from the publication of 'Dagon' Lovecraft did not produce a run of similar stories. In fact, he wrote only one other, 'Polaris', in 1918 – almost a year after the first two – so he was evidently uncertain as to whether fiction would be his forte. When Cook was unable to guarantee inclusion in *The Vagrant*, Lovecraft submitted it to another non-paying amateur periodical, *The Philosopher*, who published it just before Christmas 1920.

'Polaris' recounts the awakening of a past-life memory in the mind of the unnamed narrator who has fallen under the baleful influence of the Pole Star and is now trapped in a dream world inhabited by demons. In his earlier incarnation he had been a sentry entrusted with keeping watch for an invading army. Clearly, long nights of straining to see into the darkness have left an indelible impression on his subconscious mind. 'When I awaked, I was not as I had been. Upon my memory was graven the vision of the city, and within my soul had arisen another and vaguer recollection, of whose nature I was not then certain.'

From this point on, he is haunted by guilt for having allowed the star to lull him to sleep on duty, even as the 'squat yellow foe' advanced on the citadel. There is the suggestion that he might be ensnared in a limbo between life and death, flitting in and out of an 'unnatural dream', and that the 'memory' of an ancient marble city is a false one, but again, it is the lead character's anguish and uncertainty which lie at the core of the story and engage our interest – particularly so when we learn that the theme may have originated with a vivid dream the author described to correspondent Maurice W. Moe in May 1918. 'Several nights ago I had a strange dream of a strange city – a city of many palaces and gilded domes . . . I was in it and around it. But certainly I had no corporeal existence . . . I recall a lively curiosity at the scene, and a tormenting struggle to recall its identity; for I felt that I had once known it well . . . when something vaguely horrible had happened.'

Although he proclaimed himself a rationalist and professed disbelief in the supernatural, Lovecraft entertained the idea that writers and artists can develop an acute – even psychic – sensitivity to other realities or dimensions through the development of their imagination and so be able to access the symbolic landscape of these inner worlds of the psyche in which their fears could take on form – fears which were to haunt him throughout his brief, unhappy life.

Kenneth Grant, a disciple of Aleister Crowley, believed that Lovecraft was a natural adept who was drawn to the shadow realms of the Tree of Life in dreams and nightmares but, being unfamiliar with the Kabbalistic system, he was unable to contextualize his experiences. Instead, he constructed his own fictional netherworld inhabited by the malformed elemental creatures he had encountered. In his book *Nightside of Eden*, Grant goes so far as to assign the various deities of Lovecraft's fictional pantheon with specific spheres on the tree and the 'iridescent globes' that feature in his fiction with the fragmented Qliphoth, or shells of the imperfect tree – a symbol of God's first failed attempt to create the universe.

Ritual magicians believe that, even if the dark gods and demons of Lovecraft's stories began as mere projections of his irrational fears, any form of prolonged meditation on these dark deities would empower them with life on the inner planes. If there is any truth in such assertions, then successive generations of horror addicts might well have invested these eldritch horrors with real substance. One group of Lovecraft devotees, the Esoteric Order of Dagon – who claim to have lodges in Australia, the United States and Europe – have stated that, while they do not necessarily believe in the existence of the 'Great Old Ones' (the cosmic deities who once ruled earth but now slumber in a dreamless sleep), they find the iconography of Lovecraft's world to be a useful stimulus for gaining access to a greater reality which can be explored 'in the spirit' using guided visualisations. Doubtless, Lovecraft would have dismissed such claims, but been gratified that his creations have taken on some kind of reality beyond the printed page.

Like Samuel Taylor Coleridge before him, Lovecraft was well aware of the value of the dream-state – a limitless source of inspiration and imagery that never ceased to enrich his writings. His next story explored the thrilling possibility of producing such dreams at will. 'Beyond the Wall of Sleep', written in the spring of 1919 and published in that year's October issue of *Pine Cones*, muses on the 'occasionally titanic significance of dreams' – specifically those in which we visit an 'uncorporeal life of far different nature from the life we know'. Though its author took no active interest in the spiritualist movement, (which was not yet on the wane in America), he was certainly aware of it. He would have read newspaper reports of the poltergeist phenomena which the Fox sisters, Margaretta and Kate of Hydesville, Rochester, New York, claimed to have experienced at their farmer's farm beginning in the spring of 1848 and which spread rapidly to surrounding areas until table rappings, spectral materialisations and séances had supplanted parlour games as America's preferred after dinner amusement. Towards the end of the century the Theosophical movement established a centre in New York and high society was abuzz with talk of its charismatic founder, Madame Blavatsky and her hidden masters who channelled the ageless wisdom to her from the inner planes.

Lovecraft's repeated allusions to the existence of the soul; the possibility of possession and out-of-body experiences suggest that he found paranormal phenomena fascinating – even if he professed to not believe in them himself. 'Sometimes I believe that this less material life is our truer life, and that our vain presence on the terraqueous globe is itself the secondary or merely virtual phenomenon.' These lines might have been taken verbatim from Blavatsky's *The Secret Doctrine* (1888), but are in fact from 'Beyond the Wall of Sleep' which describes the attempts made by an asylum intern to communicate with a spirit he believes has possessed another inmate. After constructing an electric device of his own design, the intern succeeds, only to discover that the entity is not a demon or a discarnate spirit (lacking any physical form), but an extra-terrestrial which, for reasons never explained, had chosen a Catskill Mountain man as its host. Its release results in a nova in a distant galaxy, though why the entity seeks revenge against a star is never revealed.

The insight which the alien shares with his rescuer is a mash-up of science fiction (though the term was yet to be coined) and spirituality, but it is one which the initiates of any esoteric order would have recognised, although the warning is unwarranted. 'I am an entity like that which you yourself become in the freedom of dreamless sleep. I am your brother of light, and have floated with you in the effulgent valleys. It is not permitted me to tell your waking earth-self of your real self, but we are all roamers of vast spaces and travellers in many ages . . . How little does the earth-self know life and its extent! How little, indeed, ought it to know for its own tranquillity!'

If it had not been for an invitation to attend several amateur conventions in Boston and a desire to hear his new literary hero, Lord Dunsany, address a convention in the same city in October 1919, he might well have languished in that house until his mother's death. Fortunately, the temptation to meet other members of the UAPA – to which he had been not only a prolific contributor, but also first vice-president (from 1915–6) and president (1917–8) – was too great.

On a professional level, he was already moving away from amateur journalism and seriously considering investing all his energy in fiction – for which there seemed to be a growing market. Dunsany's fairy-realm fantasies appealed to Lovecraft because they conveyed a childlike sense of wonder which he considered to be the mark of the true romantic. Though Lovecraft would not have considered himself to be a romantic, this was an aspect of his nature that is evident in his dream-world tales while he could be said to have pacified the fatalist in his horror fiction. And yet listening to the charming Anglo-Irish peer read from his work in person left Lovecraft awestruck and clearly in his thrall. 'Dunsany is myself . . . His cosmic realm is the realm in which I live . . . and cherish,' he wrote in June 1923 in a letter to Frank Belknap Long.

Long is a prominent and recurring figure in Lovecraft's life. The prolific New York writer was nineteen and an active member of the United Amateur Press Association when the two struck up a regular correspondence in 1921 that would continue until Lovecraft's death. Long, whose tastes in literature and art provided great stimulus to Lovecraft, was strongly influenced in his own writing by Poe, but shared Lovecraft's scepticism in regard to the supernatural and the occult.

Lovecraft acted as a mentor and even published some of Long's work in his own amateur periodical, *The Conservative* (1915–23), as well as writing a flattering assessment of his protégé for the United Amateur in May 1924. Their association evolved into a genuine friendship after Lovecraft moved to New York in 1924 and the two formed the informal literary and discussion circle, The Kalem Club (so-called because it took the initials of its member's surnames: Rheinhart Kleiner, George Kirk, Samuel Loveman, James Morton, Everett McNeil, Lovecraft and Long). Long was the first to contribute to the Cthulhu Mythos during Lovecraft's lifetime with his tale, 'The Hounds of Tindalos' (1929) and to have his fictional creatures feature in one of Lovecraft's own tales, 'The Whisperer in Darkness' (1931).

When it came to evaluate Dunsany for his extended essay *Supernatural Horror in Literature* (1927), Lovecraft was still unstinting in his praise.

Unexcelled in the sorcery of crystalline singing prose, and supreme in the creation of a gorgeous and languorous world of iridescently exotic vision, is Edward John Moreton Drax Plunkett, Eighteenth Baron Dunsany . . . Inventor of a new mythology and weaver of surprising folklore, Lord Dunsany stands dedicated to a strange world of fantastic beauty, and pledged to eternal warfare against the coarseness and ugliness of diurnal reality. His point of view is the most truly cosmic of any held in the literature of any period. As sensitive as Poe to dramatic values and the significance of isolated words and details, and far better equipped rhetorically through a simple lyric style . . . Beauty rather than terror is the keynote of Dunsany's work. He loves the vivid green of jade and of copper domes, and the delicate flush of sunset on the ivory minarets of impossible dream-cities.

Lovecraft extolled Lord Dunsany for the 'magical prose' of his anthology, *A Dreamer's Tales* – a quality which Lovecraft found sadly lacking in his later work. 'Truly, Dunsany has influenced me more than anyone else except Poe – his rich language, his cosmic point of view, his remote dream-world, and his exquisite sense of the fantastic, all appeal to me more than anything else in modern literature. My first encounter with him – in the autumn of 1919 – gave an immense impetus to my writing; perhaps the greatest it has ever had.' (Letter to Clark Ashton Smith, 30 July 1923). In February 1921, Lovecraft wrote to Elizabeth Toldridge to warmly recommend the following Dunsany tales: 'The Gods of Pegana', 'A Dreamer's Tale', 'The Sword of Welleran', 'The Book of Wonder', and 'Time and the Gods'. 'I know of no other writer who so magically opens up the enchanted sunset gates of secret and ethereal worlds. He influenced me overwhelmingly about a decade ago. I'd be inclined to advise you to read it. It is sheer music, colour, ecstasy, and dream.'

Dunsany's influence is evident in the series of stories set in the Dream Lands. Of these tales – which became known as the Dream Cycle – the most notable were written in a white heat of inspiration in 1919: 'The White Ship', 'The Doom that Came to Sarnath' and 'The Statement of Randolph Carter'. A fourth and fifth – 'The Cats of Ulthar' and 'Celephaïs' – were written the following year and a sixth – 'The Quest of Iranon' – in 1921. To a far lesser extent there are Dunsanian elements to be discerned in the novella, 'At the Mountains of Madness', and several other tales which share this location. Lovecraft's penchant for long convoluted sentences extended by semi-colons is a direct result of his desire to emulate his literary idol, as are his detailed descriptions of fabled cities and allusions to their many marvels which his characters often view from a distance but seldom enter or obtain. It is the inaccessibility of the unspoilt land that lies 'over the hills and far away' that appealed to both writers and the promise of knowledge beyond the reach of mortal men. In that sense they were both visionaries. Dunsany even wrote in a style bordering on biblical pastiche while Lovecraft returned again and again to the theme of mythical mountains and journeys that served as a rite of passage or initiation. However, Lovecraft's dreamscape is not simply another exotic and fanciful realm of the kind envisioned by Dunsany; it's an attempt to contextualise the various levels of awareness he experienced in his own dreams. The fact that it is a largely hostile environment populated by unspeakable terrors indicates that this is how he externalised his inner-state at the time.

Of all the stories that constitute the Dream Cycle, 'The White Ship' may be slight, but it is significant for it reveals a theme underlying many of his Dunsanian tales. As with the myths and legends Lovecraft had read as a boy, these were not written and handed down merely to entertain. The quests undertaken, the temptations resisted and the challenges overcome by the ancient heroes symbolised a rite of passage that was relevant to successive generations, which is why they continue to exert a hold on us today.

The narrator of 'The White Ship', Basil Elton, is the last in a long line of lighthouse keepers whose prolonged isolation has engendered a yearning to experience the world he has never seen and a life he has never known. More truthfully, it is a longing to journey to the worlds and experience the lives that his solitude has prepared him for, like an ascetic who wanders in the desert without food or water in preparation for a vision that will bring insight and enlightenment. And this is precisely what the narrator experiences when his yearning draws the White Ship to shore.

Tellingly, the ship glides smoothly across the water regardless of how stormy the sea might be and if there is an allegorical meaning (albeit an unconscious one) then it's tempting to read the boat as a symbol of Lovecraft's desire to remain in control of his emotions (represented by the tempestuous waters). Certainly, the ship is spectral – manned by unseen oarsmen and steered by a robed and bearded man who acts as navigator and guide to strange and wondrous lands, just as the Cumaean Sibyl acted for Aeneas in his voyage to the underworld in Virgil's *The Aeneid*.

'The White Ship' reads like a Dunsanian fantasy, conceived to instil wonder (Dunsany's most popular collection was *The Book of Wonders*) and a desire for adventure, but on closer analysis reveals itself to be a thinly veiled account of a lucid dream with the titular vessel being symbolic of the soul (or astral body) and the mist through which it passes representing the gateway to the divine flanked by the two pillars of energy and matter (Crowley calls it the abyss which is precisely where Lovecraft's character finds himself). After being guided by the 'bird of heaven' to distant lands, Elton finds himself back where his journey began – at the base of the lighthouse with the wreckage of the white ship shattered on the rocks below (signifying that the experience cannot be repeated). The calendar remains unmarked, indicating that his voyage took place outside of the limits of space and time.

It is possible, of course, to read 'The White Ship' and the other Dream Cycle stories as pure fantasy, as no doubt its empiricist author intended, but if one does so, there is little beyond the evocation of the fantastic to interest one other than admiration for the author's imitation of the Dunsany style. Dunsany's decline from a once fashionable author to an obscure and acquired taste is proof that fantasy – of the fairies and unicorns variety – for its own sake is ultimately unsatisfying and ought to have at least a kernel of an idea at the core if readers are to engage with the characters, the choices they must make and the obstacles they must overcome, otherwise it is a mere vision of the impossible.

Lovecraft knew this instinctively, for there is nothing of the esoteric teachings which occultists call the Mysteries to be read into 'The Doom that Came to Sarnath' (1920), other than the pleasure of a chilling tale well told. Lovecraft may have experienced altered states during the deeper stages of sleep and glimpsed other realities in the reverie of writing, but he refused to entertain the idea that these could be imbued with any deeper occult significance. Hence, 'Sarnath' is related in the manner of a fable told by firelight for the sole purpose of sending the listener into the night with something for their imagination to gnaw upon. 'Another city stood beside the lake; the gray stone city of Ib, which was old as the lake itself, and peopled with beings not pleasing to behold. Very odd and ugly were these beings, as indeed are most beings of a world yet inchoate and rudely fashioned.'

A race of men establish their settlement within sight of the ancient stone city and slaughter the indigenous race, whose idol worship and appearance they abhor. They return with the idol, a trophy of their conquest. 'On the night after it was set up in the temple, a terrible thing must have happened, for weird lights were seen over the lake, and in the morning the people found the idol gone and the high-priest Taran-Ish lying dead, as from some fear unspeakable. And before he died, Taran-Ish had scrawled upon the altar of chrysolite with coarse shaky strokes the sign of DOOM.'

While it is true that the greater part of this tale is exposition, it is the nature of a piece whose primary purpose is to recount the origins of a myth. Character development and suspense are not essential in this context, a vivid description of the setting is all that is required, save for the malicious twist which has the hideous alien species wreak their revenge on the civilisation that had butchered their ancestors a thousand years earlier. Their revenge is all the more disturbing because it sees the overthrow of an ancient civilisation and the resurgence of primeval barbarism.

Where once had risen walls of three hundred cubits and towers yet higher, now stretched only the marshy shore, and where once had dwelt fifty million of men now crawled the detestable water-lizard. Not even the mines of precious metal remained. DOOM had come to Sarnath.

But half buried in the rushes was spied a curious green idol; an exceedingly ancient idol chiseled in the likeness of Bokrug, the great water-lizard. That idol, enshrined in the high temple at Ilarnek, was subsequently worshipped beneath the gibbous moon throughout the land of Mnar.

It is worth noting that these early tales are uncommonly brief – running to an average of 2,500 words – when compared with those of his idols. The stories of Poe, Wells and M.R. James, for example, regularly ran to two or three times that length – all of which refutes the accusation that Lovecraft was verbose, although he could be self-indulgent and prone to ostentation. In truth, he was succinct, typically introducing his protagonist in the opening paragraph, setting the scene in the next and embarking on the main theme before the reader has time to consider other options.

Even while Lovecraft remained under the influence of Lord Dunsany, he was plagued by dreams of a far more troubling nature, one of which formed the basis for his next story, 'The Statement of Randolph Carter'.

In a letter to August Derleth dated 11 December 1919 Lovecraft confessed that he did not have to embellish the dream so much as transcribe it, which may account for the episodic nature of the story. (Although it makes sense if considered as a sequel of sorts to 'The Dream-Quest of Unknown Kadath'; completed in January 1927, this story winds back the clock to when middle-aged Carter was just twenty – this according to the chronology given in 'The Silver Key'). Lovecraft had been discussing weird tales with another correspondent and close friend, Samuel Loveman, who had recommended several 'hair-raising' books that he thought might offer ideas for new stories, but before he had a chance to read them Lovecraft had a dream in which he accompanied Loveman to a neglected cemetery where they broke open an ancient tomb. The following extract from the original letter gives the gist of the story and also reveals that the tone and style of Lovecraft's private correspondence was not dissimilar to that of his prose. In the dream, Loveman insists on exploring the vault alone while his reluctant accomplice waits anxiously above.

> Beneath was a black passageway with a flight of stone steps; but so horrible were the miasmic vapours which poured up from the pit, that we stepped back for a while without making further observations.

Loveman descends into the darkness, taking a telephone and a lantern with him, uncoiling the insulated wire as he goes so he can continue to communicate with his companion. Then the glow of the lantern fades and all is still. After a few minutes the receiver crackles into life:

> 'Lovecraft – I think I'm finding it' – the words came in a tense, excited tone. Then a brief pause, followed by more words in a tone of ineffable awe and horror.
> 'God, Lovecraft! If you could see what I am seeing!' I now asked in great excitement what had happened. Loveman answered in a trembling voice: 'I can't tell you – I don't dare – I never dreamed of this – I can't tell – It's enough to unseat any mind – wait – what's this?'

More silence, then a groan followed by a piercing screech. Loveman urges his companion to save himself but Lovecraft refuses to desert a friend.

> And then came the unbelievably frightful thing – the awful, unexplainable, almost unmentionable thing. I have said that Loveman was now silent, but after a vast interval of terrified waiting another clicking came into the receiver. I called, 'Loveman – are you there?' And in reply came a voice – a thing which I cannot describe by any words I know. Shall I say that it was hollow – very deep – fluid – gelatinous – indefinitely distant – unearthly – guttural – thick? What shall I say? In that telephone I heard it; heard it as I sat on a marble bench in that very ancient unknown cemetery with the crumbling stones and tombs and long grass and dampness and the owl and the waning crescent moon. Up from the sepulchre it came, and this is what it said:
> 'YOU FOOL, LOVEMAN IS DEAD!' . . .
>
> In due time, I intend to weave this picture into a story, as I wove another dream-picture into 'The Doom that Came to Sarnath'. I wonder, though, if I have a right to claim authorship of things I dream?

When he came to compose the story, Loveman was fictionalised in the form of Harley Warren, a rather domineering occultist. Randolph Carter became Lovecraft's alter-ego, an antiquarian and explorer of the dream worlds in which he lives a second life. Warren's fate, it seems, was sealed the moment he came into possession of a grimoire, a manual of ritual magic which contained the 'barbarous words of invocation' for opening portals to other dimensions. In his eagerness to explore these alternate realities, the arrogant occultist failed to consider the possibility that demonic beings might be drawn to these gateways and gain entry into our world. Warren was therefore excluded from any further adventures.

Carter, however, would appear in a further four stories: 'The Unnamable', 'The Dream-Quest of Unknown Kadath', 'The Silver Key' and 'Through The Gates of the Silver Key' (written in collaboration with E. Hoffmann Price). He would also make what amounted to a fleeting cameo appearance in 'Out of the Aeons' (written in 1933 in collaboration with writer Hazel Heald) as a visitor to a Boston museum in the guise of Swami Chandraputra.

Lovecraft's dream cycle and his cosmic horrors (posthumously collated and named the Cthulhu Mythos by August Derleth) have somewhat overshadowed his light Dunsanian fantasies. And yet, Lovecraft named the finest of these among his personal favourites.

'The Cats of Ulthar' (1920) was written in a single day the month after the first Randolph Carter story was published in *The Vagrant*. Although it reads like the outline for a typical EC horror comic of the 1950s (which owed a great debt to Lovecraft and his *Weird Tales* collaborators), it is told in the archaic language of the Grimm fairy tales. 'In Ulthar, before ever the burgesses forbade the killing of cats, there dwelt an old cotter and his wife who delighted to trap and slay the cats of their neighbours.'

The townspeople know who is responsible for the death of their pets, but they are too afraid of the elderly couple to accuse them. Then one day a troupe of Romany gypsies passes through the town and in one gaily coloured caravan a sad-eyed boy is seen cradling a kitten. When the kitten disappears, the boy is seen to perform an invocation in the town square which draws the clouds together in ominous forms. That same night the caravan rolls out of Ulthar. No cat can be found. The next morning all the cats return, but there is no sign of the hated old couple.

> In another week the burgomaster decided to overcome his fears and call at the strangely silent dwelling as a matter of duty, though in so doing he was careful to take with him Shang the blacksmith and Thul the cutter of stone as witnesses. And when they had broken down the frail door they found only this: two cleanly picked human skeletons on the earthen floor, and a number of singular beetles crawling in the shadowy corners.

The penultimate Dunsanian fable in terms of tone and its fabulous setting was 'Celephaïs' (November 1920), though the central idea bears a strong resemblance to H.G. Wells' 'The Door in the Wall'

(1911) in that it concerns the central character's lifelong obsession with returning to the world of his childhood dreams. Wells' story offers visions of a fabulous garden, whereas in Lovecraft's tale it is an ageless paradise in which the unnamed dreamer is crowned the god-king Kuranes. But though Kuranes has attained everything he dreamt of, he grows homesick. When Randolph Carter visits his kingdom in 'The Dream-Quest of Unknown Kadath', he warns Carter to be careful what he wishes for.

If Carter was the author's fearless, but flawed alter-ego, it is tempting to see the self-pitying monarch of the changeless city as the poet-dreamer Lovecraft wished he could have become. 'His money and lands were gone, and he did not care for the ways of the people about him, but preferred to dream and write of his dreams. What he wrote was laughed at by those to whom he showed it, so that after a time he kept his writings to himself . . . The more he withdrew from the world about him, the more wonderful became his dreams.'

The last of Lovecraft's Dunsanian fables was 'The Quest of Iranon', written on the last day of February, 1921. It is an exotic fable with a simple theme; that which gives us hope, keeps us youthful. Without dreams to sustain us, life is not worth the living. Iranon is a handsome young man whose pleasant appearance and cheerful disposition endear him to everyone he meets, though they doubt his claims to having once been prince of the mythical city of Aira.

However the inhabitants of Teloth (where he chooses to settle) have no need of a workshy dreamer who seems to be expressing the author's disdain for mundane employment. 'Wherefore do ye toil; is it not that ye may live and be happy? And if ye toil only that ye may toil more, when shall happiness find you? Ye toil to live, but is not life made of beauty and song? And if ye suffer no singers among you, where shall be the fruits of your toil? Toil without song is like a weary journey without an end. Were not death more pleasing?'

After the boy befriends an outcast named Romnod the pair decide to travel in search of Aira, which Romnod believes may be the city more commonly known as Oonai. Iranon is sceptical, but agrees to join his friend on the journey which extends over many years. During this time, Romnod ages while Iranon remains unchanged.

When they reach Oonai they discover it is not Aira, but they remain because Iranon is once again celebrated for his songs and exotic tales. Romnod, however, gives in to disillusionment and despair, taking to drink while Iranon is eventually shunned by the people who once loved him because he has lingered too long in their midst; his stories are no longer novel and his songs have become familiar. When Romnod dies, Iranon continues his search for Aira, but when he comes upon an old shepherd and asks for directions he learns the truth of his lowly origins and is distraught to hear that the fabled city of his dreams was nothing but his childish fantasy which no one had believed and that is why he had run away.

The youthful visionary is revealed to be nothing more than a vain fantasist and by implication, the stern-faced citizens of the cheerless city of square plain granite are vindicated in their belief that life is nothing but suffering and toil.

If Dunsany and Lovecraft seem like unlikely travelling companions, it needs to be remembered that it was the final line in Dunsany's tale 'The Probable Adventure of the Three Literary Men' which gave rise, albeit indirectly, to the Cthulhu Mythos: 'Slith, knowing well why that light was lit in that secret chamber and *who* it was that lit it, leaped over the edge of the World and is falling from us still through the unreverberate blackness of the abyss.'

'Amateur journalism has provided me with the very world in which I live.'
Aged 25, Lovecraft poses for a formal portrait – as featured in the United Amateur
Press Association.

Clockwise from top-left: The Lovecrafts' only surviving family portrait shows proud parents Susan and Winfield with baby Howard, 1892; Dated February 1892, this is the earliest known photo of Howard, aged around six months; HPL in November 1892. His feminine dress was typical for infant sons of the middle and upper classes; Lovecraft, c. 1892: around the time the family would have been lodging with poetess Louise Guiney.

Opposite, clockwise from top-left: 'I never heard oral weird tales except from my grandfather – who used to devise all sorts of impromptu yarns about black woods, unfathomed caves, winged horrors and old witches.' Whipple Van Buren Phillips, the 'beloved' grandfather who instilled in Howard a lifelong love of gothic literature; 'The children I knew disliked me, and I disliked them.' A sailor-suit-clad Howard aged between four and five – when even second cousin Ethel found him reserved and far too serious a playmate; Lovecraft's first home at 194 Angell Street, Providence. In such grandiose surroundings, HPL began to fantasise that he was born of a long line of 'unmixed English gentry'.

Clockwise from top-left: 'With the advent of the United, I obtained a renewed will to live.' Lovecraft's United Amateur Press Association portrait, 1915; Alternate UAPA portrait, also taken around 1915; With future Kalem Club member Rheinhart Kleiner, 30 June 1919. Behind them is the house Lovecraft shared with his ailing mother at 598 Angell Street – considerably smaller than his first home at the Phillips mansion; 'Hon. L. Theobald, junr on steps of Conservative office,' scrawled HPL on the back of this photo from summer 1919 – also outside 598 Angell Street.

Clockwise from top-left: *'Theobaldus in a Georgian setting,' wrote Lovecraft on the back of this image, taken 30 June 1919; HPL labelled this 1919 photo, 'Rev. Fr. Lovecraft'; Amongst ruined columns, 4 July 1920; Lovecraft summed up this scene as: 'Theobald against a typical Georgian background'.*

Clockwise from top-left: Annie Emeline Phillips Gamwell – his mother Susan's sister and one of the two aunts who helped raise HPL after the death of his father; Sonia Haft Greene. When she first met Lovecraft in 1921, she was a single mother and a high-earning milliner. A male acquaintance described the brunette beauty as the very embodiment of a Dostoyevsky heroine; Howard and Sonia in Boston, 5 July 1921: shortly after their first meeting at an amateur press convention; In October 1921, Sonia launched The Rainbow, *an elegantly designed amateur journal to which Howard and his circle of New York intellectuals would contribute.*

Clockwise from top: *Lovecraft and William J. Dowdell, outside the Hotel Brunswick, Boston, 5 July 1921. Dowdell was publisher of* The Bearcat *and a keen member of the National Amateur Press Association. Lovecraft was active in this amateur association as well as UAPA. Though he considered himself to be a loyal 'United man' he joined the NAPA in an endeavour to bring the rival organisations together; Travelling man: Lovecraft visits Magnolia, Massachusetts in August 1922. Though frequently portrayed as a recluse, HPL was willing to leave his beloved Providence in pursuit of fresh correspondents and fascinating historical sites; The future couple pose for a second shot, 5 July 1921.*

Clockwise from top-left: Enjoying a joke with George Julian Houtain, 5 July 1921. Houtain was editor of Home Brew, *the 'vile rag' that was to publish 'Herbert West: Reanimator' the following year; Harold B. Munroe and HPL, 7 September 1921. Harold – who went on to become Deputy Sheriff of Providence – and his brother Chester were childhood friends from Howard's days at Slater Avenue; With Charles W. Heins and W. Paul Cook, July 1921.*

CHAPTER FOUR

A TRUE EPICURE OF THE TERRIBLE

'Pleasure to me is wonder – the unexplored,
the unexpected, the thing that is hidden and the
changeless thing that lurks behind superficial mutability.
To trace the remote in the immediate; the eternal in the
ephemeral; the past in the present; the infinite in the finite;
these are to me the springs of delight and beauty.'
– H.P. Lovecraft

Few writers set out to master a specific genre, although most have an inkling of what their forte might be. Lovecraft was no exception. In the spring of 1919, having experimented with supernatural horror and fantasy, he took the first tentative step into an alternative universe with 'Memory'. Weighing in at less than 1,000 words, this evocative piece of flash fiction offers a fleeting glimpse of the primeval past – or post-apocalyptic future – in the shadowed valley of Nis. Choked with 'evil vines' and 'creeping plants,' the ancient ruins described here are suggestive of decay rather than destruction. Absent are the devastated cities and technological remnants envisaged by H.G. Wells in *The Time Machine* (1895). Instead, Lovecraft conjures a menacing, Sumerian-style civilisation, filled with 'ruined palaces' of stone, broken columns, strange monoliths, marble pavements, crumbling courtyards and treasure vaults. The implication is that the fate that befell the human inhabitants of this world was nothing more than the inexorable march of the ages. Time simply ran out. It is the first indication of the author's pessimism as regards progress – symptomatic of his increasingly nihilistic worldview.

> The Genie that haunts the moonbeams spake to the Demon of the Valley, saying, 'I am old, and forget much. Tell me the deeds and aspect and name of them who built these things of Stone.' And the Demon replied, 'I am Memory, and am wise in lore of the past, but I too am old. These beings were like the waters of the river Than, not to be understood. Their deeds I recall not, for they were but of the moment. Their aspect I recall dimly, it was like to that of the little apes in the trees. Their name I recall clearly, for it rhymed with that of the river. These beings of yesterday were called Man.'

'Memory' is a self-contained fragment that doesn't qualify as a short story, but it is noteworthy for offering the first glimpse of an alternate reality presided over by indifferent gods – one Lovecraft wasn't ready to develop just yet.

At some point during the same year he wrote 'Old Bugs', the very definition of a shaggy dog story and a mildly entertaining one at that. It was not intended for publication, but to amuse his young friend Alfred Galpin who had declared his intention of sampling the demon alcohol before Prohibition made it illegal to do so and to serve as a warning of what might happen if Alfred imbibed too often. Galpin was a precocious intellectual whom Lovecraft greatly admired and was proud to acknowledge as his philosophical superior, despite being ten years his senior. When they first began corresponding Galpin was sixteen and responsible for recruiting high school students into amateur journalism. He would become a teacher, philosopher and composer, but it was the intensity of his adolescent crushes which seems to have amused Lovecraft who was inspired to write several humorous poems on the subject.

'Bugs' may be little more than an after-dinner yarn, but it demonstrates that Lovecraft could have turned his hand to the kind of tale published by the *Saturday Evening Post*, *Colliers* or *The American* had he wished to contribute to the mainstream magazine market. Had he done so, he might have cultivated a lucrative career and established a name that would have ensured publication of his books. He would have avoided the penury that plagued him in later life and might even have saved his marriage, if that had been his wish. But perhaps, of more significance to Lovecraft, it would have offered him entry into the New York intellectual elite whose fellowship might have been the making of him. It was perhaps, the single most significant lost opportunity of his life; one he didn't pursue because he suspected that he was not as great a writer as he wanted to be. 'Bugs' – however slight – suggests that he could have become another Joseph C. Lincoln, Ogden Nash, or – better still – Ray Bradbury, and still pursued his own interests.

> The disposition of Old Bugs was as odd as his aspect. Ordinarily he was true to the derelict type – ready to do anything for a nickel or a dose of whiskey or hasheesh – but at rare intervals he shewed the traits which earned him his name. Then he would try to straighten up, and a certain fire would creep into the sunken eyes. His demeanour would assume an unwonted grace and even dignity; and the sodden creatures around him would sense something of superiority – something which made them less ready to give the usual kicks and cuffs to the poor butt and drudge.

A similarly comical piece, but one that was mannered and forced is 'Sweet Ermengarde' (or 'The Heart of a Country Girl'). It is credited to 'Percy Simple' (Lovecraft's pet name for the popular writer Fred Jackson whose insipid romances he despised) and probably also originates from 1919, though it remained unpublished until 1943, when it finally appeared in the Arkham House anthology, *Beyond the Wall of Sleep*.

'The Transition of Juan Romero', written on 16 September that same year, was more serious and substantial. It began promisingly with a former British army officer and a Mexican miner investigating a rhythmic throbbing sound which emitted from a deep chasm that had opened up in their shaft. It was an early attempt at weird fiction although its author disowned the story as soon as he had completed it. It seems likely that he simply hated the fact that he couldn't think of a satisfying climax.

As he would do repeatedly over the course of his writing career, Lovecraft threw in a fleeting reference to a dreaded deity, in this case Huitzilopochtli (the Aztec god of war and human sacrifice) to suggest that the protagonists have enraged a vengeful spirit whose presence and appearance does not require further description or explanation. 'At first I beheld nothing but a seething blur of luminosity; but then shapes, all infinitely distant, began to detach themselves from the confusion, and I saw – was it Juan Romero? – *but God! I dare not tell you what I saw!* . . . Some power from heaven, coming to my aid, obliterated both sights and sounds in such a crash as may be heard when two universes collide in space. Chaos supervened, and I knew the peace of oblivion.'

Although Lovecraft resorts to what might appear to be a lazy plot device - the protagonist's suggestion that it may all have been 'a mere dream' – it is soon clear that this is not the case. The rhythmic throbbing is heard again signifying that Huitzilopochtli's vengeance has not been satiated. 'In broad daylight, and at most seasons I am apt to think the greater part of it a mere dream; but sometimes in the autumn, about two in the morning when the winds and animals howl dismally, there comes from inconceivable depths below a damnable suggestion of rhythmical throbbing . . . and I feel that the transition of Juan Romero was a terrible one indeed.'

Lovecraft's racism reared its ugly head once more in the prosaically titled, 'The Street' (1919), which would not have left such a nasty taste in the mouth had it focussed solely on the Russian anarchists' political aims and not used their bombing campaign as an excuse to attack immigration.

New kinds of faces appeared in the Street, swarthy, sinister faces with furtive eyes and odd features, whose owners spoke unfamiliar words and placed signs in known and unknown characters upon most of the musty houses. Push-carts crowded the gutters. A sordid, undefinable stench settled over the place, and the ancient spirit slept.

The story had a sound historical basis in London's Sydney Street siege of 1911, the New York parcel bombings of 1919 and the Boston

Police strike that same year, but it is his suggestion that the influx of immigrants was akin to a plague infesting American society and that immigration itself would undermine western civilisation that makes it such an uncomfortable read.

1920 marked a significant turning point in the career and fortunes of H.P. Lovecraft with the publication of his first significant stories – 'The Statement of Randolph Carter', 'The Cats of Ulthar', 'The Doom that Came to Sarnath' – and the writing of three more noteworthy tales: 'The Terrible Old Man', 'Arthur Jermyn' and 'The Picture in The House', which together established his voice and reputation as a writer to watch. His involvement in the amateur movement had evidently galvanised him, giving him purpose and a reason to write.

The year began with attempts at writing straight supernatural horror fiction and ended with the creation of what would posthumously be known as the Cthulhu Mythos (a term coined by August Derleth to denote a series of nominally connected stories which shared the same fictional locations presided over by a pantheon of elder gods known as the Great Old Ones. Cthulhu was, despite his prominence in the mythos, a lesser deity: hence his subjugation and imprisonment in the sunken city of R'lyeh. Presiding over the Great Old Ones are the Outer Gods of which Azathoth was the supreme deity. At one point Lovecraft drew up a genealogy for his own amusement which was subsequently published in *Selected Letters* as number 617. However, their creator never expressed the desire to classify them as such. Lovecraft simply referred to these stories as his Arkham cycle, as they all took place in and around the fictional town of that name, though he would also refer to them disparagingly as his 'Yog-Sothothery' whenever he felt that others were taking it all far too seriously.)

It is not known precisely when Lovecraft wrote 'The Tree', but it is likely to have preceded the quintet of conventional horror tales ('The Terrible Old Man', 'From Beyond', 'The Temple', 'The Picture in the House' and 'Facts Concerning the Late Arthur Jermyn and his Family') written that year.

'The Tree' – written in 1920 and published in the *Tryout* the following year – is a deceptively simple tale of two master sculptors in ancient Greece whose friendship is contaminated by a despot for his own perverse amusement. He commands each of them to create a sculpture knowing that it will create a bitter rivalry between them. When one of them dies from an unexplained illness, the other plants an olive twig over his sepulchre which grows into a contorted tree, suggestive of a soul in agony. After the surviving sculptor completes his statue, the heavy bough breaks killing him – the implication being that his dead friend has finally taken his revenge. However, there is no explicit reference to murder and it is this masterly understatement which makes the story so effective.

'But the olive grove still stands, as does the tree growing out of the tomb of Kalos, and the old bee-keeper told me that sometimes the boughs whisper to one another in the night wind, saying over and over again. "Oida! Oida! – I know! I know!"'

'The Terrible Old Man' is notable for its contemporary New England setting – the first time its author used the location that would become known as Lovecraft Country. The fictional town of Kingsport was just a name at this point. When it was used as the setting for 'The Festival'(October 1923) it would be described in greater detail and be modelled on the colonial town of Marblehead, Massachusetts, which Lovecraft visited in December 1922. What promises to be just another tale of grisly revenge is enriched by typical Lovecraftian touches, phenomena which are never rationalized or fully defined.

'These folk say that on a table in a bare room on the ground floor are many peculiar bottles, in each a small piece of lead suspended pendulum-wise from a string. And they say that the Terrible Old Man talks to these bottles, addressing them by such names as Jack, Scar-Face, Long Tom, Spanish Joe, Peters, and Mate Ellis, and that whenever he speaks to a bottle the little lead pendulum within makes certain definite vibrations as if in answer.'

It isn't necessary for the nature of the old man's magic to be explained. Nor does the reader expect it to be. As with the quintessentially English ghost stories of M.R. James – another master of fretful imaginings and indefinable impressions – the sense of unease is intensified, when the nature of the malevolent presence is left purposely vague.

But the tale is weakened by inconsistencies in language and an uneven tone which describes one of the thieves as 'more than ordinarily tender-hearted' and mentions that 'he did not like the hideous screams he had heard in the ancient house'. Juxtaposing so strong an adjective as 'hideous' with 'like' – a mild reaction that is more in keeping with a preference – suggests that its author did not consider it necessary to revise the text after completing the first draft. The fact that many of these early short stories were written in a single day also suggests that might have been the case. And yet again, the ending is so artless and effective that criticism of this nature seems positively churlish. 'In this idle village gossip the Terrible Old Man took no interest at all. He was by nature reserved, and when one is aged and feeble, one's reserve is doubly strong. Besides, so ancient a sea-captain must have witnessed scores of things much more stirring in the far-off days of his unremembered youth.'

Lovecraft's archaic choice of language was part of his appeal for those who appreciated such things. It was indicative of the fact that he always considered himself a man out of time, the last real gentleman in an age of the common man. It was his great conceit, the fantasy with which he justified his withdrawal from society and with which he explained the comparative obscurity under which he laboured during his lifetime. He was right, however, in one respect. The world, or at least the commercial world, was not yet ready for monsters who lived on Main Street or slavering tentacled abominations bursting forth to reclaim the realm that had once been theirs. Weird fiction was still a niche market restricted to 25-cent pulps specialising in science fiction, crime and detective titles.

'From Beyond' was a case in point, a story that would have been ideal for *The Twilight Zone* or *The Outer Limits* had TV existed in the '20s and the networks not been afraid of upsetting the sponsors. It invites comparison with H.G. Wells' story, 'The Remarkable Case of Davidson's Eyes', in which a laboratory technician is afflicted with visions of a location on the other side of the world. Only in Lovecraft's tale the scientist, Crawford Tillinghast, invents an electronic device that stimulates the pineal gland, believed by occultists to be the organ of psychic sight, and at the climax shares his visions with the narrator. 'Suddenly I myself became possessed of a kind of augmented sight. Over and above the luminous and shadowy chaos arose a picture which, though vague, held the elements of consistency and permanence. It was indeed somewhat familiar, for the unusual part was superimposed upon the usual terrestrial scene much as a cinema view may be thrown upon the painted curtain of a theater.'

Unfortunately, at this point Lovecraft attempts to ramp up the tension by having Tillinghast deliver an hysterical speech that descends into a shrill rant. 'You were afraid of the cosmic truth, you damned coward, but now I've got you! . . . I tell you, I have struck depths that your little brain can't picture. I have seen beyond the bounds of infinity and drawn down demons from the stars . . . I have harnessed the shadows that stride from world to world to sow death and madness . . . Space belongs to me, do you hear?'

The ending too, is contrived and clichéd. The narrator draws a revolver, they struggle, the gun goes off but the bullet hits the machine and destroys it, causing Tillinghast to suffer a fatal heart attack. *Twilight Zone* creator Rod Serling might have accepted it, but its author knew that it was not up to his own exacting standards.

'The Temple' could be seen as a companion piece as it shares a similar tone. It even features a fanatical central character whose comic strip dialogue ('English pig-dogs', 'superstitious Alsatian swine', etc.) makes him a caricature. Such phrases, however, constitute the only forced element in an otherwise compelling tale of retribution with an unusual variation on a well-worn theme. During World War One, a merciless German U-Boat captain is lured to his death by a mysterious artefact taken from the body of an allied seaman whose crewmates he has murdered. It affects both the crew and the navigation system of the submarine which is drawn – as by a supernatural homing signal – to the remains of a sunken city of 'immemorially ancient splendour' to which the artefact must be returned. It falls on the captain, the last survivor of the cursed U-boat, to perform this task and in doing so redeem himself. And yet, even as he prepares to meet his death, he tries to rationalise what he has seen.

What I have seen cannot be true, and I know that this madness of my own will at most lead only to suffocation when my air is gone. The light in the temple is a sheer delusion, and I shall die calmly like a German, in the black and forgotten depths. This demoniac laughter which I hear as I write comes only from my own weakening brain. So I will carefully don my suit and walk boldly up the steps into the primal shrine, that silent secret of unfathomed waters and uncounted years.

Writers invariably create their most individual work when inspired by their elusive muse – a more fanciful way of saying that their best ideas usually come when they stop trying too hard and allow the still, small voice of their subconscious to be heard. Lovecraft was no different in that respect, but there was one occasion when sheer boredom provided the basis for a good story. 'Facts Concerning the Late Arthur Jermyn and his Family' (1920) arose from a failed attempt to interest himself in the prosaic prose of 'the iconoclast moderns', specifically Sherwood Anderson whose short story sequence, *Winesburg, Ohio* almost sent him off to sleep: 'it occurred to me that I, in my weirder medium, could probably devise some secret behind a man's ancestry which would make the worst of Anderson's disclosures sound like the annual report of a Sabbath school. Hence "Arthur Jermyn,"' Lovecraft explained in a 1923 letter to Edwin Baird, the first editor of *Weird Tales* magazine.

The result was the very definition of 'weird fiction' with more than a whiff of unspeakable practices. Arthur Jermyn had descended from a long line of anthropologists and explorers whose physical appearance bore a singularly simian cast. After he commissions an agent to purchase the mummified body of a white ape, rumoured to be the goddess worshiped by the inhabitants of a lost city, Arthur discovers the awful truth of his ancestry. It is said that the truth can set you free, but in the case of Arthur Jermyn it is sufficient to drive him to self-immolation and his creator to conceive his fatalistic philosophy which he named cosmicism. Essentially an extension of Lovecraft's atheism, cosmicism states that all deities are nothing more than projections of man's own egotism, whilst stressing the insignificance of humanity. In the grand scheme of the cosmos, man's efforts are doomed to failure and his aspirations are all for nothing – in this or any other dimension.

> Life is a hideous thing, and from the background behind what we know of it peer daemoniacal hints of truth which make it sometimes a thousandfold more hideous . . . If we knew what we are, we should do as Sir Arthur Jermyn did; and Arthur Jermyn soaked himself in oil and set fire to his clothing one night. No one placed the charred fragments in an urn or set a memorial to him who had been; for certain papers and a certain boxed object were found which made men wish to forget. Some who knew him do not admit that he ever existed.

'Arthur Jermyn' gave its author the licence to tackle another taboo in his next offering: that of cannibalism. 'I had been travelling for some time amongst the people of the Miskatonic Valley in quest of certain genealogical data . . . Now I found myself upon an apparently abandoned road which I had chosen as the shortest cut to Arkham.'

So begins 'The Picture in the House', the last horror tale of 1920 (written in mid-December that year) and the first to mention two of the most important locations in Lovecraft Country. One suspects that this opening was written partly to justify the choice of setting to those who demanded a location as fantastic as the creatures that inhabit it. But Lovecraft had finally come to realise that the apparent normality of a location heightens the horror that takes place there – something which successive writers have also acknowledged and capitalised on – and continue to do so.

'Searchers after horror haunt strange, far places . . . But the true epicure of the terrible, to whom a new thrill of unutterable ghastliness is the chief end and justification of existence, esteem most of all the ancient, lonely farmhouses of backwoods New England; for there the dark elements of strength, solitude, grotesqueness, and ignorance combine to form the perfection of the hideous.'

Having tantalised us with the mention of Arkham and Miskatonic Valley, Lovecraft makes no further mention of them, leaving the reader to fear that the events he describes are not uncommon in the region and that the character at the centre of the story might have his counterparts elsewhere in that locality. Lovecraft clearly delighted in putting Yankee dialogue in the old feller's mouth and the contrast between his rustic charm and his unpleasant eating habits makes the topic more readily digestible. 'They say meat makes blood an' flesh, an' gives ye new life, so I wondered ef 'twudn't make a man live longer an' longer ef 'twas more the same.'

While incidents of cannibalism were known to have taken place in the old west (the Donner Party – a hapless group of pioneers who became stranded in the perilous mountains of the Sierra Nevada – being a particularly horrific example), the notion that a serial killer might be luring travellers to their deaths in the backwoods of New England – with a view to *eating* them – was unheard of in the twenties. The crimes of notorious grave-robbing ghoul Ed Gein and his ilk were still decades away from being uncovered and so the notion was a daringly original idea for a story. Regardless of the sensational subject matter, Lovecraft manages to maintain an atmosphere of brooding menace throughout, tightening the tension until the last paragraph when a single drop of blood falls onto the book the narrator is holding, prompting him to look up and see the red stain on the ceiling. 'I thought of the rain and of a leaky roof, but rain is not red.'

In addition to these solo efforts, Lovecraft also undertook collaborations with an array of different authors. Some were up-and-coming young authors – talented unknowns in whom he saw great promise – but he also accepted clients for purely financial reasons, some of whom were 'pathetically in need of some cheering influence' as well as 'genuine beginners who need a start'. He was never less than polite and encouraging, even to those whose prose and pamphleteering smacked of vanity and self-deception. In private, however, the worst offenders received short shrift, especially those who had exploited his good nature by refusing to settle their accounts on time. He justified his willingness to work on these by saying: 'When I revised the kindergarten pap and idiot-asylum slop of other fishes, I was, in a microscopic way, putting just the faintest bit of order, coherence, direction and comprehensible language into something whose Neanderthaloid ineptitude was already mapped out. My work, ignominious as it was, was at least in the right direction-making that which was utterly amorphous and drooling just the minutest trifle less close to the protozoan stage.'

Few of Lovecraft's collaborations were entirely successful, primarily because they were not genuine partnerships. Other people's dreams rarely make for original tales because the writer has no personal experience to draw upon, just a second-hand anecdote with little sense of the impression it had on the dreamer. His two joint efforts with Winifred V. Jackson were a case in point.

Lovecraft's chosen co-author was fourteen years his senior and a divorcee, but by all accounts a striking looking woman. Her appearance led to rumours among their amateur contemporaries that she was 'fond' of Lovecraft and that there might even be a romance in the offing. If there was any truth in this story, then Howard was a very discreet lover indeed. In his accounts of visits to her neighbourhood in Boston, he makes no mention of Winifred at all. Even supposing he was smitten and desirous of a more intimate relationship, it is extremely doubtful that she would have abandoned her long-term lover, the black poet William Braithwaite. Most intriguing of all is Sonia Greene's claim that she 'stole' Lovecraft from Jackson, although this may be a mere conceit on her part. Jackson later published two books of verse, but is chiefly remembered for being one of only two women to collaborate with Lovecraft.

Their first joint effort was 'The Green Meadow' (c. 1919), for which Jackson supplied the inspiration. It centres on the disorientation and dread experienced by an unidentified narrator who describes his arrival on a strange shoreline which is clearly not of this earth and where he senses that he is being watched by unseen malevolent beings.

'I saw clearly the *source* of the chanting, and in one horrible instant remembered everything. Of such things I cannot, dare not tell, for therein was revealed the hideous solution of all which had puzzled me; and that solution would drive you mad, even as it almost drove me . . . I knew now the change through which I had passed, and through which certain others who once were men had passed!'

The end alludes to imprisonment in eternal limbo in the dream world, although what he has done to deserve this fate is not explained. 'I shall live forever, be conscious forever, though my soul cries out to the gods for the boon of death and oblivion. . . . All is before me: beyond the deafening torrent lies the land of Stethelos, where young men are infinitely old.' (At this point, it's worth noting that the city of Stethelos is referred to in 'The Quest of Iranon'.)

Their second joint project, 'The Crawling Chaos' (1920) poses the question, 'when is collaboration nothing of the sort?' The answer being, when one of the partners does all the work and the other merely supplies the idea. In the case of 'The Crawling Chaos' the silent partner contributed the surreal imagery for the central character's drug-induced vision leaving Lovecraft to write the text. He also supplied the title which he took from the opening paragraph of 'Nyarlathotep' ('because I liked the sound of it'), although this malignant deity is conspicuously absent from the story. For this reason – and the fact that the vision does not live up to the promise of its opening – it will disappoint anyone anticipating the grotesque vistas described by Charles Baudelaire, Théophile Gautier or Gérard de Nerval.

It begins with a description of the hallucinogenic effects of opium and the fabulous vistas that those who ingest it can expect to see, before presenting the first scene in what the reader expects will be a wondrous journey. 'Gradually I realised my solitary presence in a strange and beautiful room lighted by many windows. Of the exact nature of the apartment I could form no idea, for my thoughts were still far from settled; but I noticed vari-coloured rugs and draperies, elaborately fashioned tables, chairs, ottomans, and divans, and delicate vases and ornaments which conveyed a suggestion of the exotic without being actually alien . . . Slowly but inexorably crawling upon my consciousness, and rising above every other impression, came a dizzying fear of the unknown; a fear all the greater because I could not analyse it, and seeming to concern a stealthily approaching menace – not death, but some nameless, unheard-of thing inexpressibly more ghastly and abhorrent.'

Even allowing for the fact that the foregoing is little more than an isolated fragment, there is no emotional core or drama, just a sequence of fanciful images as insubstantial as a dream, inhabited by singing cherubs who invite the narrator to ascend to the upper worlds. But then like Orpheus, the legendary musician and poet of Greek myth who ventures into the Underworld to rescue his beloved Eurydice, he ignores their warning and looks earthward whereupon he witnesses the destruction of the world.

'Around the northern pole steamed a morass of noisome growths and miasmal vapours, hissing before the onslaught of the ever-mounting waves that curled and fretted from the shuddering deep. Then a rending report clave the night, and athwart the desert of deserts appeared a smoking rift.'

This apocalyptic climax is the story's only redeeming feature, with its vivid image of global devastation from a god's perspective.

'And when the smoke cleared away, and I sought to look upon the earth, I beheld against the background of cold, humorous stars only the dying sun and the pale mournful planets searching for their sister.'

It was published in the April 1921 issue of *United Cooperative* under the pennames, Elizabeth Berkeley and Lewis Theobald, Jnr.

His only other known collaboration with a female writer was 'Poetry of the Gods', whose authorship is questionable to say the least. It simply does not sound like Lovecraft, but more like his co-author, Anna Helen Crofts, judging by its elegant drawing room character (which was not in keeping with Lovecraft's robust style) and its rambling philosophical monologues given by the great poets of antiquity. It would seem more likely that she sent him the piece for his approval and gave him co-credit for suggesting certain unspecified changes.

CHAPTER FIVE

SHADOWS RUN LIKE INK

'That is not dead which can eternal lie,
And with strange aeons death may die.'
– Abdul Alhazred, 'The Nameless City'

It's fitting that Lovecraft should name-check his erudite childhood alter-ego in 'The Nameless City' for the kernel of this story surely came from *Sinbad* and the many Arabian adventures he had entertained himself with in his grandfather's library as well as a description of the lost city of Iram that he had found in the Quran.

The nameless narrator of Lovecraft's tale comes upon a city buried in the sand. Though oppressed by a sense of foreboding, he presses on until he uncovers the entrance to a temple. The uncommonly low ceiling, inhuman proportions and odd dimensions disturb him, and he wonders if the architects could possibly have been human. On finding a second temple and descending into the impenetrable blackness, he comes upon a chamber decorated with murals of 'daringly fantastic designs', containing the mummified remains of lizard-headed creatures with forelegs similar to human hands. They are all the more grotesque because they have been dressed in robes and adorned with jewellery. He assumes they have been placed there by human inhabitants, but when he reaches the end of the subterranean labyrinth and pushes open a massive brass door, the truth is finally revealed. 'Only the grim brooding desert gods know what really took place – what indescribable struggles and scrambles in the dark I endured or what Abaddon guided me back to life, where I must always remember and shiver in the night wind till oblivion – or worse – claims me. Monstrous, unnatural, colossal, was the thing – too far beyond all the ideas of man to be believed except in the silent damnable small hours of the morning when one cannot sleep.'

The germ of the story came in a dream Lovecraft had had shortly after reading a phrase from Dunsany's 'The Probable Adventure of the Three Literary Men'. 'The unreverberate blackness of the abyss' was the line that appealed to him and as he repeated it to himself, images of the fabled lost city of Iram arose before him as if reclaimed from the desert sand.

Other authors have used this method to generate ideas during their sleep, most notably Charlotte Brontë, Robert Louis Stevenson and Graham Greene. When Brontë was asked how she could describe the effects of opium so accurately without having taken the drug, she replied that whenever she had to write about something outside her experience she would brood on it night after night in the certainty that she would live it in her dreams. Stevenson developed the art of what is now known as creative dreaming, or dream incubation, when he was in desperate need of money. He would begin a story as he lay in bed, trusting in his 'brownies' (night elves) to supply the rest in his sleep. A hundred years later, Greene would read through what he had written that day in the belief that his subconscious would revise it and provide the next chapter. A similar technique would be adopted by lucid dreamers who claim to be able to take control of their dreams once they realise that what they are experiencing cannot be real.

Decades on, master horror novelist Stephen King compared the creative process to a waking dream. 'In both writing and sleeping, we learn to be physically still at the same time we are encouraging our minds to unlock from the humdrum rational thinking of our daytime lives,' he mused in *On Writing: A Memoir of the Craft* (2000). 'And as your mind and body grow accustomed to a certain amount of sleep each night – six hours, seven, maybe the recommended eight – so can you train your waking mind to sleep creatively and work out the vividly imagined waking dreams which are successful works of fiction.'

Lovecraft practiced a similar method for incubating dreams, by reading until he was utterly exhausted. In this way, his mind became saturated with impressions from his chosen text rather than trivialities from his waking hours.

Lovecraft attempted the tale twice before finding the appropriate tone – one of eager anticipation and of profane secrets awaiting discovery – and appears to have included both opening paragraphs after seeing that they could work sequentially. The opening line of the first augurs ill for the narrator. 'When I drew nigh the nameless city I knew it was accursed.' But the beginning of the second is more evocative. 'Remote in the desert of Araby lies the nameless city, crumbling and inarticulate, its low walls nearly hidden by the sands of uncounted ages.'

Lovecraft critics have sneered at the flamboyant, self-conscious style he adopted for this story, calling it ham-fisted and seriously flawed – and there is no denying that it would have benefitted from a judicious edit to reduce the excessive exposition, excise the superfluous descriptive detail and to trim the meandering sentences that would have been more effective at half the length. Yet for all the story's shortcomings, there are many memorable images and lyrical passages to commend it. 'When I came upon it in the ghastly stillness of unending sleep it looked at me, chilly from the rays of a cold moon amidst the desert's heat. And as I returned its look I forgot my triumph at finding it, and stopped still with my camel to wait for the dawn.' It is also notable for including the first reference to Abdul Alhazred, 'the mad Arab' author of the fictitious grimoire, the *Necronomicon*.

In contrast, 'The Moon Bog' is a pleasant but inconsequential piece written for an amateur journalists' convention in Boston on 10 March 1921 – to be enjoyed with a good after-dinner cigar and a glass of fine malt whisky. It's a traditional Irish fairytale (timed to commemorate St Patrick's Day on 17 March) with little to recommend it other than its nimbleness of touch. It demonstrates that Lovecraft could indeed show restraint when the fancy took him . . .

Somewhere, to what remote and fearsome region I know not, Denys Barry has gone. I was with him the last night he lived among men, and heard his screams when the thing came to him; but all the peasants and police in County Meath could never find him, or the others, though they searched long and far.

Hapless Barry dared to drain the peat bog around his ancestral pile – a fatal move which surely invoked the vengeance of the spirits of the land. In later years it must have puzzled its author to recall that such a slight tale had been accepted for publication in *Weird Tales* when more substantial and original work – namely 'At the Mountains of Madness', 'The Shadow Over Innsmouth' and 'The Call of Cthulhu' – had been rejected.

If there is any truth in the assumption that writers' subconscious desires and fears are expressed in their work, then 'Ex Oblivione' (*c.* March 1921) can be interpreted as Lovecraft's longing for an end to a life of struggle and disappointment. But if, as seems more likely, he was simply musing on what might await us beyond death, then it can be seen as a variation on Kafka's fable, 'Before the Law', a tale warning against relinquishing our right to justice and knowledge for fear that we are not entitled to it. In the fable a man waits in a perpetual limbo outside a door in the hope of being granted access to the law beyond. Only when he is too old to benefit from it, is he told by the guard that he could have entered at any time.

Lovecraft's variation features an elderly man dreaming of a locked gate and wondering what lies behind it. He subsequently dreams of finding a parchment recording the teachings of sages who speculated on what might lie beyond and who disagreed as to whether it is a place of wonder or horror. On learning that a drug will give him access, he obtains it and in the next dream finds the gate open. On the other side he discovers that all of the sages were right, there is wonder and horror in the eternal nothingness of the void, in death.

The luxuriant language ('I walked through a golden valley that led to shadowy groves' is reminiscent of nineteenth-century Romantics like William Wordsworth) and wistful tone indicate that this is another of Lovecraft's pensive contemplations – a meditation on the serenity and release to be found in dreams. It is not the work of a man who is terrified of death, only of one beset by the nagging thought that life is futile and that blissful oblivion might be preferable to a life of suffering. As he later wrote in *In Defence of Dagon*, (Collected Essays, Volume 5): 'there is nothing better than oblivion, since in oblivion there is no wish unfulfilled'.

In stark contrast, 'The Outsider' (spring/summer 1921) provides an exercise in mock-gothic, set in a dank, cobwebbed castle in which the creations of Horace Walpole and Mary Shelley might have felt at home. Telling of a hapless creature that flees its dungeon lair, it reads like a section omitted from *Frankenstein* – except that Lovecraft's 'baroque and windy rhetoric' (his own assessment) is moderately less florid than that of his predecessor. As its author readily admitted ten years on, it was 'almost comic in the bombastic pomposity of its language', but the reveal is grimly satisfying.

If only he had ended at this point and resisted the temptation to try to out-do Poe, piling on the horrors until it seems as if he is set on self-parody. If only he had trimmed the excess fat between the penultimate and final paragraphs to create a succinct and startling revelation: that the monster and the narrator are one and the same. If only he had followed this – 'Nearly mad, I found myself yet able to throw out a hand to ward off the foetid apparition which pressed so close; when in one cataclysmic second of cosmic nightmarishness and hellish accident my fingers touched the rotting outstretched paw of the monster beneath the golden arch' – with the closing line: 'stretched out my fingers and touched a cold and unyielding surface of polished glass', omitting the overblown material between.

But he never sought the opinion of an experienced editor – and had he done so, there's every chance that he'd have made up his mind to disregard their advice . . . if his refusal to heed amateur publisher C.W. Cook is anything to go by. Cook suggested concluding 'The Outsider' with the reveal as described, but Lovecraft was in full flight and couldn't bear the thought of cutting the 'chaos of echoing images' which climax in a ride 'with the mocking and friendly ghouls on the night-wind' and a reference to 'the catacombs of Nephren-Ka in the sealed and unknown valley of Hadoth by the Nile' along with the 'rock tombs of Neb' and 'the unnamed feasts of Nitokris beneath the Great Pyramid'. Such passages have drawn derision from those who call Lovecraft 'a good bad writer', when all that was needed was a second draft and the confidence to cut the superfluous material. It is clear from Lovecraft's comments that he was not blind to the story's faults, yet the prospect of retyping it – in his laborious two-fingered manner – was more daunting than beginning a new story.

Lord Dunsany and the Nibelungen saga provided the impetus for his next offering, 'The Other Gods' – also written in a single sitting in August 1921. But here he adopts a lighter touch in keeping with a morality tale.

Barzai the Wise and his young acolyte climb to the summit of Mount Kadath to converse with the gods. Despite his appellation, there is the implication that Barzai may have succumbed to the same vice that corrupts many self-appointed spiritual and religious leaders who assume the role of mediator between man and his maker – vanity. 'Barzai knew so much of the gods that he could tell of their comings and goings, and guessed so many of their secrets that he was deemed half a god himself.'

As he scales the summit he is not humbled by the gods' proximity but emboldened to the point of arrogance. He taunts them: "'The wisdom of Barzai hath made him greater than Earth's gods, and against his will their spells and barriers are as naught; Barzai will behold the gods, the proud gods, the secret gods, the gods of earth who spurn the sight of man!'"

His pilgrimage to the peak of Mount Kadath reveals both his lack of humility and the dangers of blind faith. In truth, the gods of Earth are subordinate to more powerful and malign deities than Barzai could ever have dreamed of. Again, the theme of this tale is that a search for wisdom or for a meaning in life will only result in disillusionment and disappointment. The gods are not deserving of our devotion as they cower beneath the real overlords of the cosmos. In the eyes of these indifferent deities, we are as insignificant as insects.

The rarefied tone of 'The Other Gods' modulated into a more sombre theme for 'The Music of Erich Zann' (December 1921), one of Lovecraft's personal favourites and a story of which he was justly proud. It is another comparatively restrained tale, the recollections of an impoverished student who befriends an elderly viol player in the lodging house they share in a squalid part of Paris. We assume it is Paris because the street is named Rue d'Auseil, though 'auseil' is not a French word. Lovecraft may have chosen an unrecognisable name deliberately and omitted to identify the city to imply that it might have been a dream or delusion – a strong possibility given that afterwards the narrator can neither locate 'the street I knew', nor find anyone who has heard of the place. The fantastic theme and the fact that the street was to be found across a dark river spanned by a 'ponderous bridge' suggests a descent into the subconscious, rather than a physical location. This interpretation is more likely, given the protagonist's admission that, 'my health, physical and mental, was gravely disturbed throughout the period of my residence in the Rue'. Moreover, no friends had visited him there.

To describe a Lovecraft tale as comparatively restrained is not to imply that it is a quiet exercise in creeping unease, only that the mood is commendably restrained until the climax when the crisis is described in words befitting the danger: 'as I stood there looking in terror, the wind blew out both the candles in that ancient peaked garret, leaving me in savage and impenetrable darkness with chaos and pandemonium before me, and the daemon madness of that night-baying viol behind me'.

It is well crafted, eerily evocative and persuasive, if atypical of its author – in that it avoids identifying the source of Zann's unearthly music and its climactic scene does not involve a confrontation with an entity that must be overcome. It is an uncommonly intimate exercise in evoking the uncanny and a prime example of 'weird fiction', as evidenced by the fact that it has been included in numerous anthologies.

1921 marked a productive phase in Lovecraft's career and surprisingly so, for it was the year of his mother's death. Sarah Susan Phillips passed away on 24 May – at the age of 63 – of complications arising from a gall bladder operation. Her last words expressed her overwhelming exhaustion and despair: 'I will only live to suffer'. Her son professed to have experienced 'an extreme nervous shock' at the news of her loss, but remained 'supremely unemotional' in the belief that weeping was 'vulgar'. To assuage his grief he plunged himself into work and letter writing – all of which became a crucial outlet for his repressed emotions. In a letter to

Anne Tillery Renshaw, (an amateur journalist colleague with whom he collaborated on a treatise on English usage), dated 1 June, he expressed his desire to end his life. This time, his writing was suggestive of quiet resignation rather than maudlin self-pity. 'I do not think I shall wait for a natural death; since there is no longer any particular reason why I should exist . . . my end would cause no one more than a passing annoyance.'

Yet, within a short time his spirits picked up and his health improved 'vastly and rapidly, though without any ascertainable cause' (to quote from his letter to Maurice W. Moe) for now he was free of both her debilitating influence and responsibility for her wellbeing. It was a remarkably swift recovery from a devastating bereavement and if it was true, and he was not merely putting a brave face on things, it reveals how practiced he had become at repressing his emotions. Perhaps his reaction is simply one further indicator of Asperger's syndrome. Though people afflicted by this condition feel deeply, they don't always express their emotions openly – giving others the impression that they are insensitive. As far as he was concerned he had been a dutiful son and suffered much in silence. Now that fate had taken Susie from him, it was imperative that he not allow himself to wallow in self-recrimination and withdraw from the world. He was encouraged in this respect by invitations to attend amateur journalist conventions and family visits – none of which were sufficient to bring him out of himself. In the midst of a gaggle of enthusiastic writers he withdrew into a corner and spent the evening stroking a kitten, refusing all efforts to persuade him to sing. Lovecraft was reputed to possess a melodious voice and a good ear but he was too self-conscious to perform in public.

The year his mother died saw the reclusive and repressed author begin a tentative romantic relationship, although the courtship seems to have been one-sided. Sonia Haft Greene (1883–1972) was a Ukrainian Jew, a divorcee and a single mother. Her first child had died in infancy and her surviving daughter, Florence, was nineteen when her mother met Lovecraft at a National Amateur Press Association (NAPA) convention in Boston in July 1921. Florence would refuse to speak to Sonia after the marriage. Not only did she object to Lovecraft's blatant anti-Semitism, she also saw him as an idle sponger, content to live off her mother's money. There is some truth in this as Sonia was then a successful business woman earning $10,000 per annum as chief milliner in an exclusive Fifth Avenue fashion house. Lovecraft himself was surviving on a fraction of this income, principally from revising the work of third-rate poets, would-be authors and self-help psychologists. Sonia appears to have tolerated his racist outbursts, seeing his bigotry as no more than a mild irritant – comparable to drunkenness or gambling – and something she was confident she could curb given time.

A male acquaintance described her as the very embodiment of a Dostoyevsky heroine. She could have captivated any man she set her dark, penetrating eyes upon, but was attracted by the quiet, mild mannered author from Providence whom she thought she could loosen up and make something of. He impressed her as a self-educated intellectual: slightly straitlaced, rather self-opinionated and prematurely middle-aged in his bank-teller suit, starched collar and tie. He was taken with her evident intelligence, self-confidence and lack of artifice, but clearly didn't entertain any idea of romance after that first meeting. She, conversely, sought out every correspondent of his that she could track down and grilled them as to his character and prospects.

Satisfied that he was worth pursuing and that she had no known rivals with whom to contend, she wrote informing her intended that she would like to visit Providence in the near future and wondered if he would be so kind as to show her the historical points of interest he had mentioned at their first meeting. When he replied that he would be delighted to do so, she bought a return ticket from New York and made the half-day journey in the hope that a mutual friendship might develop into something more serious.

On returning to New York, Sonia launched an amateur journal of her own, *The Rainbow*, to which, it had been agreed, Lovecraft and a circle of New York intellectuals would contribute. It was a shrewd move for it ensured that she had a legitimate reason to maintain a regular correspondence with him and she also now had an elegantly designed quality periodical in which to present her own features and fiction to a discerning readership.

If Sonia imagined that she would be acting as a muse to a great poet and philosopher she must have been horrified to learn that her intended had embarked on a 'Grewsome Tale' for *Home Brew*, (a humorous amateur college magazine) and was knocking off an instalment a month for the princely sum of 'a guinea per tale'. This amount – Lovecraft's 'sole inducement' as far as this project was concerned – is listed as the equivalent of $5 in *Selected Letters I*. The episodic nature of 'Herbert West: Reanimator' betrayed its serial origins, but it retains a morbid fascination both as a lurid reimagining of *Frankenstein* and as a prime example of Lovecraft's pitch-black humour. It also established Miskatonic University and Arkham as key locations in Lovecraft Country.

The six instalments were written over the course of nine months from autumn 1921 and, though Lovecraft complained that it was 'enforced, laboured and artificial' hack work, the tone of his letters to friends conveys his perverse pleasure in serving up a grisly shocker that would have outraged his high-minded New England neighbours. The final instalment, in particular, with its talking decapitated head and zombie-like automatons dismembering their creator is so grotesque that one can imagine the author concocting it with tongue firmly in cheek. However the residual power of the story comes not from the macabre nature of the subject – which was hardly novel – but from the clinical tone adopted by West's unnamed friend and fellow medical student, who recounts their nocturnal grave robbing and secret experiments with the detachment of a laboratory technician. It is only at the very end when he fears that West might resort to murdering him that we share his real fear, the suspicion that everything he had described was nothing but a delusion and that the greater reality glimpsed in dreams is too much for mortals to comprehend. This is the core of Lovecraft's horror – not the tentacled monstrosities nor the vague allusions to terrors beyond description, but the suggestion that what seemed so real was in fact symptomatic of an incipient madness – the fate of which the author was so afraid and which may have fuelled both his passive hostility and the relentless activity that he hoped might prevent or at least arrest the deterioration of his mental faculties.

At key points in 'Reanimator', there is the inference that all of

SHADOWS RUN LIKE INK

the events took place in the disintegrating mind of the unnamed narrator. 'They noticed my fear; and after his disappearance used that as a basis for some absurd suspicions.' And 'it is a vicious lie to say it was Herbert West's body which I put into the incinerator.' But most damning of all: 'I told them of the vault, and they pointed to the unbroken plaster wall and laughed. So I told them no more. They imply that I am either a madman or a murderer –'

What greater horror could there be than to be rendered incapable of distinguishing delusions from reality?

While 'Reanimator' is a graphic, full-blooded reimagining of *Frankenstein*, the short story 'Hypnos', completed in March 1922, is a more elegant exercise in unease. It is a modern variation on the Greek myth of Pygmalion and Galatea in which a sculptor brings his masterwork to life and falls in love with her.

In 'Hypnos' the male sculptor offers shelter to a homeless man, not out of pity but because he imagines he perceives 'the grandeur and the terror of realms beyond normal consciousness and reality' in the stranger's eyes. Though his face is gaunt and deeply lined, the middle-aged vagrant is described in terms that border on the homoerotic – 'weirdly haggard and wildly beautiful' – as the narrator fancies he senses a mystical bond between them and declares that he has found his one and only true friend and teacher. With the aid of drugs they explore other realms of consciousness which leave them exhausted and prematurely aged. During one drug-induced astral journey the sculptor is disconcerted to see his companion surging ahead of him, but when the latter returns shaken by what he has seen, they are both afraid to fall asleep. When the police break down the door there is no sign of the older man and in his place they find a bust of the sculptor as he was in his youth. Again, as in so many of Lovecraft's most compelling tales, the entire episode appears to have been a delusion experienced by the narcissistic narrator. However those who prefer a supernatural explanation will find that it stands up to a literal interpretation.

If there is a hint of passive homoerotic attraction in 'Hypnos', it's tempting to read this as an unconscious expression of the author's own latent sexuality. While there is no definitive evidence on this matter, the terms that Lovecraft used to describe other young men

– in his fiction as well as his correspondence – are not typical for a heterosexual male of his time. This is most evident in his description of friend and acolyte Frank Long, whom he met in New York in early April at Sonia's invitation. Long, he wrote, was 'an exquisite boy . . . with . . . a delicate beautiful face' and possessed the faintest hint of a moustache – a 'tiny collection of lip-hairs – about six on one side and five on the other'. Whether Lovecraft's words are merely appreciative or inspired by some secret physical attraction, we'll never know. He would refer to another male correspondent, Alfred Galpin, as a 'delectable little imp', though such phrases might have been the result of living among women for most of his life.

If Sonia noticed anything to give her cause to question her decision to pursue the reclusive author, she didn't confide in the friends who were present on that first trip to New York – Samuel Loveman, James Morton and Rheinhart Kleiner. (Though in many ways, their relationship seems to have been more professional than personal. Kleiner and Loveman were Lovecraft's earliest colleagues in amateurdom. He'd made their acquaintances in 1915 and 1917 respectively, with Morton being added to the circle of correspondents in 1922. Morton had introduced Sonia to amateur journalism in 1917.) Nor did Sonia record it in her slender memoir, *The Private Life of H.P. Lovecraft*, published under the name Sonia H. Davis. If anything of that nature was discussed in Lovecraft's letters to his future wife, it must remain a matter of speculation, for Sonia burned a 'trunkful' of Lovecraft's correspondence after their divorce in 1926. This theory might, however, explain his unnaturally close relationship with his mother, his pathological desire for solitude and his obsessive shyness. He professed to have no interest in sex or forming romantic relationships with women, although there may, of course, have been another explanation for his reluctance and that is that he had been conditioned by his mother to regard himself as physically abnormal; ugly, awkward and a poor specimen of manhood prone to chronic, debilitating ailments.

Whatever the cause, Sonia was determined to bring him out of his shell. When a neighbour's cat came into her apartment during that first visit to New York and curled up on his lap, Sonia teased him that his affection was wasted on an animal when there were women who would appreciate it more. He replied, 'how can any woman love a face like mine?' to which she responded suggestively: 'a mother can and some who are not mothers would not have to try very hard'. Lovecraft laughed but continued to stroke the cat.

He may have been slow to read anything into Sonia's remark, but he was amenable to the idea of a further meeting on 16 June when Sonia found herself in the charming coastal town of Magnolia, Massachusetts 'on business' and free to make a stopover in Providence. After a cordial visit – with both aunts in attendance – it was suggested that Lovecraft join Sonia in Magnolia for a short two-week break, sharing the same boarding house and spending the evenings strolling together taking in the sea air. It was during one of these moonlit walks along the waterfront that they heard a distant moaning sound. Sonia immediately suggested he use it as the basis for a new tale. He agreed it would make a good story, but insisted that she write it and that he prepare it for publication. 'The Horror at Martin's Beach' tells of a huge sea creature which is caught and killed by fishermen who are subsequently dragged to their death in the deep by its vengeful mother. It has nothing to recommend it, other than the fact that it was written by the woman who was to become the first and only wife of H.P. Lovecraft and she might not have become that had he not enthused about their 'collaboration', though in truth it was nothing of the sort.

'His continued enthusiasm the next day was so genuine and sincere that in appreciation I surprised and shocked him right then and there by kissing him. He was so flustered that he blushed, then he turned pale.' The 32-year-old admitted that he hadn't been kissed since he was a child. Furthermore, he believed he would probably never be kissed again, but as Sonia noted, 'I fooled him'.

Lovecraft drew on his own disturbing dreams yet again for 'What the Moon Brings' written on 5 June 1922. It would have made an effective addition to 'Hypnos', explaining what had terrified the dreamer and fleshing out that story to a more satisfying length, but there is little doubt that 'What the Moon Brings' was intended as a stand-alone piece, brief though it is.

Intoxicated by the narcotic scent of the flowers during his

nocturnal walks, the narrator finds himself transported to another dimension. There he sees a sunken city beneath the waves where fat sea worms feed upon the dead. 'So I watched the tide go out under that sinking moon, and saw gleaming the spires, the towers, and the roofs of that dead, dripping city. And as I watched, my nostrils tried to close against the perfume-conquering stench of the world's dead; for truly, in this unplaced and forgotten spot had all the flesh of the churchyards gathered for puffy sea-worms to gnaw and glut upon.'

If the measure of a great writer is determined solely by their mastery of the mechanics of language, then Lovecraft aficionados might struggle to justify his place in the gallery of great writers. In truth, he was prone to excessive use of adjectives, overheated, melodramatic flourishes, bloated descriptive passages and overripe purple prose. Fortunately, booklovers rather than academics determine a writer's true worth by his or her ability to draw the reader into their world. And in that respect Lovecraft surely qualifies. He may not have been a great writer in terms of technical proficiency, but he was a great storyteller and he created a world as real as those envisaged by Agatha Christie, Raymond Chandler or Tolkien. It was his ability to evoke the dream-state itself which distinguishes Lovecraft from less talented writers, coupled with his facility to enrich his text with poetic phrases to give his stories an indefinable but instantly identifiable quality. 'What The Moon Brings' offers ample evidence of this restraint and of his ability to resist the urge to over-write.

'It was in the spectral summer when the moon shone down on the old garden where I wandered; the spectral summer of narcotic flowers and humid seas of foliage that bring wild and many-coloured dreams. And as I walked by the shallow crystal stream I saw unwonted ripples tipped with yellow light, as if those placid waters were drawn on in resistless currents to strange oceans that are not in the world.' And here too; 'white lotus blossoms fluttered one by one in the opiate night-wind and dropped despairingly into the stream, swirling away horribly under the arched, carven bridge, and staring back with the sinister resignation of calm, dead faces.'

The same lyricism permeates 'Azathoth' (1922), the only surviving fragment from an abandoned novel which was to be written in the florid eighteenth-century style exemplified by William Beckford, author of *Vathek*. It would be a modern myth in the manner of the *Arabian Nights* with a touch of Lord Dunsany.

In a letter to Frank Belknap Long on 9 June, Lovecraft wrote of his new project, 'I shall go out of the world when I write, with a mind centred not in literary usage, but in the dreams I dreamed when I was six year old or less – the dreams which followed my first knowledge of Sinbad, of Agib, of Baba-Abdallah, and of Sidi-Nonman.' Why he discarded it is not known, though he was to explore the same territory in 'The Dream-Quest of Unknown Kadath', so perhaps he felt he had satisfied that desire under another title. Certainly the opening promised much.

> When age fell upon the world, and wonder went out of the minds of men; when grey cities reared to smoky skies tall towers grim and ugly, in whose shadow none might dream of the sun or of Spring's flowering meads; when learning stripped Earth of her mantle of beauty, and poets sang no more save of twisted phantoms seen with bleared and inward-looking eyes; when these things had come to pass, and childish hopes had gone away for ever, there was a man who travelled out of life on a quest into the spaces whither the world's dreams had fled.

Azathoth would be used in future tales – including 'The Dream-Quest of Unknown Kadath' – as the name of the illimitable demon sultan 'whose name no lips dare speak aloud, and who gnaws hungrily in inconceivable, unlighted chambers beyond time and space amidst the muffled, maddening beating of vile drums and the thin monotonous whine of accursed flutes'. It would also be referred to in 'The Whisperer in Darkness' and is described elsewhere as a primordial deity seated on a black throne at the centre of Chaos. According to Lovecraft's own genealogy, Azathoth was the begetter of Nyarlathotep and through it the entire pantheon of elder gods including Yog-Sothoth and Cthulhu.

He made several other excursions to visit literary friends and admirers in Cleveland that summer of 1922, culminating with a long vacation in New York from mid-August as Sonia's guest. There is something quite touching and childlike in Lovecraft's letters home during this period. He tells his aunts of his sightseeing trips, of his fondness for his friends Morton, Long, Kleiner and Keil with whom he enjoyed lengthy literary and philosophical discussions, but little of his hostess who must have been hoping he would pay her as much attention as he did to George Washington's personal effects during their sightseeing excursions or the contents of the antiquarian book stores on the lower East Side. In the following letter home to his aunts, his ardour was reserved strictly for the view.

> I fell into a swoon of aesthetic exaltation in admiring this view – the evening scenery with the innumerable lights of the skyscrapers, the mirrored reflections and the lights of the boats bobbing on the water, at the extreme left the sparkling Statue of Liberty, and on the right the scintillating arch of the Brooklyn Bridge. It's something even more powerful than the dreams of the legend of the ancient world – a constellation of infernal majesty – a poem in the fire of Babylon! (. . .) Oh, my God! If only I could express the magic of the scene!

With the realisation that his future wife didn't share his liking for George Julian Houtain – the rather crude, ostentatious publisher of *Home Brew* – the tone of Lovecraft's letters shifted from indifferent to indignant. When Howard, Loveman and Sonia visited the former lawyer at his office in Brooklyn, Lovecraft dismissed her objections in no uncertain terms. 'Loveman was a bit embarrassed because Mrs Greene now hates Houtain and now resents the fact that everyone else doesn't . . . If Mrs Greene objected, she had my permission to go to hell and complain to the devil! Houtain would receive me as a guest at 1128 Bedford even if Mrs Greene should kick me out of 259 Parkside! No damn human being, however worthy and generous, can dictate to the Old Gent whom he shall associate with!'

Clearly, Lovecraft had more pressing matters on his mind than pacifying his future fiancée. Instead, he was experimenting with the incubation of dreams and had chipped off a small portion of an eighteenth-century headstone during a visit to a Brooklyn churchyard which he put under his pillow on his return to Providence in the hope that it would generate a good horror yarn. Just to be sure he read J.K. Huysmans' notorious novel *À rebours* (*Against Nature*) to nurture a sense of *ennui* that would drive his world-weary characters to plunder graves for specimens and macabre artefacts for their 'blasphemous' museum.

Lovecraft identified with Huysmans' protagonist, a reclusive nobleman whose father dies of a mysterious illness, leaving him with his neurotic widowed mother. Like Lovecraft, this character fell prey to his own overactive imagination. Duc des Esseintes, a decadent dilettante and the last of his line, suffers from an acute nervous disorder just like Poe's ill-starred protagonist Roderick Usher, with whom he in turn identifies and in whom he finds justification for his self-imposed isolation and distaste for the outside world.

Later that month while Sonia was dreaming of romance, her unlikely suitor was thinking only of how to spawn a nightmare that would furnish the plot of his next story. Like his fictional protagonists, Lovecraft shamelessly plundered the works of his literary ancestors for ripe phrases. The 'nauseous musical instruments, stringed, brass, and wood-wind, on which St John and I sometimes produced dissonances of exquisite morbidity and cacodaemoniacal ghastliness' were an echo of Roderick Usher's penchant for playing sombre ballads on the lute, while the reference to the 'baying of some gigantic hound' is a straight lift from Conan Doyle. Elsewhere there are echoes of Poe with the mention of an 'oblong box', 'a knock at my chamber door' and 'a red death'.

Lovecraft later disowned 'The Hound', describing it as a 'dead dog'. Though this seems unduly harsh, it is true that there is the impression that it is being told in undue haste, drawing rather too heavily upon Lovecraft's literary heroes – with such key events as the death of one of the main characters and the destruction of his 'blasphemous museum' mentioned only in passing, as if they are of little significance.

That said there is the gist of a good idea herein; that of a long-dead grave robber returning from his own rifled grave to wreak revenge on those foolish enough to plunder his last resting place. But it would be a mistake to see it as a deliberate parody of Poe –

THE CURIOUS CASE OF OF H.P. LOVECRAFT

or of Lovecraft's own overwrought style – for nowhere is there the merest hint of mordant humour. And if it had been intended as such an exercise, he surely would not have dismissed it with quite so much vehemence – all of which is indicative of disappointment and frustration. He did agree, however, to alter a few details, such as deleting the reference to Clark Ashton Smith as the artist of unnameable drawings collected in a portfolio bound in human skin. Smith was self-educated and multi-talented – a writer, poet and illustrator who caught Lovecraft's attention in August 1922. His book, *The Star-Treader and Other Poems* (1912), was enough to elicit an effusive fan letter from the 'Old Gent' himself.

My dear Mr. Smith:—

I trust you will pardon the liberty taken by an absolute stranger in writing you, for I cannot refrain from expressing the appreciation aroused in me by your drawings & poetry, as shown me by my friend, Mr. Samuel Loveman, whom I am now visiting in Cleveland. Your book, containing matter only chronologically classifiable as juvenilia, impresses me as a work of the most distinguished genius; & makes me anxious to see the new volume which I understand is in course of preparation.

Of the drawings & water-colours I lack a vocabulary adequate to express my enthusiastic admiration. What a world of opiate phantasy & horror is here unveiled, & what an unique power & perspective must lie behind it! I speak with especial sincerity & enthusiasm, because my own especial tastes centre almost wholly around the grotesque & the arabesque. I have tried to write short stories & sketches affording glimpses into the unknown abysses of terror which leer beyond the boundaries of the known, but have never succeeded in evoking even a fraction of the stark hideousness conveyed by any one of your ghoulishly potent designs.

I should deem it a great honour to hear from you if you have the leisure & inclination to address an obscurity, & to learn where I may behold other poems by the hand which created such works of art as Nero, The Star-Treader, & the exquisite sonnets which companion them. That I have not work of even approximately

96

equal genius to exhibit in reciprocation, is the fault of my mediocre ability & not of my inclination.

Apologising for this intrusion upon your time, & again expressing the appreciation which every renewed glimpse of your work increases, I beg the honour to remain

Yr most obedient Servt.

H.P. Lovecraft

Though 'The Hound' is arguably one of his least satisfying tales, it is notable for being the first to mention the *Necronomicon* by name. Incredible though it may seem, several cults have adopted this tome as their black bible, despite Lovecraft's admission that the 'hellish and forbidden volume is an imaginative conception of mine' (letter to Robert Bloch, author of *Psycho*, 9 May 1933) and that it had come to him in a dream. As previously mentioned, the name Alhazread (which has no Arabic root) was Lovecraft's pet name for his youthful self, whom he saw as a voracious reader (All-Has-Read). There is also the fact that no mention was made of this eighth-century text before Lovecraft alluded to it more than 1,000 years later. Moreover, in his early stories Lovecraft contradicts himself as to the nature of its contents and its use – is it a Necromancer's Grimoire or a witchfinder's handbook? Its vagueness and its creator's constant referral to other obscure and nonexistent texts would immediately arouse the suspicions of serious occultists. The very elusiveness of the *Necronomicon* is, of course, part of its appeal. Its origins have been obscured by the many veiled references to it in the works of other fantasy writers with whom Lovecraft corresponded, among them Robert Bloch, Clark Ashton Smith and Robert E. Howard (creator of Conan). But although Lovecraft had been invited to pen the accursed work himself to satisfy fans, he admitted that it was beyond him; no book could live up to their expectations. 'I wish I had the time and imagination to assist in such a project . . . one can never produce anything even a tenth as terrible and impressive as one can awesomely hint about.'

As early as November 1927 he considered it prudent to write a fictional history of the *Necronomicon* so as to ensure consistency in his own work, but also so he could provide further background for his fellow writers – all of whom were keen to reference the work in their own fiction as a homage to their friend (Appendix 1).

If Sonia was disappointed to learn that Lovecraft had sold his skills for a guinea-an-episode to *Home Brew*, (publisher of 'Herbert West: Reanimator'), she must have despaired to hear that he had condescended to write another lengthy tale for the same periodical which he now referred to as 'that vile rag'.

'The Lurking Fear', written in a sustained burst of activity during the second half of November, was competently crafted, but is far too conventional and predictable to make its author any new converts. A haunted, isolated mansion in the Catskill Mountains is revealed to be infested with the mutant descendants of its former owners – all of whom have developed an appetite for human flesh. The writing is equally uninspired, as if its author regretted accepting the commission as soon as the advance payment arrived. 'There was thunder in the air on the night I went to the deserted mansion atop Tempest Mountain to find the lurking fear. I was not alone, for foolhardiness was not then mixed with that love of the grotesque and the terrible which has made my career a series of quests for strange horrors in literature and in life.'

Seven thousand words later, the tempo has increased imperceptibly from sluggish to slow and the awful crescendo of terror that we have been promised is more of an anti-climax, a variant on the final scene in 'The Nameless City' and a rewording of the theme underlying, 'Arthur Jermyn'.

> The object was nauseous; a filthy whitish gorilla thing with sharp yellow fangs and matted fur. It was the ultimate product of mammalian degeneration; the frightful outcome of isolated spawning, multiplication, and cannibal nutrition above and below the ground; the embodiment of all the snarling and chaos and grinning fear that lurk behind life . . . and I knew in one inundating cataclysm of voiceless horror what had become of that vanished family; the terrible and thunder-crazed house of Martense.

By now he was in almost daily correspondence with Sonia, writing up to 50 pages at a time, but instead of protestations of love she had to be content with detailed descriptions of his latest excursions to Salem and Marblehead, and the epiphany he'd experienced when surveying the restored colonial architecture and narrow, cobbled streets of the latter at dusk. As the lights came on that evening in the tiny leaded windows overlooking the harbour, Lovecraft was transported back two centuries. It was 'the most powerful single aesthetic impression I have received in years,' he later wrote. 'In a flash all the past of New England . . . swept over me and identified me with the stupendous totality of all things . . . That was the high tide of my life.' Sonia must have thrilled to read that he could be so acutely sensitive and passionate, but at the same time wondered if he was capable of experiencing such profound emotion for another human being.

Fortunately for Sonia one of her greatest virtues was patience as the man she had set her sights on would take more than two years to coax into a formal partnership, having first convinced him of the benefits. Sonia would later describe him as an 'adequately excellent lover', but he was not naturally affectionate. His passion was directed toward his intellectual interests. Emotionally he was extremely reserved, even cold and very formal, though he could be considerate, kind and generous. When he finally succumbed to Sonia's entreaties to marry, it was her appeal to his reason rather than to his emotions that decided the matter. Her income would offer him financial security and stability, and her practical nature would ensure that the irksome chores associated with modern living were dealt with quietly and efficiently.

CHAPTER SIX

WEIRD TALES

*'A serious **adult story must be true** to something in life.
Since **marvel tales cannot be true** to the events of life, they
must shift **their emphasis** towards something to which they
can be true; **namely, certain** wistful or restless moods of
the human spirit, **wherein it** seeks to weave gossamer
ladders of escape from the galling tyranny of time,
space, and natural law.'*
– H.P. Lovecraft

Had it not been for *Weird Tales*, the pulp magazine launched by
publisher Jacob C. Henneberger in March 1923, H.P. Lovecraft
might have remained an obscure contributor to amateur journals
and his pantheon of primal gods and eldritch horrors unborn.

Henneberger had no personal interest in fantasy or science
fiction, but he was an astute businessman with an eye for an
opportunity. When he saw that there was a gap in the market for
a magazine devoted to 'unconventional' fiction he seized upon it,
having first secured several well-known writers who were keen to
contribute. However, when they failed to deliver, Henneberger soon
lost interest and passed the job to editor Edwin Baird. It was Baird
who accepted the first titles offered by Lovecraft, on the proviso
that they be retyped – a chore the writer was loath to do.

By a stroke of good fortune Lovecraft had only recently
discovered that aspiring author Clifford Eddy and his wife, Muriel,
lived a short walk from Angell Street and were prepared to type up

his work in exchange for advice and revisions to Eddy's own rather unpromising efforts. Lovecraft regarded Eddy as 'rather a delight' and enjoyed his company and conversation, but their friendship does not appear to have developed to the degree that Muriel later claimed. However, it seems likely that it was Eddy's enthusiasm and encouragement which led to Lovecraft submitting the first batch of stories to *Weird Tales*. Despite its reputation for publishing the best and worst weird fiction, *Weird Tales* could claim only a fraction of the circulation of its competitors, *Argosy All-Story Weekly* and *Black Mask* – which regularly sold a minimum of 300,000 copies per issue.

Lovecraft's first submission comprised five tales – 'Dagon', 'The Statement of Randolph Carter', 'Arthur Jermyn', 'The Cats of Ulthar' and 'The Hound' – as well as a letter outlining his 'weird' credentials. By his own admission, he'd read just one issue of the magazine up to then.

> My Dear Sir:
>
> Having a habit of writing weird, macabre and fantastic stories for my own amusement, I have lately been simultaneously hounded by nearly a dozen well-meaning friends into deciding to submit a few of these Gothic horrors to your newly founded periodical . . .
>
> I have no idea that these things will be found suitable, for I pay no attention to the demands of commercial writing . . . the only reader I hold in mind is myself . . .

The paltry fee of 1½ cents a word was welcome, though payment was made only on publication and these initial stories appeared at frustratingly long intervals between October 1923 and February 1926. But there would be further offers of paid work from the publisher which Lovecraft would happily accept, such as ghost writing Harry Houdini's fictitious exploits in 'Imprisoned with the Pharaohs'. However, his relationship with Baird was strained by the latter's habit of renaming any submissions that did not boast a suitably snappy title – without consulting the author beforehand. 'Arthur Jermyn' appeared under the title of 'The White Ape' which led Lovecraft to snarl, 'you may be sure that if I ever titled a story "The White Ape", there would be no ape in it!'

But if Lovecraft played the disgruntled author to ensure Baird thought twice before taking liberties with his material in the future, in private he was gratified to finally have his work accepted by a 'legitimate' professional publication – so gratified, that it led to the writing of three new tales within weeks of one another.

'The Rats in the Walls', 'The Unnamable' and 'The Festival' were all written in the autumn of 1923. Marked by a new evenness of tone, these tightly plotted new tales reflect the author's growing confidence.

The first was prompted by 'a commonplace incident'. As Lovecraft lay awake one night, listening to the cracking of the wallpaper (the day had been stifling hot and the house was still settling around him), he was reminded of a phrase from 'The Fall of the House of Usher', in which Sir Roderick is afflicted with such a 'morbid acuteness of the senses' that he fears he can hear rats in the walls – a notion Lovecraft combined with a medieval legend he had recently come across telling of a cruel Bishop, devoured by rats.

'The Rats in the Walls' begins with a simple statement of fact as a descendent of a noble family returns to England from Virginia to rebuild the ruins of his ancestral home, giving no indication of the horrors to come. The last surviving member of the de la Poer family is neither impressed nor perturbed by local legends surrounding his ancestors' alleged dabbling in the occult and unproven accusations of murder – all of which he dismisses as 'picturesque'. And so when he finally uncovers the secret that made his family name a byword for depravity, it is all the more shocking – so shocking that it drives him mad and he degenerates into a ravenous flesh-eating cannibal, devouring his friend and companion Captain Norrys. For this, he is predictably confined in a madhouse. The story concludes with his plea to be taken seriously, despite the fact that none of the attendants or doctors can hear the scurrying of the rats behind the walls of his padded cell.

Despite the hackneyed ending, the familiar gothic setting and the echoes of Poe, there is a quintessentially English tenor to the language and a chilly objectivity which invites comparison with the antiquarian ghost stories of M.R. James, specifically 'The Ash Tree'.

J.C. Henneberger was still vetting submissions when Lovecraft sent in his second batch of stories and declared 'The Rats in the Walls' the best *Weird Tales* had received to date. He was apparently unaware that it had recently been rejected by the more prestigious periodical *Argosy All-Story Weekly* and that *Weird Tales* was not its author's first choice.

Now on a roll and in need of fresh material to submit to his first professional publication, Lovecraft thought it might be a good time as any to revive his recurring character, Randolph Carter. Lovecraft's renewed confidence is evident in Carter's self-assured attitude, though he was not without his flaws.

Aspiring authors are encouraged to invest their characters with something of themselves to make them more believable and Lovecraft adhered to that, making Carter an unappreciated author who is prone to fainting spells when stressed. Not the best characteristic for a protagonist who battles hideous fiends and extraterrestrial entities, but in this latest offering Carter is shown to be strong-willed and blessed with sufficient presence of mind to extricate himself from the dangers he faces. In 'The Unnamable' (1923) Carter and his devout friend Joel Manton (a thinly disguised version of high school teacher Maurice W. Moe, with whom the author regularly corresponded) stake out a cemetery in Arkham, the fictional New England town where much of Lovecraft's fiction takes place. Carter recounts the legend of an indescribable entity which can only be perceived by the sixth sense. In due course the creature attacks, leaving them scarred and bruised by what appears to be hoof-prints.

There's a sense that Lovecraft is gently mocking his own shortcomings and the failings that others had identified. At one point he has Manton criticise Carter for his constant talk about 'unnameable' and 'unmentionable' things, which Manton calls 'a very puerile device, quite in keeping with my lowly standing as an author. I was too fond of ending my stories with sights or sounds which paralysed my heroes' faculties and left them without courage, words, or associations to tell what they had experienced'. Even so, Lovecraft provides a clear indication of how the creature would have looked a century or so earlier when it still had physical form. Once it possessed 'a face and jaw something like yours and mine', a 'blemished eye', and four-inch horns – all of which suggests the malformed issue of a local devil worshipper's pact with the horned one. Could this be the same 'screaming drunken wretch that they hanged for having such an eye'? Carter mentions finding its bones in a dilapidated house near the graveyard so it is not a nebulous entity, only an incorporeal one. How such an entity could physically injure its victims is a perplexing question never properly answered. Yet, regardless of this, the story's publication only added to Lovecraft's growing reputation.

After finishing 'The Unnamable', Lovecraft wrote 'The Festival' in October, which is generally considered to be the first entry in the Cthulhu Mythos. The story, set in the fictional town of Kingsport, had been gestating ever since he discovered the work of Arthur Machen and declared himself equally enamoured of Margaret Murray's study, 'The Witch Cult in Western Europe'. Murray, a prominent English anthropologist and folklorist, promoted the then controversial idea that witchcraft was not mere rural superstition, but had its origins in 'the old religion' which Christianity had supplanted – resulting in the loss of much valuable arcane knowledge, particularly the healing properties of certain plants. 'The Festival' is arguably one of the first truly original tale that Lovecraft ever authored, establishing the fictional town of Arkham and its environs as a centre for the convening of supernatural forces. Organised religion might have eradicated paganism and rural superstition, but those who still wished to commune with their own gods simply went underground – in this instance literally – as the inhabitants of Kingsport descend the stone steps under the church to celebrate communion with their 'alien' familiars.

Again a sombre, muted tone gives this description of the nocturnal gathering of pagan worshipers a dreamlike quality, as if the narrator has fallen under the influence of the dreaded *Necronomicon*. Indeed, he's depicted idly leafing through this same tome while waiting for the rites to begin.

We went out into the moonless and tortuous network of that incredibly ancient town; went out as the lights in the curtained windows disappeared one by one, and the Dog Star leered at the throng of cowled, cloaked figures that poured silently from every doorway and formed monstrous processions up this street and that, past the creaking signs and antediluvian gables, the thatched roofs and diamond-paned windows; threading precipitous lanes where decaying houses overlapped and crumbled together; gliding across open courts and churchyards where the bobbing lanthorns made eldritch drunken constellations.

Only the ending of the tale – at which point, grotesque winged creatures come swooping down to carry off the worshippers – seems forced. Otherwise, 'The Festival' is imbued with the ominous sense that the past and the present coexist; it takes only a shift in perception to rend the veil between the two, as Lovecraft himself had experienced during a visit to Marblehead (the model for Kingsport) in December 1922.

Such vivid evocations of place and period permeate the best of Lovecraft's fiction, offering detailed descriptions of architectural landmarks and other remarkable buildings that become as significant as the human characters. But this attentiveness to the environment was not an affectation or stylistic conceit. It was an expression of the way he saw and understood the world – as a façade behind which the past and its inhabitants continue to exist, just beyond our everyday awareness. This explains why he took every chance to visit the historical hamlets of New England at a time when he was reluctant to travel beyond the city limits to meet friends and fellow writers. These excursions offered Lovecraft the opportunity to lose himself in the past, to escape the 'blight of mutation and modernity' and the 'tyranny of mechanism' which he felt threatened to engulf the 'authentic American culture' he sought to preserve. But more significantly, this idealised past represented an alternate reality in which his own life had meaning and where a man was not measured by his wealth, status or possessions, but by the quality of his character. Such was Lovecraft's fantasy and one he realised through his writing.

It is all the more remarkable then that he agreed to uproot himself from Providence and to move to New York in the first week of March 1924, giving his aunts no hint of his intentions and himself no chance to change his mind. Perhaps he himself was not so sure what he might do when he arrived in the metropolis. Yet, it must have been liberating to cast caution to the wind, just once. He had been the dutiful son, the conscientious scholar and the industrious amateur journalist. But it was a solitary, forlorn existence and when the chance came for him to be feted in literary circles, to enjoy a Bohemian lifestyle in Brooklyn, it was more than he could resist. He had lived for his mother all his life. Now he would live for himself. He felt like a child on the eve of setting off on a great adventure. And it was all the more thrilling because it was secret. No one knew of his plans. Only Sonia. She would be his companion, his confederate, his muse, his mother, his big sister and maybe something more.

At this stage of their relationship he was evidently hoping that she would enable him to recreate the carefree and secure lifestyle he had enjoyed in the Phillips family household. In fact he expressed as much in a revealing letter to Maurice W. Moe. 'With a wife of the same temperament as my mother and aunts, I would probably have been able to reconstruct a type of domestic life not unlike that of Angell St. days.' This was his primary purpose in agreeing to the marriage. He would no longer be alone. He would leave for New York and there the two would be wed. It was only after they had cohabited that he realised their natures were incompatible; that he possessed an 'Apollonian aesthetic' that clashed with her 'Dionysian' one (letter to Maurice W. Moe, July 1929) – by which he can only have meant that she enjoyed the intimate, physical side of marriage while he did not.

Howard Philips Lovecraft married Sonia Haft Greene on Monday, 3 March 1924, at St Paul's Chapel in Lower Manhattan. After the ceremony, they retired to their four-room, first-floor apartment at 259 Parkside Avenue in Brooklyn to enjoy a quiet honeymoon. It was only days later that they printed 200 announcements to break the news to friends and family. The groom was too nervous to tell his closest living relatives what he had done without consulting them, so he wrote his aunts a convoluted letter that reads more like the confession of an undergraduate who had been 'sent down' for some undisclosed breach of the rules than a newly married man. There was no mention of romance, only respect for a fellow intellect. S.H.G., as he referred to his new wife, was a 'benevolent angel' who had driven all thoughts of suicide from his mind, a 'detailed intellectual and aesthetic acquaintance' and an 'encouraging influence' who found him 'more congenial than anyone else'. Furthermore, she had come to depend on his correspondence and conversation 'for mental contentment and philosophical enjoyment'. Marriage had been 'a decisive and dramatic gesture' entered upon in haste to overcome his 'timidity'.

Lillian read the letter several times before the import of what it contained sank in. Aged 34, her bachelor, borderline reclusive nephew had taken a wife.

If Lovecraft was in love with Sonia he did not say it, at least not outright as she might have wished. He is known to have been in financial difficulties before moving to New York and had been seriously contemplating leaving Providence, but this was not a significant factor in their decision to marry. They were extremely fond of each other and Sonia must have been hoping that once her husband was free from his aunts' constricting influence, he would find his new circumstances agreeable. She later wrote, 'I believe he loved me as much as it was possible for a temperament like his to love'.

For her part, she saw him as a 'good and beautiful soul' whom she wished to nurture until he could support himself financially. In her memoirs she admitted that she cared for him very much and that they had discussed the difficulties that might arise – which were primarily financial, specifically whether he would come to resent being supported by his wife in the event that he didn't find employment – but concluded that they would overcome them if they cared for each other. To which he 'thoroughly agreed'.

Lovecraft evidently got a kick out of such an act of impish impulsiveness. He wrote to James Morton, 'you never can tell what a guy like me is gonna do next!'

Yet, if Sonia was anticipating a romantic honeymoon she was in for a disappointment. She spent that first day and much of the night dictating from the handwritten manuscript for 'Under the Pyramids' (published as 'Imprisoned with the Pharaohs' and later 'Entombed with the Pharaohs') while her husband typed as fast as he could on a borrowed typewriter (he'd left the typescript at Union Station in Providence the day he left for New York).

Lovecraft knew a carny yarn when he heard one and as soon as Houdini had recounted his 'terrifying ordeal' – in which he claimed to have been kidnapped then bound and gagged in Campbell's Tomb – the writer asked Henneberger if he could embellish it as he saw fit, to which the publisher agreed. Lovecraft took his commission seriously, spending days researching the myths and rituals of Ancient Egypt at the Metropolitan Museum of Art, but it paid off handsomely both critically and financially. Houdini loved it, Henneberger paid 100 dollars in advance of publication and the readers of *Weird Tales* enjoyed a top-drawer tale that more than justified their subscription.

During a tour of Egypt, world-renowned escapologist Harry Houdini is lured to the top of a pyramid by his guide and a Bedouin, then overpowered, trussed up and lowered into a pit under the Great Sphinx at Giza. He manages to free himself but, after seeking a way out, he discovers that he has gone further into the tomb where he witnesses half-human, half-animal creatures preparing a ritual offering to what he assumes to be a five-headed beast. Only it is not the head of a beast but its paw.

Unusually for Lovecraft, he added a lengthy preamble which conjured up the clamour, colours and intoxicating scents of the bazaars and back streets of Cairo. 'Spice, perfume, incense beads, rugs, silks, and brass – old Mahmoud Suleiman squats cross-legged amidst his gummy bottles while chattering youths pulverize mustard in the hollowed-out capital of an ancient classic column . . .'

Although Houdini was given sole credit, regular readers and those who were already admirers of Lovecraft must have realised the author's true identity long before they reached the final paragraph. Who else but Lovecraft could have written, 'a fiendish and ululant corpse-gurgle or death-rattle now split the very atmosphere – the charnel atmosphere poisonous with naftha and bitumen blasts – in one concerted chorus from the ghoulish legion of hybrid blasphemies'?

In mid-March Henneberger surprised Lovecraft by offering him permanent employment as the editor of *Weird Tales*, but only if he was prepared to move to Chicago. Lovecraft wisely and politely declined, on the grounds that his wife was seeking a new position in New York, (she had left her job the previous month), and for one other reason – the very real prospect that *Weird Tales* would fold if its publisher continued to lose money at the current rate.

Indeed, *Weird Tales* had suffered a sharp decline in circulation – for which Baird was held responsible. That autumn he was dismissed and the editorship passed to his assistant, Farnsworth Wright. However, Wright's editorial policy seems to have been arbitrary at best. Whereas Baird had accepted everything submitted by Lovecraft, Wright would reject several of Lovecraft's most important stories ('At the Mountains of Madness', 'The Shadow over Innsmouth' and 'The Call of Cthulhu' among others), only to accept them at a later date when he was in a more amenable mood. Ironically, Baird – who had moved across to *Weird Tales*' sister pulp publication, *Detective Tales* – would reject 'The Shunned House' as being unsuitable for his new crime magazine.

In the event, *Weird Tales* stumbled on under its new editor until 1940, but it was always perilously close to going under. Ironically, its largest surge in circulation was the direct result of an unsuccessful attempt to ban its publication in the summer of 1924. Authorities in Indiana were inundated with complaints from outraged readers regarding a story in the May-June-July issue that appeared to condone necrophilia, namely 'The Loved Dead'. Though credited to C.M. Eddy, Jnr, it was rumoured to have been extensively revised by H.P. Lovecraft. A close study of the offending text, however, reveals that, while it is peppered with Lovecraftian adjectives, it is almost entirely Eddy's handiwork as it reads like a poor attempt to mimic the master, not to mention the fact that the explicit nature of the activities it describes – 'an ecstatic hour of pleasure, pernicious and unalloyed' – would have been completely at odds with Lovecraft's sensibilities. Lovecraft scholars S.T. Joshi and David Schultz are of the opinion that it was an attempt at self-parody and argue that the florid language is reminiscent of 'The Hound'.

Whatever the truth of the matter, the ban failed to stop copies flying off the shelves in Indiana or any other state and the resulting publicity saw the magazine's finances back in the black. Nevertheless Farnsworth Wright became more cautious from then on, rejecting any stories with explicit sexual content or gruesome violence.

Lovecraft may have been right to turn down the editorship, but he was in no position to refuse offers of employment. The pulps and his hack revision work paid very poorly and Sonia's prospects were showing no signs of improvement. She remained unemployed throughout the first year of their marriage. In desperation her husband applied to dozens of periodicals, at least one literary agency and even dabbled with selling insurance, a job which lasted less than a week. Positions in publishing houses and newspaper offices were not plentiful, but neither were they impossible to obtain given persistence and a personal introduction. The problem was that Lovecraft's friends were predominantly enthusiastic amateurs with no influence in the commercial publishing world. Worse still, Lovecraft's own over-elaborate style was not suitable for terse, factual newsroom prose or the gossipy conversational idiom adopted by the national magazines. Judging by a long rambling letter of application that he circulated to a dozen top-flight publications – including the *New York Times* and *Herald Tribune* – he thought himself terribly amusing and rather above mainstream journalism. His line of argument was as follows: 'The case is one wherein certain definitely marketable aptitudes must be put forward in an unconventional manner if they are to override the current fetish which demands commercial experience and causes prospective employers to dismiss unheard the application of any situation-seeker unable to boast of specific professional service in a given line.'

In other words, they shouldn't worry too much about his lack of experience and give him a chance to prove his worth. They might have done so had he not sounded so pompous and overeager to impress. Having failed to elicit a positive response by the summer, Lovecraft was forced to advertise his services in the classified section of the *New York Times*. It came to nothing as did all other efforts to secure a regular income. And in the midst of this uncertainty, Sonia was hospitalised with a gastric complaint which necessitated a long stay in the country to recuperate. When she returned to New York the couple talked the situation over and decided that they needed to economise. She would accept the offer of a job in a department store in Cincinnati, whilst he would move to a smaller apartment – where he'd await her monthly visit. The move would necessitate the disposal of some of their furniture and it must have galled her that he refused to part with some of the dilapidated pieces brought up from Providence which were of sentimental value only, while her furnishings were high quality and contemporary, including her beloved piano.

Their financial difficulties and the enforced absence put an intolerable strain on their relationship which up till then had been cordial, if not exactly passionate. Sonia was a wonderful hostess and cook but she found his stubbornness in matters relating to his appearance and his affectations a little wearing. She made considerable efforts to outfit him in modern, though not fashionable, clothes and was rewarded with foot-dragging reluctance and a petulant look as if he were a child being kitted out by a maiden aunt. She was particularly hurt when he couldn't suppress his glee at having a new coat and suit stolen by a burglar who left Lovecraft's old clothes, having presumably decided that he wouldn't be seen dead in such duds. It also became wearing for her to be referred to as 'the ball and chain' and to be the butt of his collegiate humour. Whenever he stayed out late he'd brag to his friends of having avoided 'the traditional fusillade of conjugal flatirons and rolling-pins'. She must also have found it demeaning to play second fiddle to his male writing chums – with whom he formed the Kalem Club in 1924 – and to have to force him to accompany her to the Blue Pencil Club, a Brooklyn literary society of which she was a member, but which he disliked.

The Kalem Club was an informal gathering of writers and intellectuals who gravitated around Lovecraft to pontificate on a multitude of subjects from literature, art, plays and philosophy to politics, sociology and science. The members, who he habitually referred to as 'The Boys', included James Morton, Rheinhart Kleiner, Frank Belknap Long, Arthur Leeds, George Kirk and Everett McNeil – all of whom met ostensibly to listen to Lovecraft, who would open the discussion with a lengthy discourse on anything that had taken his fancy during the previous week.

But not everyone found him charming company. The poet Hart Crane complained that he was prevented from talking with his friend Samuel Loveman during a visit to the city by that 'queer Lovecraft fellow' who Loveman had brought along to their meeting. Crane evidently found Lovecraft's obsession with all-night architectural tours wearisome and rather inconsiderate of those friends who didn't share his interest or stamina. Others expressed astonishment to hear Lovecraft's overtly racist observations in the presence of his Jewish friends and his own wife, none of whom reproved him or made their feelings known.

Finally, after eight months of revelling in his new role as husband and raconteur, he accepted that regular employment was unlikely to be forthcoming and returned to fiction. His next project was a novella entitled, 'The Shunned House', written over four consecutive days. He completed several drafts, indicating that he set much store by this piece, but after finalizing it he sent it to W. Paul Cook whose amateur imprint Reclusive Press printed just 250 copies – all of which were still unbound at the time of the author's death.

In a letter to his Aunt Lillian dated November 1924, Lovecraft explains that the story was inspired by his sight of a real house, 'a hellish place where night-black deeds must have been done . . . suffocatingly embowered in a tangle of ivy so dense that one cannot but imagine it accursed or corpse-fed'. It reminded him of the Babbit house in Benefit Street, Providence where Lillian herself had served as a companion to old lady Babbit.

The story opens with the narrator recounting the history of the house and declaring his intention to solve the mysterious deaths that have overtaken its previous owners. With the assistance of his uncle, Dr Elihu Whipple, he undertakes a scientific investigation of the cellar where the air is foul and phosphorescent fungi grows on the walls. Whatever the house is host to, it is not a ghost. 'Above the anthropomorphic patch of mould by the fireplace it rose; a subtle, sickish, almost luminous vapour which, as it hung trembling in the dampness, seemed to develop vague and shocking suggestions of form, gradually trailing off into nebulous decay and passing up into the blackness of the great chimney with a foetor in its wake.'

The most effective passages are those describing the hideous transformation of Dr Whipple who is possessed by an amorphous presence conjured up by a former owner who had dabbled in black magic and whose 'prayers were neither uttered at the proper time nor directed at the proper object'.

Whatever doubts Lovecraft may have fostered about his ability to earn a living as a writer, he surely redeemed himself in these passages.

> In that dim blend of blue and yellow the form of my uncle had commenced a nauseous liquefaction whose essence eludes all description . . . Lit by the mixed and uncertain beams, that gelatinous face assumed a dozen – a score – a hundred – aspects; grinning, as it sank to the ground on a body that melted like tallow . . . it seemed as though the shifting features fought against themselves, and strove to form contours like those of my uncle's kindly face. I like to think that he existed at that moment, and that he tried to bid me farewell. It seems to me I hiccoughed a farewell from my own parched throat as I lurched out into the street; a thin stream of grease following me through the door to the rain-drenched sidewalk.

In an echo of the final scene from 'Under the Pyramids', a squat featureless figure on the floor is revealed to be merely the elbow of some unseen monster living under the foundations which Whipple's nephew destroys by emptying six carboys of sulphuric acid into the hole that he has dug around it.

Lovecraft was evidently unaffected by the enforced separation from his wife. In his journal, he positively revels in his newfound freedom and the peace to write afforded by his bachelor's accommodation. On New Year's Eve, 1924, he moved into a spacious room on the first floor of a Victorian house on Clinton Street in Brooklyn Heights which he described as 'a pleasing hermitage for an old-fashioned man'.

The furnishings consisted of wall-to-wall bookcases (seven

in total), a desk, several chairs, a central table and a sofa-bed to which he added the items he had earlier refused to sell because they reminded him of 'home' (i.e. 454 Angell Street). The lack of cooking facilities suited him as he couldn't face the prospect of preparing meals or washing-up and the single room required little cleaning. It was not a desirable neighbourhood, but it was well served by subway trains which ran all through the night, so he could come and go as he pleased and indulge in all-night walks, alone or with one of 'The Boys'. They were more than happy to pick up the bill at an inexpensive restaurant or diner when they couldn't invite him home for a meal. Otherwise he lived frugally, spending less than five dollars a week on food by living out of cans and thick wedges of fresh bread which left change for train fare and a regular laundry service.

But by the autumn he was feeling the cold and forced to buy an oil heater which doubled as a stove so he could finally heat tins of beans, spaghetti and beef stew. He could no longer rely on natural light to wash, work and read by and was frustrated by a faulty electric light which the landlady refused to fix. And then there were the mice who kept him awake at night, foraging for crumbs and forcing him to scour the local stores for cheap traps. The novelty of his bohemian adventure was beginning to wear thin.

Sonia was in and out of work through the rest of that year, visiting her husband at infrequent intervals and staying no more than a few months in total. He fared little better, surviving on less than $200 from the sale of five stories to *Weird Tales* in the entire year leaving Sonia and his aunts to make up the difference.

If Lovecraft resented this, he never mentioned it, at least not in his letters. He still harboured hopes of securing full-time employment, but his prospects were slim. Even a short trial writing advertising copy came to nothing and he eventually ceased applying to 'situations vacant' ads in the weekend papers. He kept himself occupied for much of the year visiting his friends on an almost daily basis and exploring the less familiar districts of New York which the tourist guides did not cover. His newfound independence and the pleasure he derived from walking and talking with friends until dawn was, however, invigorating and had the added bonus of reducing his weight from a stocky 200 pounds to a lean 146 pounds. His new physique bolstered his self-esteem, as well as reinforcing the suspicion that he was better living on his own. Being 'fussed over', fed and clothed by a woman was no longer a novelty but a reminder of the cosseting he had endured as a child. However, the demands of an active social life had a detrimental effect on Lovecraft's own creativity. For nine months he wrote nothing of consequence until August 1925 when he finally penned three short stories in quick succession: 'The Horror at Red Hook', 'He' and 'In the Vault'.

The first was stimulated by his nocturnal sojourns to the back streets and alleyways of Brooklyn where he encountered 'gangs of young loafers and herds of evil looking foreigners' (extract from a letter to Clark Ashton Smith) which led him to speculate on whatever blasphemous rites they might be engaging in when not getting violently drunk and slitting each other's throats. Repellent though his bigotry is – with its repeated denunciations of 'Asian dregs', 'primitive half-ape savagery' and 'slant-eyed folk' – it must be remembered that such derogatory terms were regrettably common in pulp fiction of the period, even in the more popular Fu Manchu and Charlie Chan stories. Its undercurrent of racism aside, 'Red Hook' is a suitably ripe tale of devil worship and human sacrifice, and boasts a similar quality to the Val Lewton B-Movies that would be made for RKO in the 1940s, in particular 'The Seventh Victim', with which it shares the theme of a secret coven in a modern urban setting.

Lovecraft might have been referring to himself when he wrote of his central character, Dublin-born detective, Thomas F. Malone, 'the sense of latent mystery in existence was always present. In youth he had felt the hidden beauty and ecstasy of things, and had been a poet; but poverty and sorrow and exile had turned his gaze in darker directions, and he had thrilled at the imputations of evil in the world around.'

It's a pity he never recalled the fictional detective for further occult investigations, but perhaps the idea of a series did not appeal to him – or maybe it was the thought of being seen to emulate Conan Doyle that dissuaded him from such an idea. However, it is Dickens rather than Doyle who shapes Lovecraft's description of the teeming backstreets of Brooklyn, recalling the depiction of the nefarious Clerkenwell rookeries in *Oliver Twist*.

> From this tangle of material and spiritual putrescence the blasphemies of an hundred dialects assail the sky. Hordes of prowlers reel shouting and singing along the lanes and thoroughfares, occasional furtive hands suddenly extinguish lights and pull down curtains, and swarthy, sin-pitted faces disappear from windows when visitors pick their way through.

The reference to Dickensian alleys and byways in an earlier passage is apt – 'some of the obscurer alleys and byways have that alluring antique flavour which conventional reading leads us to call "Dickensian"' – for Lovecraft retained a Victorian outlook when it came to equating crime, poverty and swarthy-skinned immigrants for whom the morals of civilised society were to be circumvented or disregarded altogether. However, when the full horror of the demon-worshipping cult is revealed, Lovecraft pours forth a stream of consciousness that serves as a foretaste of those who would seek to emulate him. It is also one of the most intensely lyrical (and elaborate) passages he was to write.

> Avenues of limitless night seemed to radiate in every direction, till one might fancy that here lay the root of a contagion destined to sicken and swallow cities, and engulf nations in the foetor of hybrid pestilence. Here cosmic sin had entered, and festered by unhallowed rites had commenced the grinning march of death that was to rot us all to fungous abnormalities too hideous for the grave's holding . . . Goats leaped to the sound of thin accursed flutes, and Ægypans chased endlessly after misshapen fauns over rocks twisted like swollen toads.

By contrast, Lovecraft's subsequent story – the second story written that summer – is tinged with sadness and loss. Suffused by the soft radiance of the early hours and the quiet pleasure of wandering through an unfamiliar district of the city, 'He' was written early one August morning as Lovecraft sat alone in Scott Park, New Jersey after another all-night walk through the old part of New York. In a lined exercise book purchased from a kiosk on a whim, he wrote the first and only draft in a couple of hours before returning to Brooklyn, having made up his mind to leave the city as soon as arrangements could be made. Telling of the protagonist's fateful meeting with the titular 'He', it was without doubt Lovecraft's most autobiographical tale to date and the only one which betrays his feelings in the wake of his separation from Sonia and his decision to return to Providence.

'My coming to New York had been a mistake,' confesses the story's protagonist with sudden, bittersweet clarity. 'Whereas I had looked for poignant wonder and inspiration in the teeming labyrinths of ancient streets . . . I had found instead only a sense of horror and oppression which threatened to master, paralyse, and annihilate me. The disillusion had been gradual.'

It seems likely that the seed of the story was sown a year earlier when Sonia and he had chanced to meet an old man offering to show them historic parts of Greenwich Village that were off the tourist trail. Their genial host had led them through a maze of alleyways to a hidden court dating back to the Colonial period of which Lovecraft later wrote, 'beholding this ingulph'd and search-defying fragment of yesterday, the active imagination conjures up endless weird possibilities . . .'

While strolling through Greenwich Village the narrator of 'He' comes upon a stranger who invites him back to his apartment after observing that they share an interest in historic architecture. There, his host divests himself of his cloak and wide-brimmed hat. Beneath these garments, he is attired in period costume. He then relates the legend of a man who a hundred years earlier had tricked the Native American Indians into disclosing the secrets of time and space before poisoning them with bad whisky. The stranger then confesses to being that same man, though he has not aged a day since. When his guest refuses to believe such things are possible he demonstrates his powers by showing him visions of the past and future which so alarm the narrator that he screams, arousing the spirits of the murdered Indians who take their revenge.

When the protagonist confesses that, 'in those dreary days my quest for antique beauty and mystery was all that I had to keep my soul alive', it's hard not to hear Lovecraft sigh along with him. Given the many parallels between the author and his character, it seems likely that these lines were written from the heart.

In invoking the ageless fiend and having him slain by the Native Americans he had murdered, it is tempting to see it as a form of intellectual exorcism on Lovecraft's behalf so that he could be rid of the demons that had pursued and taunted him since the beginning of this unfortunate episode. 'I never sought to return to those tenebrous labyrinths, nor would I direct any sane man thither if I could . . . the city is dead and full of unsuspected horrors . . . I have gone home to the pure New England lanes up which fragrant sea-winds sweep at evening.'

If Lovecraft was mentally preparing for a return to Providence, he had not yet confided as much to Sonia, who was still hoping that their separation might be only temporary. But he was not so circumspect when it came to discussing his plans with his friends. It appears that he talked to at least one of them about a permanent separation, though not of divorce, and so it was no great surprise to 'The Boys' when he announced that he expected to be leaving New York in the spring and that he would be travelling alone. His decision, however, was delayed due to circumstances outside of his control. He could not desert Sonia unless his aunts were prepared to welcome him back home . . . Their summons would provide him with the excuse he needed to leave.

His letters home during the summer of 1924 were full of praise for Sonia, her stoicism in the face of their enforced separation, her unwavering belief in him and the support she had offered him when things looked black. Nevertheless, he now made it clear that he'd become profoundly unhappy in the city. Yet, his aunts were slow to take the hint, suggesting nothing more than a temporary return to Providence, until a suitable position could be found in New York. Lovecraft replied that such a strategy would be impractical and that a more obvious solution would be for him to return to Providence for good and for his wife to seek a permanent position in Boston, but to no avail – all of which points to the fact that perhaps they were not so keen as he to resume their earlier living arrangements.

He would become increasingly wretched as the months dragged on with no prospect of employment except at a local catalogue company, where he was paid to address envelopes for a derisory $17 a week – a job he accepted and stuck at for a fortnight until he could stand it no more.

At such times he sought solace in the companionship of his friends and in the occasional stab at fiction. On 18 September, long before he made his intentions known to Sonia, Lovecraft knocked out 'In the Vault'. A homely backwoods tale that would have appealed to Alfred Hitchcock's macabre sense of humour, the story may well have constituted an attempt to write himself out of his own black mood. The scenario may have been suggested by C.W. Smith, editor of *The Tryout*, another amateur periodical, but the morbid denouement was Lovecraft's alone.

Undertaker George Birch is locked inside the receiving tomb where coffins are stored during winter, but he is confident he can climb out through a vent if he can pile the caskets on top of one another. However, after scaling the precarious structure he slips and breaks the lid of the top coffin. Despite the pain from what he assumes to be nails or sharp wooden splinters he struggles free and escapes. Yet on close examination, his injuries suggest that he was clawed by the corpse of a client he had disliked and whose feet he had sawn off in order to fit the body in the cheap wooden box.

That winter as Lovecraft considered his options, he began a history of supernatural fiction – as commissioned by C.W. Cook – writing from morning to night on a daily basis as with any regular paying job. It was, however, a labour of love and just as well, for he would not see a cent for his time and expertise. Indeed, money was secondary to the satisfaction that this extended essay offered him, although he could ill afford to be distracted from the more urgent task of finding paid employment, or else writing new tales of his own. Nevertheless, he worked methodically through the major and minor works, re-reading entire novels to refresh his memory and to satisfy himself that he had a fair summing up of its author's qualities and shortcomings, (even if it was only to write a paragraph or two). He welcomed the opportunity it offered to reacquaint himself with his favourite authors and familiarise himself with those he had neglected or overlooked, but he was also relieved to have something constructive to occupy himself and give purpose to his otherwise 'aimless existence'.

It would be a year and a half before he would complete *Supernatural Horror in Literature* (1927), a critical survey that was as comprehensive as it was perceptive, chronicling the development of the form from its earliest known recorded examples in Graeco-Roman antiquity to those authors deemed to be 'modern masters', namely Dunsany, Poe, Machen, Bierce, Blackwood and M.R. James. Of these, only Poe, whom Lovecraft honoured as the 'fountainhead' of modern horror, has a chapter to himself.

Poe was his 'god of fiction' and principal 'model'. Yet Lovecraft was not so smitten as to be utterly uncritical. 'His themes tend to centre in limited manifestations of the terrestrially gruesome, and in sinister twists of morbid human psychology.' Despite 'deficiencies' like these, he demonstrated a 'daemonic force which no one else can even approach'. (Letter to Fritz Leiber, 9 November 1936).

Lovecraft credited Poe with 'establishing a new standard of realism' and for stressing the importance of maintaining a single mood and impression in a tale; also for the 'rigorous paring down of incidents' to those that have a direct bearing on the plot and which will figure prominently in the climax. 'Truly may it be said that Poe invented the short story in its present form.' In drawing upon the themes of disease, perversity, and decay, Lovecraft asserted that Poe influenced both the decadents and the symbolists – and in doing so aroused the urban realism and amoral sensuality of Charles Baudelaire, progenitor of 'modernity' in the literary arts and an early translator of Poe. The decadents, whose principal exponents included Joris-Karl Huysmans, Oscar Wilde and the Saltus brothers, originated in France as a reaction to the Romantic Movement. Their name was supplied by their detractors who condemned their love of artifice. While the symbolists railed against rationalism and materialism, reasoning that – as the poet Stéphane Mallarmé expressed it – 'to name an object is to suppress three quarters of the enjoyment to be found in the poem . . . suggestion, that is the dream.'

Of Poe, Lovecraft gushed, 'verses and tales alike sustain the burthen of cosmic panic . . . A Witches' Sabbath of horror flinging off decorous robes is flashed before us – a sight the more monstrous because of the scientific skill with which every particular is marshalled and brought into an easy apparent relation to the known gruesomeness of material life.'

Lovecraft made a distinction between weird fiction and Poe's tales of terror in which monomania (obsession) and 'abnormal psychology' (unusual behaviour and irrational fears) generate the disturbing visions endured by the protagonists rather than supernatural entities, and cited 'The Narrative of Arthur Gordon Pym of Nantucket', 'Metzengerstein', 'The Man of the Crowd', 'MS. Found in a Bottle' and 'The Facts in the Case of M. Valdemar' as prime examples of the latter.

Who can forget the terrible swollen ship poised on the billow-chasm's edge in 'MS. Found in a Bottle' – the dark intimations of her unhallowed age and monstrous growth, her sinister crew of unseeing greybeards, and her frightful southward rush under full sail through the ice of the Antarctic night, sucked onward by some resistless devil-current toward a vortex of eldritch enlightenment which must end in destruction? Then there is the unutterable 'M. Valdemar', kept together by hypnotism for seven months after his death, and uttering frantic sounds but a moment before the breaking of the spell leaves him 'a nearly liquid mass of loathsome – of detestable putrescence'.

Lovecraft's highest praise, however, was reserved for 'The Tomb of Ligeia' and 'The Fall of the House of Usher'.

'The Masque of the Red Death', 'Silence – A Fable' and 'Shadow – A Parable' are assuredly poems in every sense of the word save the metrical one, and owe as much of their power to aural cadence as to visual imagery. But it is in two of the less openly poetic tales, 'Ligeia' and 'The Fall of the House of Usher' – especially the latter – that one finds those very summits of artistry whereby Poe takes his place at the head of fictional miniaturists. 'Ligeia' tells of a first wife of lofty and mysterious origin, who after death returns through a preternatural force of will to take possession of the body of a second wife; imposing even her physical appearance on the temporary reanimated corpse of her victim at the last moment. Despite a suspicion of prolixity and top heaviness, the narrative reaches its terrific climax with relentless power. 'Usher', whose superiority in detail and proportion is very marked, hints shudderingly of obscure life in inorganic things, and displays an abnormally linked trinity of entities at the end of a long and isolated family history—a brother, his twin sister, and their incredibly ancient house all sharing a single soul and meeting one common dissolution at the same moment.

Poe's supreme mastery of his craft was, according to Lovecraft, due to the fact that he 'understood so perfectly the very mechanics and physiology of fear and strangeness,' investing his male protagonists – whom Lovecraft calls his 'haughty and solitary victims of Fate' – with his own peculiar psychology which involved episodic unconsciousness, seizures and paranoia. The first of these disorders he shared with Lovecraft as well as his tendency to swing from manic depression to manic productivity.

In the final chapter of his extended essay Lovecraft identified the qualities which distinguished those he considered the 'modern masters' from the purveyors of lurid gothic romances. 'The best horror-tales of today,' he wrote, 'possess a naturalness, convincingness, artistic smoothness, and skilful intensity of appeal quite beyond comparison with anything in the Gothic work of a century or more ago.'

He commended the Welsh writer Arthur Machen for his 'exquisitely lyrical and expressive prose style', for the 'strange magic' of his rural settings inhabited by pagan deities and for the 'malign witchery' of his most famous tale, 'The Great God Pan'. As far as Lovecraft was concerned, the author had effortlessly 'absorbed the mediaeval mystery of dark woods and ancient customs'. Machen's 'The White People' also comes in for fulsome praise, especially the climax where a thirteen-year-old girl is led by her nanny to witness a witch's sabbat in the Welsh Hills 'performed under an imaginative spell which lends to the wild scenery an added weirdness, strangeness, and suggestion of grotesque sentience. The details of this journey are given with marvellous vividness, and form to the keen critic a masterpiece of fantastic writing, with almost unlimited power in the intimation of potent hideousness and cosmic aberration.'

Lovecraft doesn't begrudge acknowledging a novel that had a significant influence on his own work.

> In the episodic novel of *The Three Impostors* . . . we find in its most artistic form a favourite weird conception of the author's; the notion that beneath the mounds and rocks of the wild Welsh hills dwell subterraneously that squat primitive race whose vestiges gave rise to our common folk legends of fairies, elves, and the 'little people', and whose acts are even now responsible for certain unexplained disappearances, and occasional substitutions of strange dark 'changelings' for normal infants. This theme receives its finest treatment in the episode entitled 'The Novel of the Black Seal'; where a professor, having discovered a singular identity between certain characters scrawled on Welsh limestone rocks and those existing in a prehistoric black seal from Babylon, sets out on a course of discovery which leads him to unknown and terrible things.

The cast of supporting characters includes a boy described by Lovecraft as 'retarded', the 'son of some father more terrible than mankind' (shades of 'The Dunwich Horror') and 'the heir of monstrous memories and possibilities'. With the aid of the titular black seal, the professor invokes 'the awful transmutation of the hills' causing the boy to suffer a hideous transformation. Only then are 'the horrors of his shocking paternity' revealed. Then, in Lovecraft's words, 'Professor Gregg knew the stark frenzy of cosmic panic in its darkest form. He knew the abysmal gulfs of abnormality that he had opened, and went forth into the wild hills prepared and resigned. He would meet the unthinkable "little people" – and his document ends with a rational observation: "If I unhappily do not return from my journey, there is no need to conjure up here a picture of the awfulness of my fate."'

'Black Seal' brings to mind several of Lovecraft's most memorable creations, specifically 'The Whisperer in Darkness' which shares its bleak rural setting, 'The Dunwich Horror', which features an academic investigator and 'The Call of Cthulhu' which develops Machen's theme of a sinister cult and the allure of certain mysterious artefacts.

'Machen is a titan,' he told Frank Belknap Long, 'perhaps the greatest living author – and I must read everything of his . . . there is in Machen an ecstasy of fear that all other living men are too obtuse or timid to capture, and that even Poe failed to envisage in all its starkest abnormality. As you say, he is greater than our Eddie in ability to suggest the unutterable; tho' I cannot call him so great as an artist generally, since his narration lacks the relentless force and unified impressiveness which make any work of Poe one concentrated delirium . . . I ask no more of him than to have written *The Three Impostors*.'

In a letter to Robert E. Howard dated 4 October 1930, he enthused about one of the most remarkable tales in that collection, 'The White People' calling it, 'undoubtedly the greatest, even though it hasn't the tangible, visible terrors of "The Great God Pan" or "The White Powder."'

Machen's 'The Novel of the White Powder' sees a young law student addicted to a drug that initially offers him respite from his troubles, but which ultimately destroys him. After a sticky black liquid seeps through the floor into the room below a doctor is summoned and breaks down the door to discover 'a dark and putrid mass, seething with corruption and hideous rottenness, neither liquid nor solid, but melting and changing'.

One cannot read it without being reminded of Lovecraft's own 'The Thing on the Doorstep' and 'Cool Air' and there are resonances too of the death of Wilbur Whateley in 'The Dunwich Horror' and the livid red stain on the ceiling in 'The Picture in the House'.

Lovecraft had a lower opinion of Ambrose Bierce, who is best known for his short story, 'An Occurrence at Owl Creek Bridge', in which a Confederate sympathiser escapes execution only to discover that his escape was a delusion experienced in the throes of death. Lovecraft is said to have disliked such twists and so preferred Bierce's more conventional tales of revenge such as 'The Suitable Surroundings', which subvert the genre by revealing a more prosaic explanation of events.

Lovecraft considered Bierce an author who 'seldom realises the atmospheric possibilities of his themes as vividly as Poe' and whose work was undermined by 'a certain touch of naïveté, prosaic angularity, or early-American provincialism'. Nevertheless, he opined in *Supernatural Horror in Literature* that 'the genuineness and artistry of [Bierce's] dark intimations are always unmistakable, so that his greatness is in no danger of eclipse'.

Lovecraft took his pleasures seriously – and none more so than his love of literature. He derived a particular delight in sharing his enthusiasm and literary discoveries with friends and correspondents and took the unusual step of acknowledging those authors he admired and from whom he had found inspiration in his own tales.

In a letter to Vincent Starrett dated 6 December 1927, Lovecraft ranked Algernon Blackwood highly – 'and this in spite of the oceans of unrelieved puerility which he so frequently pours forth. I am dogmatic enough to call "The Willows" the finest weird story I have ever read, and I find in the "Incredible Adventures" and "John Silence" material a serious and sympathetic understanding of the human illusion-weaving process which makes Blackwood rate far higher as a creative artist than many another craftsman of mountainously superior word-mastery and general technical ability.'

Ten years later he had not altered his opinion. In a letter to Willis Conover, dated 10 January 1937, he affirmed that: 'It is safe to say that Blackwood is the greatest living weirdist despite unevenness and a poor prose style.'

'The Willows' benefits from its isolated setting – a wilderness of islands, sand-banks and swampland off the Hungarian shore where two travellers are assailed by unsettling sensations, hallucinations and impressions. To their horror, they come to realise that they're unwitting trespassers on an unholy site. The vengeful spirit of the place can only be assuaged by human sacrifice . . .

In evaluating the work of the English journalist and author, Lovecraft noted that while Blackwood's lesser work was weakened by 'insipid whimsicality', 'no one has even approached the skill, seriousness, and minute fidelity with which he records the overtones of strangeness in ordinary things and experiences'. He also applauded Blackwood's 'preternatural insight' in developing the sensations and perceptions that accompany the altered states of awareness. 'He is the one absolute and unquestioned master of weird atmosphere . . . Above all others he understands how fully some sensitive minds dwell forever on the borderland of dream, and how relatively slight is the distinction betwixt those images formed from actual objects and those excited by the play of the imagination.' It would seem that Lovecraft found reassurance in the possibility that other creative individuals shared this facility and perhaps too his fears. However, he was less impressed by Blackwood's 'bald and journalistic style'.

But in spite of all this, Blackwood's best works evoke 'an awed and convinced sense of the immanence of strange spiritual spheres or entities'. Of these Lovecraft recommended 'The Willows', in which 'an impression of lasting poignancy is produced without a single strained passage or a single false note'.

Other tales to receive Lovecraft's approval were 'The Wendigo', 'An Episode in a Lodging House', 'The Listener' and those collected between the covers of *Incredible Adventures*, wherein 'occur some of the finest tales which the author has yet produced, leading the fancy to wild rites on nocturnal hills, to secret and terrible aspects lurking behind stolid scenes, and to unimaginable vaults of mystery below the sands and pyramids of Egypt; all with a serious finesse and delicacy . . . Too subtle, perhaps, for definite classification as horror-tales, yet possibly more truly artistic in an absolute sense, are such delicate phantasies as *Jimbo* or *The Centaur*. Mr Blackwood achieves in these novels a close and palpitant approach to the inmost substance of dream, and works enormous havoc with the conventional barriers between reality and imagination.'

He also enjoyed the quiet musty atmosphere generated by Cambridge don M.R. James, England's foremost exponent of the skin-crawling ghost story whom he credited with 'an almost diabolic power [for] calling horror by gentle steps from the midst of prosaic daily life'. Montague Rhodes James was all that Lovecraft wished to have been – a respected scholar, an antiquarian and a recognised authority on mediaeval manuscripts. It could not have escaped his attention that Dr James had attained his academic honours while earning an enviable reputation as 'a literary weird fictionist of the very first rank' (in Lovecraft's own words). It is odd that Lovecraft categorises James as a 'weird fictionist' when he is more commonly regarded as a master of the antiquarian ghost story, but he is correct in observing that James preferred a conversational tone. 'Creating the illusion of every-day events, he introduces his abnormal phenomena cautiously and gradually; relieved at every turn by touches of homely and prosaic detail, and sometimes spiced with a snatch or two of antiquarian scholarship . . . A favourite scene for a James tale is some centuried cathedral, which the author can describe with all the familiar minuteness of a specialist in that field.' In describing M.R. James as 'an artist in incident and arrangement rather than in atmosphere,' Lovecraft offered 'The Treasure of Abbot Thomas' as a prime example of the author's best work.

A British antiquarian discovers a hoard of hidden gold after deciphering clues encoded on some stained glass windows in a German abbey. Unbeknown to him the treasure is protected by an unseen guardian which wraps its arms around the antiquarian as he climbs out of the well in which the treasure has been buried. Later, after he has returned to the safety of his hotel room, the poor man is reduced to a gibbering wreck by the foetid odour of mould that wafts in under the door. In desperation the antiquarian consults a clergyman who is persuaded to replace the stone that had sealed the mouth of the treasure-vault. Just before the cleric departs he notices a Latin inscription on the rim of the well: '*Depositum custody* – keep that which is committed to thee.' No creature is ever revealed – only suggested and the story is all the more effective for that. It is this palpable sense of proximity to some unspeakable horror which Lovecraft admired so much and which has the reader looking over their shoulder or checking under their bed before extinguishing the light.

Lovecraft also names 'Count Magnus', 'The Stalls of Barchester Cathedral', 'Oh, Whistle, and I'll Come to You, My Lad' and 'An Episode of Cathedral History' as worthy of merit. 'Dr James, for all his light touch, evokes fright and hideousness in their most shocking forms; and will certainly stand as one of the few really creative masters in his darksome province.'

In the conclusion to his extended essay, Lovecraft looked to the future and predicted interesting developments for horror as a literary genre while admitting, 'it is a narrow though essential branch of human expression, and will chiefly appeal as always to a limited audience with keen special sensibilities'. In that respect, he was happily mistaken.

Supernatural Horror in Literature remains invaluable as one of the earliest surveys of the genre, complete with Lovecraft's perceptive evaluations of his contemporaries as well as his personal definition of weird fiction.

> The true weird tale has [. . .] a certain atmosphere of breathless and unexplainable dread of outer, unknown forces . . . and there must be a hint, expressed with a seriousness and portentousness becoming its subject, of that most terrible conception of the human brain – a malign and particular suspension or defeat of those fixed laws of Nature which are our only safeguard against the assaults of chaos and the daemons of unplumbed space . . . Atmosphere is the all-important thing, for the final criterion of authenticity is not the dovetailing of a plot but the creation of a given sensation . . . Therefore we must judge a weird tale . . . by the emotional level which it attains at its least mundane point . . . The one test of the really weird is simply this – whether or not there be excited in the reader a profound sense of dread, and of contact with unknown spheres and powers . . . And of course, the more completely and unifiedly a story conveys this atmosphere the better it is as a work of art in the given medium.

Ironically, as his New York adventure drew to a close in a gloomy boarding house on Clinton Street, a new phase of his writing – arguably the peak period of his creativity – was just beginning. And its first flowering was an uncharacteristically contemporary tale set in a brownstone building where the cacophony of city traffic could be heard through the open window.

'Cool Air' is one of the finest examples of the urban weird tale, and yet it was rejected by Farnsworth Wright as 'too grisly', necessitating its sale for a nominal fee to the lesser known magazine, *Tales of Magic and Mystery*.

H.P. Lovecraft
IT'S MY SILHOUETTE
By PERRY
Dated 29th Day 1925 of March
at New York, N.Y.

Clockwise from top-left: Silhouette by Perry, 29 March 1925; 'Nowhere in the animal world can we discover such Hellenic perfection of form . . . as in the felidae.' Lovecraft holding Frank Belknap Long's cat, Felis, c. 1925. HPL made no secret of his lifelong admiration of this perfectly adapted species of animal; Lovecraft, c. 1930, during the writing of 'The Whisperer in Darkness'. By this point, he had resigned himself to living off submissions to poorly paying pulp magazines.

Clockwise from top-left: Visiting the home of Arthur Goodenough, Vermont, August 1927; Signed by Lovecraft as 'Grandpa on Orton's doorstep,' September 1928; HPL and Arthur Goodenough outside the latter's home in Vermont, 21 August 1927. Lovecraft's walks through the surrounding atmospheric countryside provided inspiration and local colour for 'The Whisperer in Darkness'.

Clockwise from top-left*: Portrait printed by Sonia in* The Rainbow, *5 July 1921;
The first page of the original handwritten manuscript of 'The Case of Charles
Dexter Ward', Lovecraft's only completed novel; With the Lee boys, Vrest Orton's
neighbours in West Guilford, Vermont, 10 June 1928.*

Clockwise from top-left: Lovecraft with Vrest Orton during a two-week vacation in September 1928. Rounding up stray cows and lighting wood fires were two new skills learned by HPL while staying on Orton's newly purchased farm in Vermont; HPL in Brooklyn, 1931: the year when he began writing 'At the Mountains of Madness'; With amateur journalist 'Tryout' Smith (left), 4 October 1931; With W. Paul Cook (left), 4 October 1931.

Clockwise from top-left: With friend and protégé Donald Wandrei (left) in New York, c. 1931. *Wandrei never stopped pressing Farnsworth Wright to publish 'The Call of Cthulhu' in* Weird Tales; *Portrait by Lucius B. Truesdell, taken in Florida, June 1934; Lovecraft on one of his last vacations, possibly in Florida, 1935; Horseplay with Frank Belknap Long in Brooklyn, July 1931.*

Above: On the publication of 'The Whisperer in Darkness' in 1931, Arthur Goodenough despatched this congratulatory postcard to Lovecraft's home, complete with questions about the story. HPL mailed it straight back with answers traced over the top. *Left*: Sketch of Cthulhu by HPL, drawn for R.H. Barlow and dated 11 May 1934. At one time Lovecraft drew up a genealogy of the Great Old Ones for his correspondents to refer to when constructing fantastical worlds of their own.

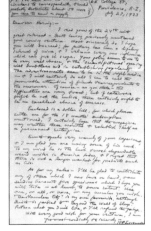

Clockwise from top: *Lovecraft was delighted by Virgil Finlay's drawing of himself as an eighteenth-century gentleman and wrote to the artist offering to write a verse. 'I could easily scrawl a sonnet to one of your masterpieces if you weren't too particular about quality'; One of seven pages of plot notes, scrawled down by HPL in the early stages of planning his 1936 novella, 'At the Mountains of Madness'; It is estimated that HPL kept in touch with as many as 75 correspondents. This letter – to one of them – is dated 27 July 1933.*

Clockwise from top-left: HPL with the Barlow family and their cat, Florida, 1935. Robert Barlow was just thirteen years old when he began corresponding with Lovecraft. They collaborated on six stories before Lovecraft made Barlow his literary executor; 'The world is indeed comic, but the joke is on mankind': Lovecraft's death certificate, 15 March 1937; Lovecraft's final resting place in Swan Point Cemetery. After his death in 1937, his name was inscribed as a postscript on the headstone of his parents. Years later, friends and admirers went to great lengths to raise funds for a memorial plaque (below right) and separate headstone (below left); HPL once referred to himself by the moniker of 'Rev. Fr. Lovecraft': here he is in St John's Churchyard, Providence, winter 1935.

In describing the storyteller Lovecraft provides a pencil sketch of himself and the situation he had found himself in. The unnamed narrator is a writer reduced to working for a cheap magazine whose salary is barely sufficient to pay for a room in a run-down boarding house. The only other tenant in whom he takes an interest is a retired physician who keeps his room at a constant temperature of 55 degrees with the aid of an ammonia cooling system which requires a regular supply of ice. When it breaks down the narrator offers to repair it, but in his absence the good doctor physically deteriorates until there is nothing left of him but a trail of putrescent ooze. It transpires that he had been on the point of death and preserving himself artificially with the aid of the cooling apparatus.

By the end of March 1926, Lovecraft was writing to his aunts to tell how he'd been 'screaming in sheer desperation and pounding the walls and floor' in despair every morning that he awoke in that accursed lodging. His state of mind was of great concern to his friend Frank Long who enlisted the help of his own mother in writing to Lillian and apprising her of her nephew's precarious condition and expressing the fear 'that he might go off the deep end'. Two days later a small cheque for the purchase of a railway ticket was delivered to a man whose greatest fear was that he would not be allowed to go home.

He returned to Providence on the afternoon of Saturday, 18 April 1926, in a state of euphoria, no wiser than when he had left it. He was also somewhat bruised and despondent at having failed to make a future for himself and his wife. He still harboured a vague hope that Sonia might join him later on and that she would find a position in Providence that would allow them to live as a couple in a house to be shared with his now widowed aunts, but it was not to be. Clearly he entertained an unconventional idea of matrimony, one in which a wife coexisted in domestic harmony with her husband's relatives as one extended family ruling out any chance of privacy or – more significantly – intimacy.

In the meantime, being low on funds, he rented a room on the ground floor of a three-storey Victorian house at 10 Barnes Street – west of his former family home – for the sum of ten dollars a week. His Aunt Lillian took a room on the second floor. The house clearly made an impression upon him. This same address is also cited as the home of Dr Willett in 'The Case of Charles Dexter Ward', appearing at the head of the ominous letter he writes to foreshadow Charles' escape from hospital.

In correspondence with Frank Belknap Long (on 1 May 1926), Lovecraft makes further mention of the place. 'I have a fine large ground-floor room (a former dining room with fireplace) and kitchenette alcove in a spacious brown Victorian wooden house at the 1880 period – a house, curiously enough, built by some friends of my own family, now long dead.'

But if Lovecraft returned to Providence in ignominy (as he saw it), he brought with him the outline of a story that would ensure his place among the greats of American literature and one which exemplified the weird tale as no other would do: 'The Call of Cthulhu'.

CHAPTER SEVEN

THE CALL OF CTHULHU

*'Fear best lends itself to the creation of
nature-defying illusions.'*
– H.P. Lovecraft

'The Call of Cthulhu' (written in the summer of 1926 on Lovecraft's return to his hometown) is the product of a singular mind and a feverish imagination, formed and informed by its author's aversion to a hostile world, a world from which he had fled, fearing that if he lingered he would lose his tentative hold on reality and be cast adrift on those 'black seas of infinity' – as were his mother and father before him.

'Cthulhu' is Lovecraft's psychosis made manifest – a lord of chaos slumbering in the subconscious that is subdued by its creator's rational mind – in the hope that if he can articulate his fear, he may yet master it. But if he were to cease writing and attempt to restrain his intense, irrational anxieties through some other means such as drink or narcotics, he could unleash those inner demons that exist 'not in the spaces we know but between them', just below the thin shell of civilised society and reason.

This eruption of 'the other' into ordered existence in one form or another is a recurring theme in many of his earlier stories, but never more explicitly expressed than in 'The Call of Cthulhu'. The darkened premise of this tale is encapsulated in the opening lines: 'The most merciful thing in the world . . . is the inability of the human mind to correlate all its contents. We live on a placid island of ignorance in the midst of black seas of infinity, and it was not meant that we should voyage far.'

After opening with this – one of the most arresting lines in modern literature – the story unfolds through the discovery of several seemingly unrelated documents. Presented together, they uncover a truth that would cause widespread panic if it was made public knowledge. The first reveals that a monstrous creature, Cthulhu, has been slumbering for millennia in a city beneath the sea (a clear reference to the Greek myth of the Kraken and its Scandinavian variant). Its re-emergence has been sensed in the dreams of certain hypersensitive individuals who are tormented by their visions of the scaly, winged abomination, described as being a cross between a dragon, an octopus and a hideously deformed human being. The second source, an account of an investigation undertaken by a Louisiana police inspector into the disappearance of squatters in the swamps of New Orleans, describes the breaking up of a voodoo cult which worshipped the same deity. A third paper records a witness statement written by a seaman who saw the creature with his own eyes, he being the sole survivor of a ship whose crew explored the uncharted island where the monster had been imprisoned. After unwittingly releasing it, his boat is pursued by the 'gelatinous green immensity' which survives being rammed by reconstituting itself. This is arguably the one weak point in the entire story, reducing the ageless Old One to the level of a cheesy B-movie creature that can be fought with conventional weapons.

The narrator ends his investigation by resigning himself to the inevitable – a dreadful death at the hands of the Cthulhu cult who by now must be aware that he knows too much. And this is the twist of the knife in the gut of the tale: not the awakening of Cthulhu, but the narrator's realisation that death – even a violent death at the hands of the cult – is preferable to living with the knowledge that everything is meaningless and that all our efforts are futile.

This piecing together of the evidence by a respected academic (albeit a fictional one) not only invests the tale with a sombre authority, but also parallels the process of psychoanalysis – in which successive layers are peeled back to reveal repressed emotions, archetypal personalities and suppressed memories. The descent into the psyche begins in this instance with a young sculptor's dream, symbolising the superficial persona or ego, then the account of the primitive cult representing the primal urge just beneath surface and finally the confrontation with the id, or shadow-self at the core – personified by Cthulhu and his savage acolytes. This stifling sense of uncertainty, confusion and disorientation is brilliantly conveyed by Lovecraft, explaining why his writings appeal particularly, but not exclusively, to adolescents.

Like the neurotic and eccentric young sculptor Henry Wilcox – whose glimpse of a terrifying reality leads him to fashion a bas-relief of Cthulhu – Lovecraft was a 'psychically hypersensitive' individual whose experiences of the lower worlds occurred not in mediumistic trance, but in his dreams, when the 'ordinary mind', as Zen Buddhists call our waking consciousness, was powerless to prevent these primal forces from breaking through to torment him.

The greatest horror Lovecraft could imagine was the violent emergence of the savage self – as exemplified by the bestial worshippers of an imaginary malign deity, whose real-life counterparts were the 'foreign' hordes who threatened to overrun his precious homeland. Hence, Lovecraft never stopped fighting to suppress his emotions; instead he strove to divert his energies into intellectual pursuits. By cultivating a superior intellect, he believed he could contain the inner, inferior man; the primitive, uncultured, ignorant brute whose baser instincts disturbed him so violently that they could only be exorcised by projecting them onto 'inferior' races.

It is true that elements of the story are borrowed from the work of other authors – namely the Louisiana swamp scenes of cult worship and the piecing together of a narrative from recovered fragments, documents and witness statements – but the cumulative effect of these incidents ensures its enduring popularity. Lovecraft created an authentic modern myth, something that he would not have been aware of at the time, or believed if anyone had suggested as much, but he must have sensed that he had produced something extraordinary.

They worshipped, so they said, the Great Old Ones who lived ages before there were any men, and who came to the young world out of the sky. Those Old Ones were gone now, inside the earth and under the sea; but their dead bodies had told their secrets in dreams to the first men, who formed a cult which had never died.

This faux-biblical language is crucial to Lovecraft's myth making, as is the preponderance of archaic phrases elsewhere in the text which gives the impression of having been written by an authority with something profound to impart. There are numerous examples of affectation which are simply self-indulgent and 'Cthulhu' is not immune from these. On hearing of his great uncle's death and its probable cause, the narrator remarks: 'At the time I saw no reason to dissent from this dictum', instead of simply stating that he saw no reason to disagree, or to question it. Similarly, he indulges in long convoluted passages for the perverse pleasure it gives him to lead the reader by the most circuitous route.

A further example: 'That tenebrousness was indeed a positive quality; for it obscured such parts of the inner walls as ought to have been revealed, and actually burst forth like smoke from its eon-long imprisonment, visibly darkening the sun as it slunk away into the shrunken and gibbous sky on flapping membranous wings.'

For someone as well-read as Lovecraft this degree of ostentation can only be deliberate.

Lovecraft's own evaluation of 'Cthulhu' is characteristically modest, calling it 'full of cheap and cumbrous touches', an assessment which may have been influenced by Farnsworth Wright's initial rejection of the tale. Fortunately, he was persuaded to reconsider and 'The Call of Cthulhu' was published eighteen months later in February 1928.

'Cthulhu' is the ultimate expression of its author's nihilistic philosophy which states that we exist in an amoral universe and that ignorance of this fact is our best defence. As T.S. Eliot declared, 'human beings cannot take too much reality,' a theory that Lovecraft understood instinctively. His pessimism was not in keeping with the spirit of the time, but would be wholeheartedly embraced just half a century later, when recreational drugs and a change in consciousness gave his cosmic horrors a suitable context. The altered states he described and the characters he created no longer seemed outlandish to a generation tripping on

LSD, casting off their constraints to the accompaniment of mantric rock music and threatening to overthrow civilised society. The Age of Aquarius would give way to the cult of Cthulhu, the occult revival and the destruction of institutionalised religion overseen by the gods of chaos.

'The Call of Cthulhu' forms the foundation of Lovecraft's reputation and rightly so, but it is doing its author a disservice to identify it as the cornerstone of the Cthulhu Mythos, which as previously stated, was the invention of another, August Derleth, who contrived a device to link unrelated stories by the most tenuous connection. Authors frequently allude to fictitious incidents, characters and locations in related works and Lovecraft was no different. Although he amused himself by drawing up a genealogy of his gods, there is no evidence that he worked out a unified system or pored over maps to create a viable world for his characters to inhabit as Tolkien would do. It may provide hours of pleasure for some to speculate on how these various elements interact (an exercise which can enhance many of the Lovecraft-themed role playing games) but Lovecraft himself was wilfully indifferent in such matters. He relocated Arkham, for example, at various sites in subsequent stories and is likely to have used the same name in different stories, not for one moment imagining that a century later his readers would be attaching great significance to each and every one. He could be maddeningly inconsistent; inspired, spontaneous and dynamic one moment and in the next calculating, precise and formal, as he slipped in and out of the light trance-like state that engenders creativity, the subconscious driving the former and the intellect the latter. Yet disparities like these are entirely in keeping with the shifting mental and emotional states of his protagonists. Even the blasphemous *Necronomicon* was merely a convenient repository of ancient lore, most of it unspecified, though there have been several attempts to publish completed editions, some as a scholarly exercise, some to capitalise on Lovecraft's cult status and others incorporating genuine magical rituals.

Lovecraft himself couldn't have held 'The Call of Cthulhu' in any special regard for once he'd finished this story, he immediately embarked on a standard tale of the supernatural, albeit one that plays out in a realistic Boston setting and delivers a satisfying twist. Though it is almost never remarked on, Lovecraft's incredible facility for adopting different voices lends his tales variety, making nonsense of the criticism that all his stories sound the same. For 'Pickman's Model' (September 1926) – the story of an artist who paints horrors 'from life' – he adopted a conversational tone in keeping with its anecdotal nature. Thurber, the narrator, remarks, 'I remember your asking Pickman yourself once, the year before you went away, wherever in thunder he got such ideas and visions.'

This monologue form also gave Lovecraft the opportunity to vent his personal opinion on a subject close to his heart.

> Only a real artist knows the actual anatomy of the terrible or the physiology of fear – the exact sort of lines and proportions that connect up with latent instincts or hereditary memories of fright, and the proper colour contrasts and lighting effects to stir the dormant sense of strangeness. I don't have to tell you why a Fuseli really brings a shiver while a cheap ghost-story frontispiece merely makes us laugh. There's something those fellows catch – beyond life – that they're able to make us catch for a second. Doré had it. Sime has it. Angarola of Chicago has it. And Pickman had it as no man ever had it before or – I hope to Heaven – ever will again.

He is also generous in name-checking real fellow writers and illustrators who he believed were deserving of wider public acclaim. 'There was none of the exotic technique you see in Sidney Sime, none of the trans-Saturnian landscapes and lunar fungi that Clark Ashton Smith uses to freeze the blood.' This was not the first mention of Smith who had become a close personal friend of Lovecraft's.

Lovecraft is not out to terrify his readers, nor nauseate them with graphic descriptions of visceral horrors, but to unsettle them and leave them with a suffocating sense of unease so that they will not look on the world as they once did. This is his particular – or peculiar – gift. The unveiling of Pickman's latest portrait even gives Thurber, a hardened war veteran, cause to shudder. 'It was a colossal and nameless blasphemy with glaring red eyes, and it held in bony claws a thing that had been a man, gnawing at the head as a child nibbles at a stick of candy' – an allusion, perhaps, to Goya's painting, *Saturn Devouring His Son*.

It is a curious contradiction that whilst Lovecraft was highly critical of his own work, he also imagined himself a literary authority, well qualified to criticise the work of others who paid him to edit and revise their manuscripts prior to publication, a sideline he had begun in 1918. One young hopeful, however, came to resent his mentor's 'interference'. Wilfred Talman, a staff writer at the *New York Times*, objected to Lovecraft's dialogue – which he thought 'stilted' – and to his 'gratuitous' editing, though he seems to have little cause for complaint, for his story 'Two Black Bottles' was duly published in the August 1927 issue of *Weird Tales*. Apparently the matter did not sour their working relationship. Soon after, Talman was appointed editor of the *Texaco Star*. Once he'd assumed this new post, Lovecraft did not hesitate to pitch 'descriptive travel-treatises' to his former protégé. Yet, after careful consideration, Lovecraft himself dismissed the idea as an unsuitable sideline, citing his archaic writing style, his penchant for out-of-the-way locations and his aversion to 'commercial' writing on principle as reasons for revoking his offer.

Instead he turned to his most ambitious undertaking to date, *The Dream-Quest of Unknown Kadath* (1926), a novel that its author considered unsatisfying in many respects and so remained unpublished during his lifetime. It reads like the first draft of a new Greek odyssey, but with a modern world-weary tone as the despondent Randolph Carter searches in vain for the unattainable. But there are jarring anomalies among the quasi-biblical text such as the use of the anachronism term 'harassed' in this sentence. 'In light slumber he descended the seventy steps to the cavern of flame and talked of this design to the bearded priests Nasht and Kaman-Thah. And the priests shook their pshent-bearing heads and vowed it would be the death of his soul. They pointed out that the Great Ones had shown already their wish, and that it is not agreeable to them to be harassed by insistent pleas.'

Lovecraft was all for disowning it saying, 'it isn't much good; but forms useful practice for later and more authentic attempts in the novel form'. He also admitted that Carter may have outstayed his welcome as an unlikely hero, especially when he spends much of the 'adventure' in quiet contemplation or running from danger and is of little use in a scrap. There is also the suspicion that piling on one fantastic scenario after another must have produced ennui in the average reader.

It is tempting to see this tale as analogous to Lovecraft's personal search for success and meaning in a life that had come down to endless stretches of unpaid work – with little to no critical acclaim. Carter has been given glimpses of a celestial city but each time it fades before he can reach it. After appealing to the gods to allow him to enter, the visions stop altogether, leaving Carter to make his own way without a map or guides.

Carter's experiences and encounters in 'The Dream-Quest' have frustrated many of Lovecraft's most devoted admirers who see no cohesion or sense in its apparently random images and are put off by the banal names given to the various species and cultures (specifically the ghasts, the gugs and the zoogs). But as an impression of the dream-state it is mesmerising, distinct from the author's more celebrated work and quite charming. 'Vaguely it called up glimpses of a far forgotten first youth, when wonder and pleasure lay in all the mystery of days, and dawn and dusk alike strode forth prophetic to the eager sound of lutes and song, unclosing fiery gates toward further and surprising marvels.'

Most striking of all is the changeless city of Celephais (originally the subject of a short story with the same title written in 1920), which had been dreamt into being by its monarch King Kuranes who became a permanent inhabitant of the dream lands after his death. If this is not an allusion to the Universal Laws of the esoteric tradition linking death and dreams, conception and creation, willpower and imagination, it reduces the novella to a mere fairy tale – and one not worth the telling. However, read as a spiritual quest, the various stages of Carter's journey begin to make sense with the final revelation that the gold and marble city of wonder is only the sum of what he had seen and loved in youth. 'This loveliness, moulded, crystallised, and polished by years of memory and dreaming, is your terraced wonder of elusive sunsets; and to find that marble parapet with curious urns and carven rail, and descend at last those endless balustraded steps to the city of broad squares and prismatic fountains, you need only to turn back to the thoughts and visions of your wistful boyhood.'

Carter's journey ends when he realises that he has been directed to a place of no return by the deceitful Nyarlathotep, a malign deity from the story of the same name, and saves himself by recalling that he is dreaming. After leaping from the giant bird that is taking him to the realm of no return he feels he is falling but has no fear. Anyone familiar with the sensation of falling prior to waking is thought to be experiencing the return of the dream body (also known as the astral body or etheric double) to the physical shell, a sensation that Lovecraft must have had many times and so incorporated into this story even if he was unaware of its significance.

It ends with Carter waking in his own bed in time to gaze on a wondrous sunrise like that of his visions and the realisation that he had been in the 'right' place all the time. Lovecraft seems to be saying that there is no point in believing in gods for they do not exist and if they did, they would not help us. What we seek is here before us and always has been. We only have to perceive the world in a different way to realise that, but often we need to go deep within ourselves and explore our dreams, before we come to this realisation.

He was evidently in an introspective mood, for his next tale continued this mystical, questing theme, that of an inner journey and the search for the true self.

On 9 November Lovecraft returned – in spirit – to Kingsport, (the fictional town that was the setting for 'The Festival'), for a moral fable that is rich in esoteric symbolism. 'The Strange High House in the Mist' has been built on a cliff that appears unapproachable to all but a philosopher named Thomas Olney. Weary of teaching the same 'ponderous things in . . . college' year upon year, Olney yearns for some form of genuine insight and experience. He scales the cliff face only to discover that the door is on the 'other' side. While he ponders what to do a bearded figure appears at the window and invites him to climb in. His host is kindly and dressed in ancient garments such as might adorn a magician. At his invitation they talk for hours. Olney listens to him as if in a trance.

At length the philosopher returns to the world below, but he is not the same man who left Kingsport that morning. It is said that he left his spirit in the High House and that the only person he can share his experience with is the Terrible Old Man who is shunned by the other inhabitants of the town.

The ending is deliberately ambiguous, but the implication is that there now dwell two kindred spirits in the Strange High House and that it is a happier place for it. The world below is just as empty and cheerless as before. It is a world where Olney's wife and children pray to 'the bland proper god of Baptists' and where his soulless shell walks dutifully beside them, while the world in which Olney's spirit now resides is one of wonders illuminated with laughter and music learned from the Elder Ones.

'The Strange High House' leaves the reader with a sense of paradise lost, as did the other wistful fantasy penned by Lovecraft that month: 'The Silver Key'. Lovecraft was at that time still absorbed in his ambitious and not entirely successful epic *The Dream-Quest of Unknown Kadath*, which he completed at the end of January 1927. It preoccupied him more than any other tale because he identified with Carter who was more than a fictional alter-ego. Lovecraft often remarked that he felt as if he was an old man occupying a young man's body prompting him to refer to himself as 'grandpa' and the 'old gentleman' and to address his adult male acquaintances as if they were his children. And that young man, that persona, was Carter, an unsuccessful author who shared several of his creator's characteristics and interests including his preference for antiquarian literature. Since childhood Lovecraft had dreamt of characters whose bodies he felt he could enter, but he had always awoken before he had mustered the courage to attempt it. In conceiving Carter, Lovecraft finally had an individual he could live through and explore the inner landscape of his psyche at will. Carter has the ability to wander through the dream-worlds, to determine events and interact with its inhabitants, unlike his creator who simply viewed the terrain and felt himself at the mercy of forces he was incapable of controlling. Though Carter is a mere observer when we first encounter him (in 'The Statement of Randolph Carter'), he matures and grows bolder with each adventure until he is able to confront – and to triumph over – the 'night gaunts' that so terrified the young Lovecraft, enlisting them as allies in his quest. With his tormentors subdued, it would remain only for Carter to conquer time, another of Lovecraft's obsessions, in his final appearance ('The Silver Key') and fulfil Lovecraft's most cherished dream – the return to childhood.

By the winter of 1926 Lovecraft's struggle to reconcile rationality and scientific certainty with the irrational and intuitive world of dreams found expression in the fourth Randolph Carter story, 'The Silver Key', in which the middle-aged Carter loses his ability to enter the dream-lands of his youth due to his preoccupation with the mundane responsibilities of 'waking life'. But on a visit to his childhood home in Massachusetts he recovers a key inscribed with Arabic symbols which enables him to return to the past as a ten-year-old boy who can foretell the future.

There are allusions to Lovecraft's increasing disillusionment with life and the sense that he too may have lost the childlike sense of wonder by insisting that there must be a rational explanation for his all too vivid dreams.

Wonder had gone away, and he had forgotten that all life is only a set of pictures in the brain, among which there is no difference betwixt those born of real things and those born of inward dreamings, and no cause to value the one above the other. Custom had dinned into his ears a superstitious reverence for that which tangibly and physically exists, and had made him secretly ashamed to dwell in visions . . . They had chained him down to things that are, and had then explained the workings of those things till mystery had gone out of the world.

The author may indeed have grown world-weary in his thirty-sixth year, but his alter-ego was now back at the Phillips house with his beloved grandfather, his doting mother and aunts. And the transformation from man to boy was achieved with the deftest stroke of the pen. 'And when he danced back to the house that night he offered no excuses for his lateness, nor heeded in the least the reproofs he gained for ignoring the noon-tide dinner-horn altogether.'

Perhaps sensing that he had not achieved what he had set out to do with *Kadath* – in failing to make the dreamscape so real and alluring that readers would be induced to accompany Carter on his inner journey, and fearing that he might have overwhelmed them with a 'plethora of weird imagery' – he immediately began outlining what was to become his longest work of fiction. *The Case of Charles Dexter Ward* (January to March 1927) remains his only full-length novel, a tale of ritual magic that transposes the witch hunting hysteria of eighteenth-century Salem to contemporary Providence. It is tempting to see yet another autobiographical reference in Lovecraft's description of the main character.

> Charles Ward was an antiquarian from infancy, no doubt gaining his taste from the venerable town around him, and from the relics of the past which filled every corner of his parents' old mansion in Prospect Street on the crest of the hill. With the years his devotion to ancient things increased; so that history, genealogy, and the study of colonial architecture, furniture, and craftsmanship at length crowded everything else from his sphere of interests. These tastes are important to remember in considering his madness . . .

When Ward learns that he is a direct descendant of Salem warlock Joseph Curwen he becomes determined to unearth the truth of the accusations made against what he believes to be his unjustly maligned forbear. But after his attention is drawn to their physical resemblance, curiosity intensifies into obsession. He becomes fascinated with alchemy and 'cabbalistic' magic, specifically with the rumours concerning Curwen's use of 'essential saltes' to resurrect the dead. After performing the accursed ceremony himself, Ward is murdered by the resurrected Curwen who assumes his identity. It is only then that Curwen's evil intentions are laid bare by the family physician, Dr Marinus Willett, whom Ward has entrusted with his suspicions. Willett is left to confront Curwen who has been confined to a madhouse after conducting diabolical rites in the basement of his house where a malformed creature is to be found writhing in a noisome pit. 'What the thing was, he would never tell. It was like some of the carvings on the hellish altar, but it was alive. Nature had never made it in this form, for it was too palpably *unfinished*.'

The two men face off in Curwen's cell and engage in a magical duel which Willett wins, by invoking the malign deity, Yog-Sothoth, who reduces Curwen to dust.

The novel, published posthumously in *Weird Tales* in two instalments in May and July 1941, profited from Lovecraft's decision to take the supernatural element seriously, researching the subject of ceremonial magic as diligently as the historical background he had woven into the tale in order to give it an air of authenticity. Ward's mansion is modelled on a house the author was familiar with – the Halsey house at 140 Prospect Street – and other details and personalities are taken from Gertrude Kimball's survey, *Providence in Colonial Times* (1912). The story was first suggested by Aunt Lillian who sent her nephew a newspaper clipping concerning an alleged haunting at the Halsey house, while Lovecraft's recent rediscovery of Walter de la Mare's *The Return* (1910) had furnished the theme of possession, which Lovecraft substituted for one of murder and substitution. But his masterstroke was to present 'Ward' as a patient's case history with the supernatural element revealed only at the very end.

Sadly, he didn't give himself the luxury of re-reading or re-evaluating the manuscript. After completing his critical history of supernatural literature he judged his latest offering to be substandard, condemning it as a 'cumbrous, creaking bit of self-conscious antiquarianism' (as he wrote to R.H. Barlow in March 1934). He consigned it to a drawer in disgust, a fate it did not deserve.

Turning his back on horror, at least temporarily, he tried his hand at science fiction, believing that he might make a name for himself if he could bring something new to the bourgeoning genre. 'The Colour Out of Space' (March 1927) succeeded in this objective, introducing an alien presence that was a genuine departure from the stereotypical humanoid creatures so familiar to readers of early science fiction. Rather than focus on this crude cliché (which had already given sci-fi something of a bad name), Lovecraft's tale explores the impact of the arrival of an alien life-form in an isolated community to the west of Arkham. A surveyor relates the coming of a strange meteorite with the leisurely air of a man with time on his hands, a chaw of tobacco in his cheek and a good yarn to spin.

'They had uncovered what seemed to be the side of a large coloured globule embedded in the substance. The colour, which resembled some of the bands in the meteor's strange spectrum, was almost impossible to describe; and it was only by analogy that they called it colour at all.'

Perhaps it was this easy, back-porch manner that endeared it to Lovecraft who named it his personal favourite among all his work.

People vowed that the snow melted faster around Nahum's than it did anywhere else, and early in March there was an awed discussion in Potter's general store at Clark's Corners. Stephen Rice had driven past Gardner's in the morning, and had noticed the skunk-cabbages coming up through the mud by the woods across the road. Never were things of such size seen before, and they held strange colours that could not be put into any words . . . That afternoon several persons drove past to see the abnormal growth, and all agreed that plants of that kind ought never to sprout in a healthy world.

Ironically, the story's greatest strength can also be seen as its fatal weakness. While, the absence of the obligatory bug-eyed alien is to be welcomed, the menace of Lovecraft's 'moving colours' is simply too abstract to be threatening. However, it is very effective if taken as an example of a 'scientific romance' – in which the alien visitation puzzles the inhabitants of a sleepy community and causes them to scratch their heads in wonderment. The reaction of those who witness the departure of the strange phosphorous life form might have been lifted intact from H.G. Wells.

The shock served to loosen several tongues, and embarrassed whispers were exchanged. 'It spreads on everything organic that's been around here,' muttered the medical examiner. No one replied, but the man who had been in the well gave a hint that his long pole must have stirred up something intangible. 'It was awful,' he added. 'There was no bottom at all. Just ooze and bubbles and the feeling of something lurking under there.'

To its author's delight, the story was immediately accepted by *Amazing Stories*. Unfortunately, payment was slower in coming. Having lost his enthusiasm for writing anything 'on spec' (without a firm commitment to publish), Lovecraft resolved never again to submit his work to the magazine. A glimmer of compensation was offered by the story's inclusion in Edward O'Brien's *Best Short Stories of 1928*, which Lovecraft regarded as a singular honour. The American author and anthologist claimed to read 8,000 short stories a year and only chose those he considered demonstrated a development of the form.

Even if Lovecraft's waking life was not panning out as he had hoped, his dreams were eminently more interesting. One in particular would have made a compelling short story, but remains no more than a detailed anecdote in his private correspondence. In a letter to Frank Belknap Long dated 1 November 1927, it is given in outline only, but in a second account, given to Bernard Austin Dwyer, it has been elaborated upon. In the third and final version – as told to Donald Wandrei – there is sufficient material for a story, suggesting that Lovecraft was already developing it along those lines.

In the dream he is Lucius Caelius Rufus, a provincial Roman official serving in a region of what is now Spain, where every year the dark folk (miri nigri) come down from the hills to raid the settlement for citizens to sacrifice in their strange rituals. But they have not been seen since they came to trade and were involved in a dispute which left several of their number dead. Rufus suspects the dark folk may be planning an attack and so insists the garrison march on their encampment to slaughter them before they can organise another raid. After a long and tiring march – remembered with all the monotony and anxiety that would accompany a journey into hostile territory – the Romans approach the edge of the hills. 'All the torches now began to dim, and the cries of frightened legionaries mingled with the unceasing screams of the tethered horses. The air grew perceptibly colder, more suddenly so than is usual at November's brink, and seemed stirred by terrible undulations which I could not help connecting with the beating of huge wings.'

The dream ends with their guide committing suicide for fear of what approaches and the horses stampeding, killing many of their riders. Lovecraft woke with a start with Lucius' last words ringing in his ears: 'Malitia vetus – militia vetus es – venit – tandem venit' – which roughly translates as, 'the old affliction – the battle it ends'. The mystically inclined would no doubt interpret it as the recollection of a past life – a theory that Lovecraft, ever the 'mechanistic materialist', would have scoffed at. But even he had to admit such intense dreams may originate from deep regions of the mind. 'It was the most vivid dream in years, drawing upon wells of the subconscious long untouched and forgotten.'

In late April 1928 he very reluctantly agreed to make a return visit to New York at Sonia's request. Though he regarded himself as being on 'alien soil' and loathed it 'like poison', he felt obliged to offer her moral support while she attempted to establish her own millinery business within walking distance of her third-floor flat at 370 East 17th Street in Brooklyn and to make himself amenable. He spent six weeks in the city, but was rarely 'home', preferring the companionship of his male friends, with whom he talked and dined until the early hours, often bringing them back to greet his wife as she prepared to leave for a day of meetings. It was clear to her that he regarded her new apartment as a convenient base for sightseeing and his wife as nothing more than one of his circle of friends.

He extended his absence from Providence to three months by accepting invitations from various acquaintances to visit Washington DC, Wilbraham, Massachusetts and Vermont. On his return, there was more routine revision work from budding writers to keep him occupied. In this way he passed a year and a half without writing anything new – unless one counts the gently self-mocking 'Ibid', a sly dig at pompous scholarship, as worthy of more than passing interest. 'Ibid' traces the journey of a fictional Roman consul's skull as it passes through various hands, until it comes to be used as a beer-stein by a drunken Milwaukee settler. If nothing else, the piece reveals Lovecraft's erudition and the gently mocking humour which was rarely displayed in his fiction.

Such a prolonged drought of creativity might have driven other writers to drink, or to believe that their muse had forsaken them, but Lovecraft was possessed of uncommon patience. He once said, 'I never try to write stories, but I wait until a story wants to be written. Whenever I set out deliberately to write a tale, the result is flat and of inferior quality.'

But finally he was taken with the notion that ripened into 'The Dunwich Horror' (August 1928), one of the most original and imaginative works in the entire horror canon.

It incorporated one of the New England legends he had heard during his stay in Wilbraham which told of the whip-poor-wills who are said to capture the disembodied soul. Indeed, the description of the country around Dunwich is taken almost verbatim from Lovecraft's letters describing Wilbraham and its surroundings. The name of the fictitious town of Dunwich was derived from combining Greenwich and Dana, two picturesque villages in North Central Massachusetts to which Lovecraft took a fancy on his travels, while its plot appears to have been derived from Arthur Machen's 'Novel of the Black Seal' and 'The Great God Pan' which Lovecraft had been re-reading for his history of supernatural fiction. But 'Dunwich' owes only a nodding acknowledgement to its source and is as fine an example of sustained imagination as will be found in horror fiction.

In rural Massachusetts the Whateley family have been shunned by their neighbours since the birth of a son, Wilbur, whose paternity is unknown. The boy, who is unnaturally tall and uncommonly intelligent, is raised by his deranged grandfather who introduces Wilbur to books of forbidden lore (inviting speculation that the youth is a fictional surrogate for the author, though he confessed to 'identifying' with the aged scholar who appears toward the end of the story). The old man hints that Wilbur might be the offspring of an unholy union between his absent mother, Lavinia, a deformed albino, and the god, Yog-Sothoth, an antecedent of 'the Old Ones' who seek to reclaim the Earth.

With his dying breath his grandfather urges Wilbur to consult the *Necronomicon* which is held at Miskatonic University library so that he can open the cosmic portal for the Old Ones. When the librarian, Henry Armitage, refuses to let the boy see it, Wilbur attempts to steal it, but is savaged to death by a dog leaving only a foetid pool of tarry stickiness and a pungent odour. Lovecraft delights in offering a detailed description of the foetid remains.

It was partly human, beyond a doubt, with very manlike hands and head, and the goatish, chinless face had the stamp of the Whateleys upon it. But the torso and lower parts of the body were teratologically fabulous, so that only generous clothing could ever have enabled it to walk on earth unchallenged or uneradicated.

With the mischievous glee of a child seeking to shock his parents, he relishes every opportunity to offer graphic descriptions of the process of putrefaction, but in this particular instance he overdoes it and it works against him. It draws attention to his excessive verbiage and gives his critics evidence of his lack of restraint and subtlety.

The back was piebald with yellow and black, and dimly suggested the squamous covering of certain snakes. Below the waist . . . the skin was thickly covered with coarse black fur, and from the abdomen a score of long greenish-grey tentacles with red sucking mouths protruded limply.

Their arrangement was odd, and seemed to follow the symmetries of some cosmic geometry unknown to earth or the solar system. On each of the hips, deep set in a kind of pinkish, ciliated orbit, was what seemed to be a rudimentary eye; whilst in lieu of a tail there depended a kind of trunk or feeler with purple annular markings, and with many evidences of being an undeveloped mouth or throat. The limbs, save for their black fur, roughly resembled the hind legs of prehistoric earth's giant saurians, and terminated in ridgy-veined pads that were neither hooves nor claws.

From this point on, Dunwich is terrorised by an invisible presence which demolishes buildings, kills those unlucky enough to get in its way and leaves massive footprints. Armitage investigates and discovers a journal kept by old man Whateley in which the magician wrote of invoking a race of 'terrible elder beings from another dimension'. Enlisting the assistance of two companions, the librarian arms himself with the requisite incantations and a powder that will render the creature visible, if only for a moment. The three rush to a mound opposite Sentinel Hill where it is finally revealed in its true form and perform the rite that destroys it. In its death agony it cries aloud for its father Yog-Sothoth. The invisible creature was Wilbur's twin brother and the spawn of the god.

Lovecraft expected Farnsworth Wright to reject it on the grounds that it was 'too fiendish', but Farnsworth did publish the story in April 1929 paying a substantial sum – $240 – for the privilege.

On 24 January 1928, Lovecraft reluctantly applied for a divorce on the grounds that Sonia had deserted him – a strategy they had both agreed upon in order to end the relationship officially. It had been her idea to make the break having finally accepted that he was willing to make no effort to be reconciled with her and that she had effectively lost him to his first love, Providence. It was one of the many ironies of his life that the decree was not finalised before his demise. In fact, the committed bachelor died a married man. (When Sonia remarried many years later she was still legally Mrs Lovecraft). The prospect of divorcing Sonia saddened him, as he believed that it was unbecoming for a gentleman to do so while he still 'appreciated' his wife, but it was only fair to release her from her obligations if he had no intention of honouring his. This odd attitude reveals that he viewed their marriage as little more than a formal arrangement and that he was concerned to be seen to have done the right thing by her by divorcing her, if that was her wish.

They would meet for the last time in March 1933 in Hartford, Connecticut when Sonia invited her husband to join her to explore the colonial town she had found so charming. On parting the first night she asked for a kiss to which he is said to have replied, 'No, it is better not to'. The next day they went sightseeing before Lovecraft bid her goodbye for the last time.

'Some of us awake in the night with strange phantasms of enchanted hills and gardens [. . .] and then we know that we have looked back through the ivory gates into that world of wonder which was ours before we were wise and unhappy.' – H.P. Lovecraft, 'Celephaïs'

CHAPTER EIGHT

AT THE MOUNTAINS OF MADNESS

'Heaven knows where I'll end up – it's a safe bet I'll never be
at the top of anything! Nor do I particularly care to be.'
– H.P. Lovecraft

Eighteen months passed between the completion of 'The Dunwich Horror' and the commencement of Lovecraft's next original work of fiction, 'The Whisperer in Darkness' (begun in February 1930). During the winter of 1928 and the whole of the following year he had been engaged in activities which kept him occupied but distracted from his true calling. These included the now customary travels to places of interest (among them Vermont, Wilbraham and Virginia) visits to old friends, writing voluminous letters (the longest running to 70 pages), revision work for lesser authors, chasing payment and toying with various business and employment prospects which invariably came to nothing. In rare cases these 'revisions' were so extensive as to almost qualify as Lovecraft originals, the plot of 'The Mound', for example, being the only element supplied by the tale's original 'author' Zealia Bishop. As her agent, Frank Belknap Long confirmed, 'that brooding, sombre and magnificently atmospheric story is Lovecraftian from the first page to the last'. In all he toured ten states in the south enjoying a life of leisure, but not of luxury for he was acutely aware that he had to make his meagre funds last until the next cheque arrived. When not staying with favoured correspondents and their families, he would be reduced to renting a room in a cheap boarding house for as little as a dollar a night.

Another factor which accounted for his low productivity is the demoralising effect of repeated rejections. Self-confidence and the will to commit to creating something new seemed to be more than Lovecraft could muster at this particular moment. Time and again his tales were returned by magazine editors and book publishers with polite refusals or standard rejection slips – all of which rankled with the acutely sensitive and all too readily discouraged writer. His fellow writers would think nothing of resubmitting a piece of theirs after making some perfunctory changes, while Lovecraft took rejection as the final word on the matter. He was not fishing for compliments or exhibiting false modesty when he wrote: 'there are probably seven persons, in all, who really like my work; and they are enough'. The last remark could be seen a text-book defence mechanism by a man who took set-backs and criticism too personally.

Although he wished to see his work in print and to be paid for it, he was not ambitious in the sense that he did not crave wealth or acclaim, only recognition and a readership that would appreciate his work. These, he felt, were his due and to be deprived or denied these – as well as the prestige of having his work published in book form by a major publisher – must have been a source of great disappointment to him. So low were his expectations that he did not promote himself as actively as he might have done – limiting his submissions to mainly amateur publications and rarely approaching national magazines, book publishers or literary agents. And that was his undoing. He knew his work was exceptional, even if he expressed disappointment with it on occasion, but he couldn't bring himself to believe that its merits would be recognised by the commercial publishers. It took the effort and enthusiasm of others after his death to bring his work to the attention of a wider readership. If this audience had been hitherto unaware of his existence, it was simply because Lovecraft didn't possess the same talent or energy for self-promotion that brought lesser authors to prominence. He appeared to be satisfied to be the centre of a small circle of young admirers – his peers in the world of amateur journalism. It was as if he thought it unbecoming of a gentleman to sing his own praises and call attention to himself. Such activities were for carnival barkers, theatricals and hucksters; not respectable gentlemen from 'good families'.

Whenever he became disheartened, he would immerse himself in a furious bout of letter writing, spilling out his frustration to any one of up to 75 regular correspondents (Lovecraft's own estimation) until he had recovered his equilibrium. By late 1930 these included Texas-born Robert E. Howard, creator of Conan the Barbarian and originator of the whole sword-and-sorcery subgenre. In a letter to Frank Belknap Long, (his correspondent for a startling seventeen years), Lovecraft explained why he placed such value on maintaining a regular and lengthy written contact with his fellow writers.

> An isolated person requires correspondence as a means of seeing his ideas as others see them, and thus guarding against the dogmatisms and extravagances of solitary and uncorrected speculation. No man can learn to reason and appraise from a mere perusal of the writing of others. If he live not in the world, where he can observe the public at first hand and be directed toward solid reality by the force of conversation and spoken debate, then he must sharpen his discrimination and regulate his perceptive balance by an equivalent exchange of ideas in epistolary form.

Although Lovecraft did not write any new fiction during this period, he produced his most intriguing verse cycle that winter; 36 individual 'pseudo-sonnets' under the collective title *Fungi From Yuggoth*. Lovecraft appears to have resumed his love affair with poetry while revising Maurice W. Moe's critical history of verse, *Doorways to Poetry*, which was never published. It seems likely that it motivated him to consider writing a slim volume of weird verse, but after a week of sustained creativity his enthusiasm had run its course. He hadn't abandoned the idea entirely, however, speaking only weeks later of his willingness to add a dozen more if there was a chance that they might be published.

Attempts have been made to find a single unifying theme linking these verses to the Cthulhu Mythos, but they are clearly self-contained and their allusions to earlier work obviously intended to tease those readers of *Weird Tales* who would be writing in to enquire if these were intentional and to ask if the author could explain the contradictions!

The fact that he employed a variety of metres and styles – aping Dunsany here and Poe there – confirms that the verses are not part of a single work. Add to that the knowledge that he allowed individual poems to be published in isolation without any further explanation seems to put paid to the notion that it was a cohesive work. However, if one were determined to put it in the context of the mythos, the diversity of styles employed by Lovecraft could reflect the dissimilar nature of the visions and the worlds experienced by the anonymous occultist who has stolen a book of ancient lore that provides him with the key to the dream-world and to other dimensions.

> I had the book that told the hidden way
> Across the void and through the space-hung screens
> That hold the undimensioned worlds at bay,
> And keep lost aeons to their own demesnes.

It appears that he attempted to adapt the first three verses into a full-length story judging by a surviving fragment entitled 'The Book' which was written later that year. In the first vision the narrator sees himself being sacrificed to Yuggoth, the god after whom the cycle is named. This is followed by impressions of various locations from Aylesbury to Arkham by way of Innsmouth before Lovecraft ventures into the realm of shadows charted by Machen and Poe.

> They took me slumming, where gaunt walls of brick
> Bulge outward with a viscous stored-up evil,
> And twisted faces, thronging foul and thick,
> Wink messages to alien god and devil.

The mood is interrupted by a series of rustic vignettes which mimic the homespun horror of 'The Colour Out of Space'.

> Farmer Seth Atwood was past eighty when
> He tried to sink that deep well by his door,
> With only Eb to help him bore and bore.

Then the tone shifts again for a run of languid verses in Dunsanian style, before Lovecraft plunges his narrator into the nightmares of his own youth.

> Out of what crypt they crawl, I cannot tell,
> But every night I see the rubbery things,
> Black, horned, and slender, with membraneous wings,
> And tails that bear the bifid barb of hell.

The final verses imply that he has emerged from an initiation rite with a new understanding of the nature of reality.

> There is in certain ancient things a trace
> Of some dim essence – more than form or weight;
> A tenuous aether, indeterminate,
> Yet linked with all the laws of time and space.
> A faint, veiled sign of continuities
> That outward eyes can never quite descry;
> Of locked dimensions harbouring years gone by,
> And out of reach except for hidden keys.

When a publisher for the *Fungi* verse cycle failed to materialise, he returned to fiction. 'The Whisperer in Darkness' occupied him on and off throughout the spring and summer, before being completed in September.

There is a lot to be said for building suspense, but if the opening doesn't hook the reader they won't have the opportunity to find out exactly how well this aspect has been developed. Lovecraft was a past master of the 'hook', offering a tantalising preview of the horrors awaiting the reader within. The second paragraph of 'The Whisperer in Darkness' is just one example.

> The whole matter began, so far as I am concerned, with the historic and unprecedented Vermont floods of November 3, 1927. I was then, as now, an instructor of literature at Miskatonic University in Arkham, Massachusetts, and an enthusiastic amateur student of New England folklore. Shortly after the flood, amidst the varied reports of hardship, suffering, and organized

relief which filled the press, there appeared certain odd stories of things found floating in some of the swollen rivers . . .

As various scholars have suggested, this story too owes a considerable debt to Arthur Machen's 'The Novel of the Black Seal', which also begins with the discovery of what appears to be a human body in the water, making the most of its desolate setting. The two stories also share a central premise: the discovery of a non-human elder race whose existence is unknown to the wider world and which leads to the death of a central character. Lovecraft himself acknowledges as much in the text when his narrator refers to 'the fantastic lore of lurking "little people" made popular by the magnificent horror-fiction of Arthur Machen'. This nod to Machen allows Lovecraft to recycle elements from 'The Black Seal' without being accused of plagiarism. It could be argued that it was Machen's work that convinced Lovecraft that it was possible to write 'weird fiction' without having to resort to the supernatural or the occult. Remote regions of the Earth might conceal dreadful secrets or mysterious artefacts whose discovery would have alarming consequences. Yet, even allowing for the thematic similarities between the two stories, the tone and execution of 'The Whisperer in Darkness' is pure Lovecraft.

Lecturer Albert N. Wilmarth scorns local legends that blame a race of monsters for a spate of unexplained disappearances and deaths. But then he receives a letter from a reclusive Vermont academic, Henry Wentworth Akeley, forcing him to reassess his assumptions. Akeley writes to inform him that: 'I have certain evidence that monstrous things do indeed live in the woods on the high hills which nobody visits'. These beings, he goes on to claim, are responsible for the bodies found floating in the river after the flood. This race of extra-terrestrial beings is worshipped by a cult whose members have been heard to chant the names of the deities Cthulhu and Nyarlathotep. Akeley manages to secretly record one of these ceremonies using a wax cylinder gramophone and sends the disc to Wilmarth.

I hardly need say that I gave that shocking record many another playing, and that I made exhaustive attempts at analysis and comment in comparing notes with Akeley. It would be both useless and disturbing to repeat here all that we concluded; but I may hint that we agreed in believing we had secured a clue to the source of some of the most repulsive primordial customs in the cryptic elder religions of mankind. It seemed plain to us, also, that there were ancient and elaborate alliances between the hidden outer creatures and certain members of the human race.

Akeley sends further documentary evidence to Wilmarth, before he's attacked by the cult members. He survives, but then inexplicably retracts his accusations, claiming that he has met with the aliens and determined that they are benign. Their home planet, he has discovered, is Yuggoth at the very edge of our solar system. 'But Yuggoth, of course, is only the stepping-stone. The main body of the beings inhabits strangely organised abysses, wholly beyond the utmost reach of any human imagination. The space-time globule which we recognise as the totality of all cosmic entity is only an atom in the genuine infinity which is theirs.'

Akeley asks Wilmarth to visit him, to see for himself, but his insistence that the lecturer brings all the documentary proof with him arouses Wilmarth's suspicions. Nevertheless, he agrees to do so.

In the most unsettling scene, Wilmarth finds Akeley sitting in the darkness of his cabin and speaking deliriously of the aliens who have perfected a method of deep space travel which involves transplanting their brains into metal receptacles to avoid their bodies aging during the voyage. Akeley has agreed to subject himself to the operation because it will grant him knowledge few men could possess. It is then than Wilmarth notices a canister with Akeley's name on it.

When Wilmarth returns the next day with the police he is horrified to find Akeley's dismembered head and hands which the aliens must have used to deceive him into believing that Akeley was still alive. With the discovery of Akeley's brain in the canister comes the realisation that his friend was already dead.

Those fans who are dismayed at the amount of time Lovecraft 'wasted' on his travels may be consoled by the knowledge that he incorporated large portions of his description of the Vermont countryside in 'The Whisperer in Darkness', lending the story a naturalistic, ominous atmosphere. It also benefited from significant changes made as a result of his friends' reactions to personal readings some months later which led to 'considerable condensation throughout' and a markedly subtler ending. This reveals that Lovecraft was not adverse to constructive criticism from those he respected and whose judgement he trusted. Despite – or maybe because of – its protracted gestation, the finished tale is one of Lovecraft's finest and fully realised works of fiction. It also earned him an appropriately large financial reward for his time, originality and craftsmanship – $350 and the satisfaction of having the 26,600-word novella published intact in the August 1931 issue of *Weird Tales*.

Having seen such a substantial work published unabridged in a single issue, Lovecraft naturally assumed that Farnsworth Wright would be willing to purchase a second story of similar length for the same sum, given a decent interval. In that positive frame of mind he began one of his most substantial and influential tales, 'At The Mountains of Madness' in the Spring of 1931, unaware that it would be almost five years before it would see publication in *Astounding Stories*, having been rejected by the editor of *Weird Tales* as 'unconvincing' and far too long even for serialisation.

It is conceivable that there would be no *Alien*, *The Thing* or any of their myriad imitations had screenwriters Dan O'Bannon and Ronald Shusett and novelist John W. Campbell not been so enamoured of Lovecraft and of 'At The Mountains of Madness' in particular. For although both script and novel bear only a superficial resemblance to Lovecraft's source novella, they share the same central premise; the uncovering of a horror that has been in hibernation for millennia and is unleashed upon the world by the unwitting members of a scientific expedition.

Film director Guillermo del Toro has been quoted (in 2008's *Lovecraft: Fear of the Unknown*) as saying, 'I think there is a huge Lovecraftian influence, and a huge "At the Mountains of Madness" influence on the first Ridley Scott *Alien*. The idea that they find a derelict, city-sized ship, dead denizens in it, and something that is very much alive and waiting and then takes over the humans. That's essentially, you could say very much, in the "Mountains of Madness".'

The story begins with a presentiment of impending tragedy as Professor Dyer of Miskatonic University is compelled to relate his horrifying experiences in Antarctica in order to dissuade the leaders of a major scientific expedition from exploring the same mountainous region. Dyer explains that he had led an earlier expedition which uncovered the ruins of a vast, ancient stone city and the remains of its non-human inhabitants. An advance party had recovered perfectly preserved specimens of a life form that appeared to have evolved beyond anything like it on Earth, but by the time Dyer and his team reached the camp, their colleagues had been murdered and the preserved life forms had disappeared. Only one of the advance team was found – and he had been dissected.

On exploring the city Dyer and a young colleague called Danforth discovered hieroglyphic murals depicting the coming of the Old Ones millions of years ago, the history of their civilisation, the building of the city with the aid of shape-shifting protoplasmic entities called Shoggoths and their destruction after the Shoggoths developed a will of their own and turned against their masters. 'The Cyclopean massiveness and gigantism of everything about us became curiously oppressive; and there was something vaguely but deeply unhuman in all the contours, dimensions, proportions, decorations, and constructional nuances of the blasphemously archaic stonework. We soon realized, from what the carvings revealed, that this monstrous city was many million years old.'

The survivors of this superior Elder race waged war with other alien races who came to colonise the Earth (the fungi from Yuggoth and the progeny of Cthulhu) then migrated to the ocean floor as they fled an unidentified evil that lived beyond the mountains and it is the sight of that entity that drove Danforth out of his mind as the two men finally fled to safety.

Had it been written by one of Lovecraft's contemporaries it would have exercised a certain frisson on account of its originality, the unusual setting and the then novel concept of an ancient alien race predating man on Earth. But in all likelihood it would have been competent rather than astonishing. Lovecraft brought an epic grandeur to the horror tale that none of the other 'modern masters' could have matched. He had been fascinated by the theme of Antarctic exploration since his childhood, when he'd read several accounts of early expeditions. He had also written his own essays on the subject and so when he came to set his story in the still largely uncharted continent he was able to generate a vivid impression of its bleak grandeur and the forbidding sense of isolation felt by those who had trekked across a landscape as alien as any to be found on Earth. He was inspired by the fossils unearthed between 1928 and 1930 by American aviator and explorer Richard Evelyn Bird, whose expedition by boat and plane formed the basis of Dyer's fictional Miskatonic enterprise. Secondly, he had by this time created a fantastic though credible mythology which he was able to introduce into his fiction with all the conviction of a classical scholar, imparting indisputable scientific fact. Indeed, so persuasive was Lovecraft's vision that only the most unresponsive reader could fail to be drawn in.

If the tale has any flaws, it is that the scientific data becomes gratuitous after the first couple of paragraphs and the appearance of giant albino penguins is likely to raise an unintentional titter, but otherwise the seamless blend of fact and fantasy has few equals.

His next novella was far more sombre in tone, the result no doubt, of his failure to find a publisher for 'At the Mountains of Madness' – although this tale was subsequently sold to *Astounding Stories* by an agent, Julius Schwartz, whom Lovecraft had met at a literary gathering. It would be the one and only occasion when Lovecraft allowed himself to be professionally represented, having been dissuaded from ever doing so again when the magazine heavily edited his copy. Although the edits were made by the magazine, Lovecraft blamed Schwartz for failing to protect his 'property'. 'So many important details, and impressions and touches of sensation are missing,' he complained. 'I'll be hang'd if I can consider the story as published at all.'

If despondency ever found full expression in fiction it is in 'The Shadow Over Innsmouth' (November to December 1931), set in the familiar confines of New England and Lovecraft Country. An oppressive atmosphere hangs like a pall over the melancholy seaport to which a young man, Robert Olmstead, finds himself diverted en route to Arkham. Local rumours tell of an unspecified epidemic which claimed a large number of lives and left the surviving townsfolk deformed.

As for the Innsmouth people – the youth hardly knew what to make of them. They were as furtive and seldom seen as animals that live in burrows . . . They seemed sullenly banded together in some sort of fellowship and understanding – despising the world as if they had access to other and preferable spheres of entity. Their appearance – especially those staring, unwinking eyes which one never saw shut – was certainly shocking enough; and their voices were disgusting . . .

After plying an old man with liquor he learns of the legendary sea captain, Obed Marsh, who in 1846 returned from the South Seas in a ship laden with gold and precious gems. It was said that these had been given to him by creatures that were half-fish and half-frog in exchange for human sacrifices and for the right to mate with the inhabitants of Innsmouth, begetting human-alien hybrids condemned to live for an unnaturally long span of years. Olmstead disregards the old man's story as a sailor's yarn . . . until he is confronted by a group of mutants 'surging inhumanly through the spectral moonlight'. He manages to elude them, but during his research he uncovers evidence of his own family connection and after dreaming of an undersea city he wakens to discover that he has succumbed to the curse and is now a 'blasphemous abnormality' with an irresistible compulsion to swim out to the Cyclopean city and live among the Deep Ones beneath the waves.

A brief summary of the plot cannot convey the pervasive strangeness of the tale and the bleakness of its ending, which counters Olmstead's elation with the hideousness of his appearance and the loss of his humanity. Rarely has Lovecraft achieved this degree of personal tragedy in his fiction and one can only assume it is because Olmstead cuts such an innocent, impotent figure. The inheritor of a mutant gene, he is powerless to prevent the hideous transformation that overcomes him. In many ways, his story represents Lovecraft's own deepest fears. What if his neurotic mother was proven right and he succumbed to the same fate that befell his father and his father's cousin – a victim of some unspeakable disease passed down to him at birth? 'Innsmouth' represented the borderland between life and death with the sea and its cold, dark fathomless depths symbolic of the abyss that would swallow him if he shared that fate. And then there is the colourful local dialect which gives the impression of real people, living and breathing somewhere in this godforsaken part of the world.

'That refinery, though, used to be a big thing, and old man Marsh, who owns it, must be richer'n Croesus. Queer old duck, though, and sticks mighty close in his home. He's supposed to have developed some skin disease or deformity late in life that makes him keep out of sight.'

It was perhaps inevitable that Lovecraft would, at some point, attempt a synthesis of the various elements he had been developing throughout his career. For 'The Dreams in the Witch House' (February 1932) he melded his own brand of cosmicism, science fantasy, lucid dream trips and old school occultism in a story that sees a Miskatonic University mathematics student, Walter Gilman (whose surname, gill-man, may be a sly allusion to the previous tale), staying in a house that is reputedly haunted by a seventeenth-century Salem witch. The odd geometry of Gilman's attic room and the cryptic designs he finds smeared across the walls facilitate inter-dimensional travel to a dream world where he encounters the disembodied spirit of Keziah Mason, a witch who had been held captive in that very house when it had served as the town gaol. In the dream he prevents her from sacrificing a baby by wresting the knife from her hand and fending her off with a crucifix – only to discover upon waking that an infant had been abducted that night.

Gilman vainly attempts to resist Keziah's subsequent psychic attacks, but after several encounters he suffers a breakdown and is hospitalised. On his discharge he returns to the house and is brutally murdered there in full view of another lodger who witnesses Gilman's frantic writhing and screaming as his heart is torn out by a rat, leaving a gaping wound in his chest. After his death, the house is demolished – and the remains of the witch's skeleton, her rodent familiar and a hoard of children's bones are unearthed together with a book of black magic, a sacrificial knife and a star-headed statuette uncannily similar to that of the Old Ones, whose baleful influence appears to have been behind Keziah's sacrificial rites all along.

Many Lovecraft aficionados consider this to be amongst the author's weaker stories, with too many aspects unexplained and others left deliberately vague, although *Weird Tales* columnist Kenneth Hite has called it 'one of the purest and most important examples of sheer Lovecraftian cosmicism'. Gilman's hallucinations induce an appropriately nauseous sensation by conveying his sense of disorientation as he shifts in and out of consciousness unable to determine what is real and what is imaginary, but his impressions of the astral dimension are too abstract for the reader to truly visualise – with allusions to colours, geometric shapes and bubbles. Evocative of neither fear nor a shift in sense perception, these descriptions are merely abstruse and incomprehensible. Had Lovecraft taken a leaf from the experiences of Thomas De Quincey and other eminent opium-eaters he might have captured the sense of disorientation and delirium that he was seeking. Even those who believe the vagueness is entirely in keeping with the theme of altered states and astral projection must admit that the story reads as if Lovecraft is trying too hard to squeeze everything in, that it is contrived and a little tired – a shortcoming that Lovecraft could be said to share with his protagonist. 'Possibly Gilman ought not to have studied so hard. Non-Euclidean calculus and quantum physics are enough to stretch any brain, and when one mixes them with folklore, and tries to trace a strange background of multi-dimensional reality behind the ghoulish hints of the Gothic tales and the wild whispers of the chimney-corner, one can hardly expect to be wholly free from mental tension.'

There is also an all too familiar ring to the introduction with a narrator who is verging on the edge of a nervous breakdown, beset by fearful imaginings and an acute sharpening of the senses, oppressed by his sinister surroundings and tormented by the sound of rats scampering behind the walls. It's as if he has rifled through his own notebook of 'Weird Story Plots' (in which he had summarised his favourite tales) for a suitable opening when a little more thought might have brought forth something more engaging. This notebook, along with his 'Commonplace Book' of ideas for possible tales, ensured that no potential story idea was overlooked.

Whether the dreams brought on the fever or the fever brought on the dreams Walter Gilman did not know. Behind everything crouched the brooding, festering horror of the ancient town, and of the mouldy, unhallowed garret gable where he wrote and studied and wrestled with figures and formulae when he was not tossing on the meagre iron bed. His ears were growing sensitive to a preternatural and intolerable degree, and he had long ago stopped the cheap mantel clock whose ticking had come to seem like a thunder of artillery. At night the subtle stirring of the black city outside, the sinister scurrying of rats in the wormy partitions, and the creaking of hidden timbers in the centuried house, were enough to give him a sense of strident pandemonium. The darkness always teemed with unexplained sound – and yet he sometimes shook with fear lest the noises he heard should subside and allow him to hear certain other fainter noises which he suspected were lurking behind them.

Lovecraft himself described it as a 'miserable mess', but the passages which focus on the occult elements are as powerful and enigmatic as any that he wrote.

He must meet the Black Man and go with them all to the throne of Azathoth at the centre of ultimate chaos. That was what she said. He must sign the book of Azathoth in his own blood and take a new secret name now that his independent delvings had gone so far. What kept him from going with her and Brown Jenkin and the other to the throne of Chaos where the thin flutes pipe mindlessly was the fact that he had seen the name Azathoth in the *Necronomicon*, and knew it stood for a primal evil too horrible for description.

Had it not been for August Derleth taking the initiative and submitting it to *Weird Tales* without its author's knowledge, the story might have remained in a drawer and never seen the light of day. Its acceptance and publication (in 1933) was critical since Lovecraft was seriously considering abandoning fiction – if this comment to Derleth was made in earnest. 'The whole incident shews me that my fictional days are probably over.'

His despair cannot be attributed solely to the low opinion he had of some of his own work, (which was doubtless due to simple fatigue and familiarity), but to a general malaise at the thought that he was labouring in a field that was unworthy of his talent. In a letter to Edgar Hoffmann Price, a regular contributor to *Weird Tales*, he explained his objections. 'I dislike this trade because it bears a mocking external resemblance to the real literary composition which is the only thing (apart from ancestral traditions) I take seriously in life.' It demeaned him to be working for the pulps and especially for publishers whose critical faculties and business practices he frowned upon. While he welcomed the cheques, he was ashamed for his name to be seen in the company of so many third-rate hacks (a reference to formulaic writers such as Fred Jackson who he had earlier lampooned). But it wasn't only the contrived plots and prosaic prose that offended his refined taste. His nineteenth-century sensibilities were appalled by the lurid, erotic artwork which adorned the covers and illustrated the submissions – so much so that he was relieved when his work was printed without the customary illustration. There were exceptions in both artwork and prose which met with his approval, but they were rare. Howard Brown's illustrations for 'At the Mountains of Madness' in *Astounding Stories* and anything drawn by Virgil Finlay – whose artwork Lovecraft greatly admired – are two rare exceptions.

In an effort to raise standards and to finally fulfil his ambition to become a tutor, (a career from which he'd been hitherto excluded, due to his lack of a university education) he began mentoring a dozen or so promising young writers, taking the time to send them annotated notes praising the positive aspects of their work, but not shrinking from constructive criticism. James Blish and Fritz Leiber benefited greatly from their correspondence with Lovecraft, with Leiber later remarking that Lovecraft was second only to Shakespeare in terms of influence. But of all of Lovecraft's protégés, Robert Bloch profited the most from the master's guidance, His comments on Bloch's work are particularly revealing, warning the young writer of the temptation to indulge in 'too much overt inculcation' and the piling on of 'monstrous adjectives, malign nouns and unhallowed verbs,' which Lovecraft confessed was 'an early and scarcely-conquered habit of my own'. Bloch's 'The Shambler from the Stars' was to inspire Lovecraft's final work of fiction, 'The Haunter of the Dark' to which Bloch would write a sequel, 'The Shadow from the Steeple'.

Writing down, as he saw it, for the pulps had had a detrimental effect on the quality of his own work and that he resented most of all. Writing to C.L. Moore on 7 February he complained: 'Every magazine trick and mannerism must be rigidly unlearned and banished even from one's own subconsciousness before one can write seriously for educated mental adults'. Although writing of A. Merritt, he inferred that he too had learned the 'trained-dog tricks too well and now he can't think and feel fictionally except in terms of the meaningless and artificial clichés of 2-cent a word romance'. He would later admit to Clark Ashton Smith that he believed his own work suffered from a 'general crudeness' and that the finished piece rarely reflected the subtlety of the vision that had inspired it being 'forced, awkward, childish, exaggerated and essentially inexpressive. I have staged a cheap melodramatic puppet show . . .'

One wonders then, why he didn't explore a different genre, but he had committed himself to so many projects – including revision work, ghost writing, amateur journalism and correspondence – that he simply couldn't afford the luxury of experimentation or writing in another area 'on spec'.

There were unexpected benefits, however, to be had from his association with *Weird Tales* – specifically the relationships he was able to forge with fellow contributors. Randolph Carter might have remained in limbo had it not been for Edgar Hoffmann Price, who suggested a sequel to one of his favourite Lovecraft creations, 'The Silver Key', after meeting its author in New Orleans in the summer of 1932.

The description Price gives of Lovecraft at this time is worth recording.

'His face was thin and narrow, longish, with long chin and jaw . . . His speech was quick and inclined to jerkiness. It was as though his body was hard put to keep up with the agility of his mind.' Price noted that his new friend slouched which made him appear less imposing than his height and the breadth of his shoulders would suggest (a posture he adopted in the mistaken belief that he had developed a curvature of the spine after hours of star gazing), but that he strode quickly, revealing a vitality that was evidently hard to contain. His mental energy was boundless and kept them talking almost continuously for 28 hours.

Price didn't find Lovecraft pompous or pretentious, but observed that even casual remarks were expressed in a formal, academic vernacular and that it was natural for him to do so. Contrary to the impression others have had of him, Price saw that Lovecraft possessed an 'enormous enthusiasm for new experience' and a capacity for ideas that Price called 'mental greed'. 'A glutton for words, ideas, thoughts. He elaborated, combined, distilled, and at a machine gun tempo.'

Lovecraft was initially reluctant to resurrect a character he hadn't given any thought to for six years. Yet after Price produced a 6,000-word draft of the tale he was proposing, Lovecraft couldn't resist adding his revisions until, Price claimed, there were fewer than 50 words of his original remaining. Lovecraft's version, which added a subplot that saw Carter's discarnate spirit possess the body of another being, ran to 14,000 words but he had retained key plot elements and thematic strands such as the theosophical concepts that Price, a student of the occult and esoteric, had introduced. In acknowledgment of this, Lovecraft agreed that both their names should be credited as authors when 'Through the Gates of the Silver Key' was published in the July 1934 issue of *Weird Tales*. The pair had, at one time, planned to collaborate on a regular basis producing 'a million words a month', according to Lovecraft who was in one of his more impulsive moods when he made this boast. In fact, it had taken him nine months to re-write their first collaborative effort, but it was rich in memorable imagery and Lovecraftian lore.

It opens with the reading of Carter's will at which a Swami recounts the events that followed his disappearance. If what he tells the heirs is true, it appears that Carter used the silver key to explore higher dimensions during which the nature of reality was revealed to him. He was then offered the chance to pass through the Ultimate Gate and incarnate on a distant planet where he would learn the fate that befell an alien race that he had been dreaming about. But Carter becomes trapped in the body of magician having neglected to memorise the incantations that would have given him dominance over his alien counterpart. Instead the two become locked in a struggle for control of the body which Carter eventually wins with the use of narcotics before returning to Earth to reclaim his Estate. Or does he? For Lovecraft this outcome fulfils another yearning, to recover the life of leisure, domestic bliss and financial security that he had enjoyed in Angell Street.

The twist, however, leaves room for an entirely different interpretation of the preceding events, although a postscript suggests the swami had been telling a version of the truth.

Lovecraft's despondency was compounded by the death of his Aunt Lillian on 3 July 1932. In the six years since his return to Providence, the two had been living in the same house and her loss led him to remark that, 'it will be impossible for me to get concentrated on any project of moment for some time to come'. Instead he set off on another round of travels (taking in Boston and Newbury in the company of Paul W. Cook before embarking alone for four days of sightseeing in Montreal and Quebec) during which he lived on nervous energy and ate very sparingly, returning home a shadow of his former self.

Paul W. Cook was so shocked on seeing his old friend in such a state that he immediately took the walking scarecrow to a restaurant and commenced feeding him up. He later wrote that Lovecraft had withered almost beyond recognition. 'Folds of skin hanging from a skeleton. Eyes sunk in sockets like burnt holes in a blanket. Those delicate, sensitive artist's hands and fingers nothing but claws.'

Cook had declined an invitation to join his friend as he knew he would be sleeping on buses and trains to avoid having to pay for lodgings and that he would be averse to eating out for the same reason. Their excursion to Newbury had shown Cook that when Lovecraft went sightseeing he was determined to see every building and street that might be of interest and would stop for nothing until he had taken them all in.

With architecture dating back to 1608, majestic cathedrals and awe-inspiring vistas of the Saint Lawrence valley from the cliff bordered plateau, Quebec was a natural destination for the obsessive antiquarian. He was so impressed with the city that it led to the writing of his longest work, the 130-page travelogue entitled, 'A Description of the Town of Quebeck in New-France, Lately Added to His Britannick Majestie's Dominions'. After offering a condensed history of the 'priest-ridden' province he provides a virtual tour for visiting Americans. This is so meticulously detailed that readers must have considered saving their fare and allowing Lovecraft to give them an exhaustive guided tour, street by street, from the comfort of their armchairs.

By February the following year Lovecraft's finances were in such desperate straits that he left his room at Barnes Street (where the rent was ten dollars per week) and moved in with his widowed Aunt Annie, the two of them sharing a five-room apartment in a house on College Street for half of what each had been paying. It was a very fortunate move and one which delighted him, for the house was built in the colonial style popular just prior to the Civil War and furnished like a living museum. It was situated in a pleasant neighbourhood near Brown University and backed on to the John Hay Library. 'After admiring such all my life, I find something magical and dreamlike in the experience of actually living in one,' he mused. It would be his last home.

By late August his mood had improved considerably, prompting an attempt at a new story. 'The Thing on the Doorstep' is hardly deserving of the drubbing it has received from those who consider themselves Lovecraft's most ardent admirers. The opening, for example, is admirably terse and engrossing: 'It is true that I have sent six bullets through the head of my best friend, and yet I hope to show by this statement that I am not his murderer.'

Again, there is the suspicion that Lovecraft is drawing on his own experience to render his characters more human and that perhaps he may be using them to acknowledge his own shortcomings. 'In self-reliance and practical affairs, however, Derby was greatly retarded because of his coddled existence. His health had improved, but his habits of childish dependence were fostered by over-careful parents, so that he never travelled alone, made independent decisions, or assumed responsibilities. It was early seen that he would not be equal to a struggle in the business or professional arena, but the family fortune was so ample that this formed no tragedy.'

Although Lovecraft did not acknowledge the probable source, it is uncannily reminiscent of H.G. Wells' 'The Story of the Late Mr Elvesham' (1896), though it is possible that the resemblance is coincidental as Lovecraft was not particularly impressed by Wells and had read little of his work.

'Elvesham' relates an encounter between a student and an old man who offers to bequeath his wealth to the youth if the latter agrees to adopt the old man's name and take a potion that he has prepared. Indulging the old man, the student does as he is asked only to find that the drug has facilitated an exchange of consciousness so that he now occupies the old man's decrepit body and vice versa.

The denouement to Lovecraft's story is lifted from W.W. Jacobs' much anthologised 'The Monkey's Paw' (1902), in which a couple are granted three wishes, the last of which they use to bring their dead son back to life and ends with an ominous knock on their front door. In Lovecraft's version we are given a graphic description of what awaits on the other side of the door.

The caller had on one of Edward's overcoats – its bottom almost touching the ground, and its sleeves rolled back yet still covering the hands. On the head was a slouch hat pulled low, while a black silk muffler concealed the face. As I stepped unsteadily forward, the figure made a semi-liquid sound like that I had heard over the telephone – 'glub . . . glub . . .' – and thrust at me a large, closely written paper impaled on the end of a long pencil.

What they finally found inside Edward's oddly-assorted clothes was mostly liquescent horror. There were bones, too – and a crushed-in skull.

It is Lovecraft's obvious relish in communicating such noisome abominations that have endeared him to connoisseurs of the macabre. The final plot was developed from an outline taken from a journal Lovecraft called his Commonplace Book in which he recorded ideas for possible stories. The entry that gave rise to 'The Thing on the Doorstep' read: 'Man has terrible wizard friend who gains influence over him. Kills him in defence of his soul – walls body up in ancient cellar – BUT – the dead wizard (who has said strange things about soul lingering in body) changes bodies with him . . . leaving him a conscious corpse in the cellar.'

The final draft takes the form of an account by one Daniel Upton of the bizarre transformation that overtakes his friend, Edward Derby, a cultured and psychically sensitive aesthete, after the latter falls in love with Asenath Waite, the daughter of an infamous occultist. Derby and Asenath exhibit very distinctive personalities, (he being weak-willed and she the opposite), but these characteristics are reversed, leading Upton to suspect that Asenath can swap bodies at will. Only it is not Asenath but her father who is in possession of her body. Desperate to be free of her influence Derby kills Asenath and is confined to an asylum, but 'she' had projected her consciousness from the grave into his body and his into hers, leaving him 'a foul stunted parody' of a man. It is this mute walking corpse which knocks on Upton's door and hands him a written explanation of all that has preceded it prompting Upton to visit the asylum and kill the occultist, who is now in possession of Derby's body.

> The patient rose to greet me, extending his hand with a polite smile; but I saw in an instant that he bore the strangely energized personality which had seemed so foreign to his own nature – the competent personality I had found so vaguely horrible, and which Edward himself had once vowed was the intruding soul of his wife. There was the same blazing vision – so like Asenath's and old Ephraim's – and the same firm mouth; and when he spoke I could sense the same grim, pervasive irony in his voice.

That October, Lovecraft was to have another vivid dream which could have been developed into a story, but which sadly remains a lengthy description in a letter to Bernard Austin Dwyer. It can be found in Lovecraft's bibliography under the title, 'The Evil Clergyman'.

A similar premise is at the centre of his penultimate novella, *The Shadow Out of Time* (February 1935) which was three months in the making and was the first new work to be produced in over a year, excluding revisions. The plot is a simple one – Nathaniel Wingate Peaslee, a professor at Miskatonic University suffers a severe mental collapse resulting in acute amnesia, but eventually recovers physically after which he demonstrates amazing mental agility, spending five years in intense scientific research that seems beyond normal human understanding.

> My sojourns at the universities were marked by abnormally rapid assimilation, as if the secondary personality had an intelligence enormously superior to my own. I have found, also, that my rate of reading and solitary study was phenomenal. I could master every detail of a book merely by glancing over it as fast as I could turn the leaves; while my skill at interpreting complex figures in an instant was veritably awesome.

As with the best of Lovecraft's fiction, the plot is propelled by a bizarre incident, remarked upon with curiosity and concern by those who are there to witness it. Nevertheless, life goes on with the threat of something unearthly and abominable simmering just beneath the surface.

> About the middle of August I returned to Arkham and re-opened my long-closed house in Crane Street. Here I installed a mechanism of the most curious aspect, constructed piecemeal by different makers of scientific apparatus in Europe and America, and guarded carefully from the sight of any one intelligent enough to analyse it.
>
> Those who did see it – a workman, a servant, and the new housekeeper – say that it was a queer mixture of rods, wheels, and mirrors, though only about two feet tall, one foot wide, and one foot thick. The central mirror was circular and convex. All this is borne out by such makers of parts as can be located.
>
> On the evening of Friday, 26 September, I dismissed the housekeeper and the maid until noon of the next day. Lights burned in the house till late, and a lean, dark, curiously foreign-looking man called in an automobile.

The addition of small intriguing details (the apparatus with no known purpose, the arrival of an unidentified caller) effects a subtle shift from the ordinary to the extraordinary, creating a hint of the uncanny. A secondary theme – the transfer of consciousness across the aeons – challenges our complacency by questioning our understanding of the nature of time and space.

With his research completed, the professor succumbs to a second breakdown which wipes his memory of all his remarkable recent achievements and restores him to his old self. But in his dreams he is plagued by images of an alien life form which had taken over his body in order to perform the research while his mind had been entrapped in its body. It is only when describing the Great Race that Lovecraft fails to produce a credible concept and the reader is reminded of the low-budget aliens that afflicted episodes of 1960s sci-fi series. 'The Great Race's members were immense rugose cones ten feet high, and with head and other organs attached to foot-thick, distensible limbs spreading from the apexes. They spoke by the clicking or scraping of huge paws or claws attached to the end of two of their four limbs, and walked by the expansion and contraction of a viscous layer attached to their vast, ten-foot bases.'

Peaslee is convinced the dreams are symptomatic of his recent illness until he is contacted by an Australian explorer and archaeologist who leads him to the remains of an ancient city where the troubled academic recovers the record he had written in English in his own hand 150 million years ago while supposedly 'out of his mind'.

By autumn 1936 Lovecraft was in a pitiable state financially. It had been two years since he had been able to sell a story and he was now reduced to economising on ink – surely the most demoralising situation any writer could find themselves in. 'I was never closer to the breadline than this year,' he told J. Vernon Shea that December. Then – just when it looked like he might have to petition friends for a loan to see him through the winter – he received almost $600 for the sale of two tales to *Astounding Stories* ('At the Mountains of Madness' and 'The Shadow Out of Time'), the latter submitted by a friend, Donald Wandrei, without the author's knowledge.

He began what was to be his last tale on 5 November and

completed it four days later. 'The Haunter of the Dark' centres on a young author, Robert Blake, (modelled on Robert Bloch, to whom the story is dedicated), who takes up residence in Providence in the very house that Lovecraft himself occupied on College Hill. Lovecraft wrote it as a friendly repost to Bloch who had killed off the leading character in his story 'The Shambler From the Stars' (1935), an antiquarian who was clearly based on Lovecraft and died when he accidently summoned an extra-dimensional bloodsucker. Bloch had written to Lovecraft to obtain permission to create a character that would be recognisable as a caricature of himself – to which Lovecraft enthusiastically agreed. But he also suggested that Bloch use the Latin title for his fictional grimoire, *De Vermis Mysteriis* (which translates as 'Mysteries of the Worm') and provided an extract of Latin text to be quoted. Lovecraft subsequently referred to the book in several of his own stories. Other writers followed suit, so that *De Vermis* achieved a near-mythical status comparable to the *Necronomicon*. Bloch in turn wrote a sequel, 'The Shadow From the Steeple' (1950) as a homage to his avuncular mentor.

Gazing out of his study window Blake is drawn to a derelict church on Federal Hill and eventually can't resist the urge to visit it.

> More and more he would sit at his westward window and gaze at the distant hill and the black, frowning steeple shunned by the birds. When the delicate leaves came out on the garden boughs the world was filled with a new beauty, but Blake's restlessness was merely increased. It was then that he first thought of crossing the city and climbing bodily up that fabulous slope into the smoke-wreathed world of dream.

There he finds books of occult lore, a metal box containing a curiously shaped, luminous stone and the remains of a journalist whose notes record the activities of a satanic group who performed unholy rites in the church during the nineteenth century. From the notes he learns of a malevolent entity that shuns the light and of a Shining Trapezohedron, brought to Earth from Yuggoth by the Old Ones, which acts as a portal to other dimensions and whose radiance keeps the bat-winged entity confined to the shadows of the church. In panic, Blake flees, closing the lid of the box and freeing the creature which is said to be an avatar of Nyarlathotep. Blake comes to believe that the entity is taking possession of him and struggles to retain his sanity. 'His entries dwell monotonously on certain terrible dreams, and of a strengthening of the unholy rapport in his sleep. There is mention of a night when he awakened to find himself fully dressed, outdoors, and headed automatically down College Hill towards the west. Again and again he dwells on the fact that the thing in the steeple knows where to find him.'

At the critical moment, both the entity and Blake are electrocuted by a freak lightning bolt. The next morning Blake's rigid body is found seated at his desk with 'glassy, bulging eyes and the marks of stark, convulsive fright on the twisted features'.

> Cautious investigators will hesitate to challenge the common belief that Robert Blake was killed by lightning, or by some profound nervous shock derived from an electrical discharge. It is true that the window he faced was unbroken, but nature has shown herself capable of many freakish performances. The expression on his face may easily have arisen from some obscure muscular source unrelated to anything he saw, while the entries in his diary are clearly the result of a fantastic imagination aroused by certain local superstitions and by certain old matters he had uncovered.

The all-too-convenient *deus ex machina* aside, 'The Haunter of the Dark' is one of Lovecraft's most effective tales, immersing the reader in a credible location where the dread of the dark is more unsettling than any sudden scare. It boasts several atmospheric scenes, namely the description of the city at night as seen from Blake's study, his exploration of the interior of the church and the hunt for the creature after it has withdrawn inside the belfry and attempted to block the light coming in through the windows.

Feeling satisfied with himself and much relieved by the unexpected infusion of funds, Lovecraft permitted himself a visit to his friends in New York over the Christmas vacation. Shortly after his return though he found himself strangely lethargic – to the point where he could not put it down to mere travel fatigue. More worryingly, he began to experience headaches, nausea and painful stomach cramps. At a time when he should have been attending to his own health he was instead acting as 'nurse, butler and errand boy' to his Aunt Annie who had been diagnosed with breast cancer. Such an assessment of his role suggests a certain resentment on the part of her nephew, for after she was transferred from hospital to a convalescent home, he was again reduced to eating out of tins due to his lack of basic culinary skills as much as to a lack of funds. His health improved sufficiently in the coming weeks to see him playing the genial host to old friends and returning to revision work which had been piling up since Annie's illness. She returned home for Christmas which cheered him, but by February his own health had deteriorated to the point where he was in constant pain and only able to digest liquids. He sought medical advice and was prescribed medication, primarily painkillers, but was evidently hoping it was only a temporary condition as he wrote a brief postcard to a friend informing him that he was 'very ill and likely to be so for a long time'.

In fact, he was terminally ill with cancer of the small intestine and kidney disease, both thought to be caused, or aggravated, by a high-fat diet. He was informed of the fact on 27 February and is said to have taken the news philosophically, keeping a diary of his condition until 11 March – one day after he was admitted to Jane Brown Memorial Hospital. His diary came into the possession of Robert Hayward Barlow, the teenage correspondent and collaborator whom Lovecraft named as his literary executor shortly before his death. Barlow carried the diary on his person until his suicide in 1951, after which it was lost. Unfortunately for posterity the contents were not copied before its disappearance, although Barlow quoted brief extracts in letters to August Derleth.

Prior to being hospitalised, Lovecraft had taken to sitting in a hot tub to alleviate the pain and sleeping fitfully in a chair as it was too agonising to lie down. By this time his abdomen had swollen, prompting his Aunt Annie to recall Lovecraft's personal physician, Dr Cecil Dustin, who in turn consulted a specialist, Dr William Leet. It was Leet who advised Annie to call an ambulance in view of a worrying new development; by this point, the patient was unable to eat or even drink.

Annie wrote to Barlow on 12 March informing him that, 'Howard is so pitifully ill and weak' and that he has been 'pathetically patient and philosophical'. The following day, when Harry Brobst and his wife came to visit, Lovecraft could barely summon up the strength to smile. Brobst, a voracious reader of weird fiction, had been a regular visitor to Lovecraft's rooms and a frequent companion on his evening strolls since the autumn of 1931, when he obtained Lovecraft's address from Farnsworth Wright.

On 14 March the patient underwent a stomach tap. The aim was to drain away the fluid and reduce the swelling in his abdomen. But by now he was unable to take liquids – even intravenously – without vomiting, and suffering 'unbearable pain'. He grew weaker until, at 7.15 on the morning of 15 March 1937, Howard Phillips Lovecraft passed quietly away.

The next day the *New York Times* reported 'Writer Charts Fatal Malady' in reference to the diary he had kept of his final days. It was perhaps fitting, given the nature of his work, that Lovecraft attained in death the recognition he had been denied in life. Two years earlier he had written, 'Nothing is really typical of my efforts . . . I'm simply casting about for better ways to crystallise and capture certain strong impressions (involving the elements of time, the unknown, cause and effect, fear, scenic and architectural beauty, and other seemingly ill-assorted things) which persist in clamouring for expression.'

The funeral was held at noon on 18 March in the chapel of the Horace B. Knowles' Sons Funeral Home on Benefit Street. It was attended by a small circle of acquaintants including Harry Brobst and Lovecraft's one surviving close relative, Aunt Annie who was comforted by her best friend Edna Lewis. None of Lovecraft's regular correspondents were present as they didn't learn of his death until they read the obituaries or were informed by fellow correspondents. For some, it would be several weeks before they heard the news.

After the service the mourners made their way to Swan Point Cemetery where they were joined by Lovecraft's second cousin, Ethel Phillips Moorish and her husband Edward Cole. It was a poor showing, but sadly not the last indignity. His name would be inscribed as a postscript on the headstone he shared with his parents until fans and admirers raised sufficient funds to erect a separate headstone forty years later.

Clark Ashton Smith spoke for both friends and fans when – one week later – he wrote to August Derleth of the man neither had met. 'It saddens me as nothing has done since my mother's death'. This genuine and profound sense of loss was echoed by many who had only exchanged letters with Lovecraft – and is fully understandable when one realises that the genuine psychic bond that they shared with him.

Over the following weeks and months *Weird Tales* was inundated with letters from fans and fellow writers, while the amateur world offered its tributes, of which W. Paul Cook's 75-page 'In Memoriam' (Driftwood Press, 1941) was arguably the most heartfelt.

When Howard Philips Lovecraft died I was a great many miles from New England, my address was not widely known, and it was some time after the funeral when I received the news from several sources in one mail. Reaching into the pigeon hole of unanswered letters I pulled out not one, but three, from Lovecraft. Spreading the letters out before me, I went into a black spell of self-recrimination. It made no difference in my feelings that there was nothing in the letters requiring immediate reply. I had shown, to say the least, an unpardonable discourtesy to one of the truest gentlemen and staunchest friends I have ever known.

Cook's tribute was limited to less than 100 copies, but the extent to which Lovecraft's untimely death affected his admirers could not be measured solely by the number of pages various publications devoted to his passing. A number of poets composed moving elegies to their friend, including Derleth, Smith and Long – all of whom expressed the sadness that had overtaken them and who now regretted that they had not done more to support him in life, in whatever way they were able.

While they wrung their hands, the nineteen-year-old Robert Hayward Barlow hopped on a bus from Kansas City arriving in

Providence too late for the funeral (the journey by bus took several days), but not too late to carry out Lovecraft's dying wish, to seize all of Lovecraft's papers and step into the role of Lovecraft's literary executor. Barlow had been in regular correspondence with Lovecraft for more than six years and had played host when his friend and mentor had visited Florida in the summers of 1934 and '35, staying in the family home for two months on each occasion. The pair had also collaborated on half a dozen stories, but it was nevertheless a shock to Frank Belknap Long and other close associates to learn that Barlow was Lovecraft's executor of choice and that this young man was already in possession of all of Lovecraft's personal effects, scrapbooks, notebooks and original manuscripts.

Barlow had been first on the scene because Annie had informed him of her nephew's death by telegram that very evening. The teenager had earlier written to enquire if he should make the journey, having been informed that Howard had made him executor shortly before his death. The document, entitled 'Instructions in Case of Decease' had no legal binding and could never have superseded Lovecraft's will made in 1912. Yet Annie felt obligated to honour this, her nephew's last wish.

On March 26, just a week after the interment, Annie formalised Barlow's position by having a contract drawn up under which he would arrange for publication of the manuscripts at his own expense. She was to receive all receipts, less a three percent commission of the gross amount. But while Barlow's claim may have been entirely legitimate, he was forced to acknowledge that he had neither the time – nor the expertise – to catalogue all of the material bequeathed to him. Hence, he donated much of it – including Lovecraft's letters – to the John Hay Library at Brown University.

Nevertheless, Barlow was seen by some – Clark Ashton Smith and Donald Wandrei in particular – as a fan who had first ingratiated himself with Lovecraft, then seized the personal papers of a man whose legacy might have been more faithfully administered by themselves. It is true that Barlow failed to see much of the material entrusted to him in print, but he did contribute to the first Arkham House publications and the manuscripts he donated to John Hay have been an invaluable source for Lovecraft scholars ever since.

CHAPTER NINE

THE HAUNTER OF THE DARK

*'I felt myself on the edge of the world; peering over the rim into
a fathomless chaos of eternal night.'*
– H.P. Lovecraft, 'Dagon'

Few outside the confines of Arkham Asylum would disagree that
Lovecraft's creations are the very definition of the 'weird' tale.
However, the true meaning of the term – as derived from 'wyrd', the
Anglo-Saxon word for fate or destiny – only covers one element in
his work. A more accurate term might be *sui generis* (of its own kind
or unique in its characteristics), for he revived and re-imagined the
genre he called 'fear-literature' by eliminating lumbering monsters
and supernatural creatures from these tales and replacing them with
beings which are far less easy to define and describe – because they
are powerful symbols of our deepest fears. In *Supernatural Horror
in Literature* (1927) he makes an important distinction between
'the literature of mere physical fear and the mundanely gruesome'
and 'the literature of cosmic fear in its purest sense'. Like no other
author, Lovecraft exemplifies the latter.

Lovecraft himself characterised the weird tale as having
'something more than secret murder, bloody bones, or a sheeted
form clanking chains'. The true weird tale, he wrote in the
introduction for *Supernatural Horror in Literature*, is suffused
with 'a certain atmosphere of breathless and unexplainable dread
of outer, unknown forces . . . there must be a hint, expressed with a
seriousness and portentousness becoming its subject, of that most

terrible conception of the human brain – a malign and particular suspension or defeat of those fixed laws of nature which are our only safeguard against the assaults of chaos and the daemons of unplumbed space.'

The evil visited upon humanity in Lovecraft's fiction is not that spawned by the devil, but the chaos unleashed by man's insatiable thirst for knowledge and new experience – that which tempts him to explore regions or mysteries best left undisturbed. Once liberated, the malevolent entities or predatory creatures cannot be banished by the simple expedient of brandishing a crucifix or performing a rite of exorcism. There is no divine intervention in a materialist universe (although lightning can strike at the most convenient moment), and yet Lovecraft's old fashioned morals led him to visit terrible biblical-style retribution on characters whose only true transgression was inquisitiveness. Their punishment therefore is always worse than death. It is oblivion. For Lovecraft could conceive of nothing worse than the loss of one's reason.

Many of those who knew him described Lovecraft as modest, kind and undeniably generous with his time and talent. He valued his family and his friends, but he was sorely lacking in empathy – a core symptom of what would now be labelled Asperger's syndrome (though Lovecraft's aversion to checking and revising his tales hardly chimes with the meticulous tendencies typically associated with this condition). Asperger's people are said to struggle to identify the emotions of those around them and this would certainly explain why so few of Lovecraft's characters are fully fleshed out. 'The people of a place matter absolutely nothing to me except as components of the general landscape and scenery,' Lovecraft explained in a letter to his aunt Lillian, on 29 March 1926. 'My life lies not in among people but among *scenes.*' In truth, his characters are mere ciphers, serving only to convey facts to the reader – which is why they frequently speak through surviving notes, documents and diaries. In this regard he breaks the first rule of dramatic fiction, which is to identify the characters' desires and then contrive obstacles for them to overcome. There is rarely conflict in Lovecraftian tales, only confrontation. It's true that there are occasional rivalries, but the protagonists themselves are not conflicted. They pursue the truth, all the while suspecting that it will only confirm their worst fears and when it does, it invariably drives them insane.

It is the foreknowledge that tragedy will overtake the narrator and that nothing will intervene to save him that elicits an emotional response from the reader. It is not necessary for them to identify with the protagonist – only to share the fear that the past is catching up with them in one form or another, or that they are being punished for overreaching – one of the few sins that humans can commit in an amoral universe. Another is to have been born to degenerate parents; after the hapless offspring is faced with the terrible truth of its origins – as in 'Arthur Jermyn' and 'The Rats in the Walls' – insanity is the only sentence that can be meted out. In Lovecraft's amoral, atheistic universe there is no redemption, no forgiveness and no divine intervention. Thus, the sins of the father are always visited upon the son. It is as if, in visiting terrible retribution upon his characters, Lovecraft is enacting a kind of penance of his own, attempting to expunge the shame and guilt he felt in having a father who had contracted a socially unforgiveable and unspeakable disease. Whatever the nature of the illness that killed him – whether it was syphilitic or not – Lovecraft could never shake the impression that it had led to his mother and himself being cast out from polite society. Indeed, it's hard not to see his father's untimely death as the source of the family's subsequent misfortunes. From then on, Lovecraft lived as one under a curse, both in reality and in his fictional life through his ill-fated protagonists. Perhaps this explains his pessimism, the crushing conviction that his literary efforts would be in vain.

A variation on this theme underlies 'The Dunwich Horror' and 'The Shadow over Innsmouth' in which miscegenation results in hideous mutations – except that the afflicted in these stories suffer different fates. Again, so extreme is the punishment for physical relations outside of marriage or one's race – the birth of deformed progeny, evisceration, annihilation – that it can only have been an expression of the most intense, internalised pain and rage.

It is not unreasonable to see these tales as Lovecraft's attempt to work through the trauma of his father's 'shameful' affliction and the subsequent mental collapse suffered by his mother.

The interbreeding and 'unnatural appetites' that lead to the degeneration of several accursed individuals in his fiction also helped him to address his fear of racial 'contamination' – the kind he imagined would arise if cultured Aryans bred with 'primitive', 'degenerate' or 'inferior' races. Even the transference of mind and body which underpins 'The Shadow out of Time' and 'The Thing on the Doorstep' implies a subconscious desire to be free of a body that may fall prey to disease and decay.

Revulsion on witnessing the corruption of what was once wholesome, mute astonishment at the deterioration of what had been vigorous and gibbering awe upon discovering the ruins of once great civilisations – these are the horrors at the heart of Lovecraft's desolate universe. Romance and material possessions have no place in his world, though the acquisition of ancient relics, books and documents play a vital role.

The world his almost exclusively male characters inhabit places no value on human relationships and that is why his stories appeal primarily, but by no means exclusively, to those who identify with their lone protagonists. The one major female figure, Asenath Waite in 'The Thing on the Doorstep', is literally an empty vessel, possessed by her father's spirit, while Lavinia, the deformed mother in 'The Dunwich Horror' is off-stage long before the action begins.

Lovecraft's male characters offer each other vital information or moral support when one of them ventures into a potentially dangerous situation, but they do not share their aspirations with each other, bemoan their situation or voice their opinions on mundane matters, as fleshed out characters do in much mainstream fiction.

The most unsettling aspect of Lovecraft's fiction is the notion that there are no absolutes or certainties and that knowledge is more likely to corrupt or drive the recipient insane than to enlighten them.

If he did not create cosmic horror – a term Lovecraft never applied to his own work, but to the Scandinavian sagas in which the universe is ruled by a pantheon of gods – he certainly popularised the form. More significantly, he purged fantastic fiction of its suffocating Victorian morals and the simplistic struggle for men's souls personified by the climactic showdown between a virtuous hero and a black-hearted villain. Unlike the Victorian scientific romances of Verne and Wells, there is no moral centre to which Lovecraft's characters can gravitate or even seek sanctuary. Faith in a greater good and even in one's fellow man is not only unrewarded but exposed as foolishness. Self-sacrifice and courage are invariably in vain.

It is tempting to see all his doomed male protagonists as victims whose knowledge cannot save them from oblivion, or at the very least a traumatic shock that will leave them psychologically damaged for the remainder of their purposeless lives. As such they could be seen as being representative of the author who felt similarly victimised by life.

Unable, or unwilling to confront his feelings for fear of being overwhelmed by them, he instead internalised the hurt, loss, disappointment and – most of all – the fear that what had been taken from him was lost forever, specifically privilege, prestige, domestic stability and financial security. Yes, he derived considerable pleasure from his sightseeing visits and from socialising with friends – like-minded individuals and fellow artistic spirits – but it was not so much their friendship he sought as their company, for he needed to belong and be accepted and it was the company of men that provided this. Women he considered his intellectual inferiors – despite having been brought up by his mother and aunts. Though some would claim that he modified his opinion in later life, they remained a mystery to him. Being in the company of young single men, however, allowed him the illusion of not having grown up, although he was acutely aware of the disparity in their ages and often referred to himself as 'grandfather' or the 'old man'.

One of the reasons why his horrors defy description could be because he was unsure what precisely it was that terrified him in life. Being reluctant to brood on such matters, he put it down to an antipathy to modernity, justifying his alienation by telling himself that he was born out of time, 'a stranger in this century', as he put it. But self-recrimination brings only self-loathing and ultimately self-destruction – unless it can be deflected. Hence, Lovecraft projected his frustrations and his fears onto those who would not retaliate or challenge his unfounded and irrational prejudice: strangers – specifically 'foreigners' or 'aliens' – whose unwelcome presence threatened to corrupt and destroy the impossibly perfect world exemplified by his hometown of Providence and its colonial cousins.

For Lovecraft, writing offered a means of retreating from a hostile world and returning, a childhood of wonder and of terror. But even the terrors of childhood nightmares were preferable to the very real horrors of the adult world for he knew he would wake up from the one, but not from the other.

It was partly for this reason that he sought out historic colonial towns, sites and architecture with such inexhaustible enthusiasm, walking for hours without fatigue. The mere existence of these places confirmed that something of humanity survives when the individuals who built them have gone. It suited his saturnine, self-pitying temperament to profess himself an 'indifferentist' – labouring under the belief that existence is given meaning through aesthetic appreciation alone – but for all his avowed pessimism he harboured a desperate hope that life was not futile, that something of what we create can remain unchanged, unsullied and uncorrupted by time. That we do not dream in vain. If that were not the case, he would have written nothing – nor exchanged his beliefs on so many matters and at such length with his correspondents. While one may write out of despair for a short period, writing over a lifetime constitutes a kind of purpose – a way to validate one's own existence. While his sojourns to places of historical interest provided him with the physical evidence that it was possible for something of ourselves to resist the rigours of aging and decay which had deprived him first of his father, then his beloved grandfather and finally his mother. They also provided a tangible link to the past that he felt he could tap into if he could only be present in the right location at the right moment, as he had done in Marblehead when he had what psychologist Abraham Maslow called a peak experience, that is a transcendental moment when mindfulness of the material world gives way to a sense of something eternal. For some it's a spiritual experience, a momentary realisation of the connectedness of all things, for others a sense of ecstasy when they triumph over adversity or are liberated from the limitations of the body. For Lovecraft it was liberation from the reality which he found oppressive to the point that it made him physically ill and drained his vitality. For him these tours were a secular pilgrimage and the effect on him was as rejuvenating as that experienced by a religious man on reaching a sacred site. To be present at these locations, to see them intact and not as ruins (a prime source of horror in his fiction) and to have this confirmed each time at various locations was sufficient to compel him to venture forth from his self-imposed exile from society. In short, visiting the unspoilt eighteenth-century towns of New England throughout his adult life sustained him and renewed his will to live.

Having stopped believing in God at an early age, he came to abhor organised religion as nothing more than institutionalised superstition and to put his faith in the immutable laws of science. These could be measured and proven, but provided him with a sense of awe and mystery such as others might find in religion or some form of spiritual philosophy. Being a self-confessed indifferentist appealed to Lovecraft's intellect, but provided scant comfort when he was left alone to contemplate the meaning and purpose of life – to which his only answer can have been creativity. Believing in nothing of significance outside of himself, he retreated deeper within, creating his own reality – in which resourceful men of knowledge were confronted with indefinable horrors intent on eradicating insignificant beings who had the temerity to believe that what they did, thought and created actually mattered. Life may be futile in Lovecraft's universe but death does not bring insight, only the dreamless sleep of non-existence. Self-sacrifice and heroism do not bring redemption or release from the forces that unleash chaos in his hostile universe.

Reason dictates that we should not like Lovecraft's tales as he offers no hope and no reward for courage, ingenuity or even the acquisition of knowledge. But that is the paradoxical character of human nature – we are sometimes attracted to that which we know is not good for us but we simply can't resist it. Lovecraft is the darkness to which we are drawn when our instincts warn us to leave it be. Here be dragons, or worse, but we can't resist the urge to peek through the curtain and see it for ourselves. Lovecraft was no different, only he was able to articulate our morbid fascination as few writers have been able to do before or since.

Those who come to Lovecraft expecting scares are invariably disappointed because he considered cheap shudders to be beneath him, although he served up more than his share of repulsive images. Delivering shocks was the business of pulp hacks, not a well-read literary figure of his calibre. His remit, as he saw it, was to peel back the membrane that insulated the material world from the abyss and reveal the awful truth of our insignificance. The greatest shock he could conceive of for a man of his sensibilities was the discovery that one was ordinary. He struggled to rise above all that was commonplace and mundane, by immersing himself in the most obscure, unfashionable and arcane literature, by rejecting those he considered 'modernist' authors and by summoning forth a bestiary of primordial entities that symbolised the forces of chaos that his New England neighbours feared. Only a mind as morbidly neurotic as Lovecraft's could have conceived of such horrors, just as Poe's bouts of manic depression manifested in tales that were informed by his fears.

Lovecraft's intellect and imagination empowered him, setting him apart from many of his contemporaries whose motivations were a mystery to him. On the other hand, it could also be said to have restricted his readership and limited his appeal. Lovecraft's psychosis, his hang-ups, fixations and phobias, were manifold but the one closest to home, so to speak, was his revulsion for the body that he felt he had been trapped in. Perhaps even more so than the fear of aging or disease, the thought of intimacy with another human being was truly repellent to him. The clues to this particular neurosis can be found festering just beneath the surface of almost every one of his stories. In 'The Shunned House', he tells of the 'white fungous growths' erupting in the cellar and discharging a 'viscous yellow ichor'; in 'The Colour Out of Space,' the rustics are infected by a puss-like globule that seeps from a meteorite, leaves their land barren, drains their bodies of vitality and drives a farmer's wife mad so that she has to be confined to the attic – an allusion perhaps, to his mother's mental and physical disintegration.

Physical contamination by contact with alien or 'lower races' is an underlying theme in much of his fiction. 'The Horror at Red Hook' describes 'the root of a contagion destined to sicken and swallow cities, and engulf nations in the foetor of hybrid pestilence'. In 'The Shadow over Innsmouth', it is the slimy skin of the phallic fish people that repels him so violently. The very sight of fish left Lovecraft feeling physically sick and he could not bear to be in the same room as someone eating it. 'I have hated fish and feared the sea and everything connected with it since I was two years old,' he confided in Donal Wandrei. Sigmund Freud could not have wished for a more challenging patient. His tales abound with genital substitutes. Preoccupied with ravenous fish-headed gods, predatory tentacled entities, rigid pillars and columns (invariably and revealingly in ruins), yawning abysses (caverns, wells, shafts, gaping mouths and cosmic portals), and explorations and ascents of mysterious mountains, Lovecraft presents a textbook case for the theory of displacement.

This revulsion is an extreme reaction to the emotional turmoil associated with adolescence, a phase Lovecraft never fully grew out of. It seems likely that his obsession with time – and most specifically the need to arrest decay and degeneration – stems from his desire to return to the past as he remembers it. He had no yearning for the fantasy of time travel as he did not wish to revisit the past as an adult, but as a child – the pampered child who lived with his mollycoddling mother, appreciative aunts, and indulgent grandfather on Angell Street. As L.P. Hartley observed, 'the past is a foreign country, they do things differently there'. Lovecraft never stopped mourning the loss of that life.

Lovecraft – A Question of Style

'If you look at the way critics describe Lovecraft . . . they often say he's purple, overwritten, overblown, verbose, but it's un-put-downable. There's something about that kind of hallucinatorily intense purple prose which completely breaches all rules of "good writing", but is somehow utterly compulsive and affecting. That pulp aesthetic of language is something very tenuous, which all too easily simply becomes shit, but is fascinating where it works.' – China Miéville, *Science Fiction Studies*

There may be some truth in the assertion – made by a number of Lovecraft's most ardent admirers – that his greatest literary legacy are his letters, which not only attest to his prodigious gift for language, but also encapsulate his thoughts on a diverse range of subjects shared at length with his correspondents. His amateur journalism, essays, scientific articles and poetry are also each deserving of a volume to themselves. However, it is his fiction on which his reputation rests and which has proven a pervasive influence on popular culture. And still, he divides opinion more than any other author.

Lovecraft came in for a considerable amount of criticism for his excessive use of adjectives, for long convoluted and incomprehensible passages congested with purple prose and for describing a mood of terror rather than evoking one. The fantasy author Lin Carter singled out 'The Nameless City' in her critical appraisal of Lovecraft's work, *A Look Behind The Cthulhu Mythos* (1972), as being one example in which the air of escalating horror is 'applied in a very artificial manner' and reproved him for overwriting and overdramatizing when a more subtle approach might have proven more effective. Carter observed, 'the valley in which the city lies is "terrible"; the ruins themselves are of an "unwholesome" antiquity; certain of the altars and stones "suggested forbidden rites of terrible, revolting, and inexplicable nature" . . . Decking them out with a variety of shuddersome adjectives does not make them intrinsically shuddersome . . . it is the flaw of the amateur.'

Carter makes a valid point, but Lovecraft was a poet by inclination and imbued everything he wrote with a lyricism lacking in writers of strictly narrative prose. The internal rhythms and phrasing of his best prose are those of a poet, informing his work with a distinctive voice, although it is arguable that he was an intuitive talent, well-read certainly, but untutored. He articulates a stream of consciousness as if channelling the thoughts of his central characters to produce a synthesis of prose and poetry. Sometimes a word is chosen for its sound rather than its meaning. 'Squamous', 'cacodaemoniacal', 'proboscidian' and 'gelatinous voice' give a stronger impression of what is being described than if he had used some more mundane comparison. Every writer enjoys playing with words, no matter how serious their subject might be, and Lovecraft was no different. He liked the sound of his own 'voice' and he clearly derived enormous pleasure from bending words into odd and curious shapes until he found something that appealed to or appalled him. It was permissible to be perverse and provocative, just so long as he wasn't being predictable.

When reading the disparaging comments made by his critics one is reminded of a scene in the film *Dead Poet's Society* in which the professors of a prestigious public school subject the work of approved poets to a rigorous line-by-line evaluation according to strict academic criteria until they have determined what is good and what is bad verse, thereby reducing art to a formula.

Tellingly, Lovecraft complained bitterly of the punctuation and paraphrasing arbitrarily applied to 'At the Mountains of Madness' in *Astounding Stories* – to his meticulous mind, these edits destroyed the flow and cadences of certain key sentences. For there is a brisk energy in the original, unmangled version, especially in those stories that were based on his dreams because they were, in effect, dictated by his subconscious immediately upon waking, scribbled down hastily before the impressions vaporised. This immediacy would be lost if subjected to a rigorous revision, rendering them lifeless and stilted.

Like Lord Dunsany before him, Lovecraft doesn't describe a scene in photographic detail. Instead, he provides his central character's emotive impression of that scene. If they are disturbed by it, the language will naturally reflect their agitated state of mind. If the city is 'terrible' and the ruins 'loathsome' it is because this is the way the central character perceives them; it tells us what they are feeling at that moment, not what the objects look like, or what characteristics they possess. Such adjectives are therefore not superfluous but essential to convey the narrator's subjective experience of the supernatural, or of the surreal nature of their dreams. By resisting the urge to give specific details he encourages the reader to elaborate upon what can only be suggested, hinting at the even greater horrors to come.

By informing the reader that the stones in 'The Nameless City' arouse revulsion in the narrator, Lovecraft is implying that the narrator understands the nature of the rites that were practiced at the site in ancient times and that he is sickened by them. Moreover, it reveals that the unnamed character is acutely sensitive to atmosphere and so what follows may be the result of the oppressive surroundings on his overwrought imagination. If the ruins made no impression on him, there could be no ambiguity and no possibility that the narrator had lost his mind and imagined subsequent events. It is regrettable that Lovecraft resorted to the hackneyed 'insanity' defence so often, but it lends credibility to his characters' claims. Their accounts must be valid and the creatures they encountered must be real, for no rational person could have experienced such horrors and remained sane.

No one can accuse Lovecraft of subtlety. He painted in broad, livid strokes and in thick daubs of primary colours unlike the diffuse atmosphere of impending dread favoured by the likes of M.R. James, Algernon Blackwood and Arthur Machen whose style might be compared to pen and ink washes or misty watercolours. But he has endured while many great writers – or at least those once lauded by the literary establishment – are no longer read, or even in print. And he has done so largely because he speaks to our twenty-first century malaise; our insecurities and vulnerability, our irrational fears and our loss of faith in organised religion, in authority and in the infallibility of science to cure all our ills.

As to the question of why Lovecraft became better known than many of his contemporaries, it has been argued that the sheer volume of his correspondence may be a significant contributing factor. In effect, he was networking almost a century before social media became the method of establishing a presence in the consciousness of fans and fellow writers. As noted earlier, he was also the first to create a fictional universe to which all were invited to contribute, thereby ensuring his characters' longevity.

Lovecraft irritated literary critics not so much because he refused to conform to their standards of expression, but because he did not see the need to explain the irrational elements in his work. However, his wilful refusal to describe the object in question is perfectly in keeping with the testimony of a madman, or a man whose sanity is questionable and whose experiences are beyond description . . .

but he's going to attempt to put them into words regardless. Don't then be surprised if he descends into an inarticulate barrage of adjectives and superlatives as he describes the dissolving corpse which visited him and said nothing but 'glub, glub'. This deliberate misuse of language is not only excusable, but entirely appropriate as it reveals the protagonist's hysterical mental state.

In short, it is a mistake to read Lovecraft as one reads his contemporaries. He has a language all his own and it is the language of a visionary who does not fully understand what it is that he has seen. Why else would he use such impressionistic phrases as 'the primal white jelly', 'the moon ladder' and 'the windowless solids with five dimensions', not to mention 'Yog-Sothoth' and a host of similarly named beings? It is as if he is admitting that language is incapable of describing what his characters have experienced and what he himself had seen in his dreams.

His solution to this predicament was simple but ingenious. He invented his own language to express the intangible, either mangling or manipulating words and phrases to suit his needs. This is not to say that he did not respect and understand literary conventions; only that he saw no need to conform to them slavishly when writing of events outside his experience.

Like Poe before him, he delighted in orchestrating passages using consonance, assonance, alliteration and other literary effects to drive his narrative, giving it forward momentum, modulation and dynamics. Although he was a stickler for the correct use of syntax and sentence structure when revising the work of other writers and when offering advice to aspiring authors in his essays on literary technique, (see appendix 2, 'Notes on Writing Weird Fiction') he would often deliberately flout the rules of grammar to produce a particular effect. Some of this would have been consciously crafted, but much was achieved intuitively as he had a well-tuned 'ear' for the sound of words and a gift for combining them to create the desired impression. The following passage from 'The Dunwich Horror' is typical of his signature style:

The speaking impulse seemed to falter here, as if some frightful psychic struggle were going on. Henry Wheeler strained his eye at the telescope, but saw only the three grotesquely silhouetted human figures on the peak, all moving their arms furiously in strange gestures as their incantation drew near its culmination. From what black wells of Acherontic fear or feeling, from what unplumbed gulfs of extra-cosmic consciousness or obscure, long-latent heredity, were those half-articulate thunder-croakings drawn? Presently they began to gather renewed force and coherence as they grew in stark, utter, ultimate frenzy.

Only a prose-poet would have substituted a line as impressionistic as, 'the speaking impulse seemed to falter here,' for a plain statement of fact to the effect that they were mute with fear. But he also demonstrates a visual sense that is almost cinematic as the close-up suggested by the straining eye pulls out to take in a long-shot of the three figures in the middle-distance. And there is drama too in having the narrator observe his companions who he cannot hear but who he sees gesticulating furiously which conveys both their vulnerability and his inability to help them.

The repetition of the phrase 'from what . . .' accentuates the awe and incomprehension that overcomes the narrator as he grapples with something outside his experience. The use of consonance (repetition of the same consonant in short succession) is evident in 'speaking impulse' and in 'seem' and 'some', with an internal rhyme in 'their incantation drew near its culmination' which emphasises the mantra-like nature of their chanting.

Alliteration (repetition of the initial consonant) is easily overdone, but when used sparingly it can generate a mood and emphasise the importance of the events being described as in 'fear or feeling', 'cosmic consciousness', 'psychic struggle', 'long-latent' and 'utter, ultimate'. The first coupling underscores the nature of the fight the characters are engaged in (it's not a physical battle but a test of their resolve); the second underlines the arcane nature of the incantation and the third conveys the state of near hysteria that they had worked themselves into.

Assonance (the repetition of a vowel sound in non-rhyming words) is often used for musical effect as in 'strained his eye' and 'began to gather'. In fact, the rhythm of this first line is more akin to verse than prose. In following it with the longer sentence the second acts like an answering phrase to compliment and develop the theme introduced by the first as counterpoint augments a musical theme.

The musical effect is heightened by the proliferation of strong sequential 'S' words within a short space to generate a rhythmic pulse (speaking; seemed; some; psychic struggle; strained; saw; silhouetted; strange) which give way to a conspicuous lack of words beginning with this letter when the point of view shifts from action to contemplation before returning to action in the final line.

Finally, the staccato effect achieved by forcing a pause between 'stark', 'utter' and 'ultimate' enforces the intensifying panic that accompanies the climax of the incantation and the imminent appearance of the Dunwich Horror itself.

These quirks and affectations were integral to his distinctive, deliberately archaic personal style, ensuring that Lovecraft's 'voice' is instantly recognisable from the opening paragraph.

The Dream-Quest of H.P. Lovecraft

'I believe that – because of the foundation of most weird concepts in dream-phenomena – the best weird tales are those in which the narrator or central figure remains (as in actual dreams) largely passive, & witnesses or experiences a stream of bizarre events which . . . flows past him, just touches him, or engulfs him utterly.'
– H.P. Lovecraft

In a dark recess at the back of one of London's antiquarian bookshops, where the casual browser is unlikely to stray, stands a rack of remarkable postcard-sized prints that no sane tourist would consider sending home. For each depicts a hideous pen and ink sketch of an insect-like creature that would give even the most dedicated naturalist nightmares. But if a customer were to enquire what these might be the balding, bespectacled owner would take great pleasure in explaining that they are elementals – rudimentary life forms that the writer H.P. Lovecraft had encountered on the astral plane.

Lovecraft called them 'night-gaunts', the winged demons of his childhood nightmares that took him on wild, terrifying flights over 'dead and horrible cities' and vast mountain regions, down into the depths beneath the waves where sunken cyclopean ruins testify to the ravages of time and upward into the vast, infinite blackness of space where he was overwhelmed with the sense of his own insignificance.

But when he returned to consciousness he rationalised his experience, dismissing the possibility that they had been lucid dreams which give the dreamer a glimpse of an alternative reality, a mental dimension which they are able to manipulate at will, or perhaps even an out-of-body experience in which the dream body (the finer etheric double) is able to explore the astral plane, one level higher than the physical world. Had he not been a stubborn rationalist, cynic and 'mechanistic materialist' – and instead given some credence to the beliefs of theosophists, occultists and practitioners of Yoga and eastern philosophy – he might have interpreted those uncommonly vivid dreams in an entirely different way.

It is significant that he made a distinction between such dreams and those which evaporated upon waking. In a letter to Maurice Moe he described the former as being 'as real as my presence at this table,' adding, 'I am, or was, actually and indisputably an unbodied spirit hovering over a very singular, very silent, and very ancient city . . .'

Those who have experienced such disembodied states invariably describe them as liberating and exhilarating. Temporarily detached from the physical body, the individual is also free from all earthly anxiety and fear. Some look back at their lifeless physical shell and cannot identify with it for they are now truly awake and their 'real' self. But Lovecraft, it seems, did not awaken in the dream body and explore his surroundings like a living apparition (commonly known as out-of-body or near-death experiences, a phenomenon that has been well documented). Instead, he merely became conscious that he was dreaming – a state which understandably terrified him when he was young. From his descriptions of the dream-state it would appear that his fear had restricted him to the shallow end of sleep where he became conscious that he was dreaming but could not take control of it, or had limited control leaving him at the mercy of those entities that symbolised his anxieties (as Jung would have interpreted it), or elementals (as occultists would have it). And the more he feared them, the more he empowered them. Not being aware of the true nature of what he was experiencing, he resorted to the only course open to him – he sought to write them out of his mind.

Had he studied theosophy or any other spiritual discipline rather than dismissing them out of hand, he would have discovered that what he assumed to be a sense of insignificance was instead an awareness of being an infinitesimal but vital part of a greater reality. Vital in the sense that becoming aware of the existence of one's immortal True Self (also known in the esoteric tradition as the Higher Self) cannot but engender a positive attitude and end the illusion of the 'suffering' – as Buddhists call it – which stems from our temporary separation from the divine source. It is the realisation that the notorious magician Aleister Crowley expressed in the maxim: 'Every man and every woman is a star'.

And the knowledge that while we may be physically separate from other sentient beings, we are at our very essence part of what Jung called the collective unconscious, or what esotericists term the universal mind. It is this shared pool of past experience and accumulated knowledge that Lovecraft appears to have glimpsed in the deepest phase of sleep. In creating his dark pantheon of gods and monsters he gave form to his readers' fears of the unknown, both in this world and the one beyond.

As the American author Joyce Carol Oates observed in the *New York Review of Books*, 'despite Lovecraft's expressed contempt for mysticism, clearly he was a kind of mystic, drawing intuitively upon a cosmology of images that came to him unbidden, from the "underside" of his life: all that was repressed, denied, "defeated"'.

From an early age Lovecraft was an intuitive practitioner of what Jung called creative visualization. As a child of seven or eight he admitted to being so enamoured with Greek mythology that he 'half-believed' in the existence of the dryads or nature spirits and by brooding on them intently he claimed to have eventually seen them. 'Once I firmly thought I beheld some kind of sylvan creatures dancing under autumnal oaks, a kind of "religious experience" as true in its way as the subjective ecstasies of a Christian . . . I have seen hoofed Pan.' And yet, in letters to friends and admirers he readily admitted that his 'black pantheon' of nameless horrors was 'one hundred percent fiction', for he feared that if he admitted – even to himself – that such visions could be anything more than pure imagination, he might come to doubt his own sanity.

'Poe and Lovecraft – not to mention Bruno Schulz or Franz Kafka – were what the world at large would consider extremely disturbed individuals. And most people who are that disturbed are not able to create works of fiction. These . . . are people who are just on the cusp of total psychological derangement. Sometimes they cross over and fall into the province of "outsider artists". That's where the future development of horror fiction lies – in the next person who is almost too emotionally and psychologically damaged to live in the world but not too damaged to produce fiction.' – Thomas Ligotti, American horror author

CHAPTER TEN

GRAPHIC CLASSICS, REEL HORRORS AND MORE

'A master craftsman, Lovecraft brings compelling visions of nightmarish fear, invisible worlds and the demons of the unconscious. If one author truly represents the very best in American literary horror, it is HP Lovecraft.'
– John Carpenter, director

Re-Animated! Lovecraft on Film

Lovecraft's world and its creations are said to be unfilmable and yet, that has not dissuaded moviemakers from trying. Sadly, many of their progeny have emerged malformed; hideous abominations that would have been incomprehensible to their creator. It is a curious fact that, of the numerous films that claim to be based on Lovecraft's stories, few could be said to be faithful adaptations, while those which betray his influence most strongly – such as *Alien* (1979) and *The Thing* (1982) – are far closer to his vision and his misanthropic philosophy.

Until the 1960s filmmakers hadn't even considered adapting his stories for the big screen because his fiction had not been widely published. When Roger Corman adapted 'The Case of Charles Dexter Ward' for the screen in 1963, the distributor, UIP, insisted that it be billed as Edgar Allan Poe's *The Haunted Palace*, partly to capitalise on the popularity of their Poe cycle, but also because they didn't see Lovecraft being a box-office draw. That wasn't entirely true as his tales were already being eagerly consumed by college students, but they were only a small part of the drive-in

197

audience for the low-budget B-movies that Corman produced. Another reason for Lovecraft's absence from the cinema screen – despite the perennial popularity of horror movies – was that his 'indescribable' eldritch horrors were considered unfilmable. Until the advent of CGI, even the most resourceful special-effects departments couldn't do justice to his numinous creations – a fact which deterred the studios who knew that audiences demanded a monster worth screaming at. That said, *The Haunted Palace* was an effective and handsome-looking movie (courtesy of Daniel Haller's art direction) which boasted a muted performance by Vincent Price and a solid supporting role from Lon Chaney, Jr. The credit to Poe was rationalized by the inclusion of a few lines from the titular poem at the very end, but it was a Lovecraftian film from the opening scene to the final credits, with mentions of the *Necronomicon* and invocations of Cthulhu and Yog-Sothoth. The action was also set in Arkham.

At least it proved that successful Lovecraft adaptations do not depend entirely on budget or effects. Atmosphere is everything, as RKO B-movie producer Val Lewton demonstrated in the forties when lumbered with ludicrous titles and minimal resources. Choosing the right location and making the most of it is a vital element, if a movie is to evoke the required mood. Plot is secondary to a keen sense of place. Quite simply, there is no place comparable to Lovecraft country in horror fiction with its tree-lined avenues and dignified academic institutions, isolated fishing villages and rural backwoods – each the very picture of normality – an idyllic setting whose tranquillity will be destroyed with the unexpected incursion of unimaginable horrors. If the town or village isn't decimated by the rampant monster, as it is in 'The Dunwich Horror', or infested by flesh-eating predators in various forms as in 'The Rats in the Walls', it will be corrupted by the lingering presence of the defiler – as Providence was to be in 'The Shunned House'.

And what would these settings be without their inimitable inhabitants? Any Lovecraft adaptation worthy of the name has to pay particular attention to casting. Actors have to look the part, not simply reel off their lines. Professors have to be pillars of respectability; young leads must be bookish, but inquisitive; rustics gnarled and cantankerous and madmen tragic and deluded rather than drooling, ranting loons.

If only the producers of such missed opportunities as 'The Colour Out of Space' (released as *Die, Monster, Die!* in 1965), 'The Dreams in the Witch House' (*The Crimson Cult* aka *Curse of the Crimson Altar*, 1968), (*The Dunwich Horror*, 1970) and 'The Shadow Over Innsmouth' (*Humanoids from the Deep*, 1980) had remained faithful to the source material they might not have done their author such a disservice. Significant elements were altered for no discernible reason and the cast were encouraged to overact to compensate for the lack of adequate production values and the absence of the titular beasties.

Die, Monster, Die! (aka *Monster of Terror*), for example, was relocated to contemporary England to explain Boris Karloff's heavily enunciated accent and an American teenager and his girlfriend were imported to provide the obligatory love interest, but like all Corman pictures of the period it looked suitably garish.

Karloff again lent gravitas to *Curse of the Crimson Altar*, but by now his health was in decline and the real interest lies in appearances by Christopher Lee and Mario Bava's leading lady Barbara Steele.

The Dunwich Horror starring Dean Stockwell, was more faithful to the story in terms of plot, but committed the unforgivable sin of trying to be 'trendy' with a gratuitous sex scene and cheap 'psychedelic' lighting. As such it has curiosity value as a tacky artefact of the late sixties, but scores poorly on every other front. The casting of Sandra Dee as a helpless sacrificial victim who apparently serves no purpose other than to be rescued at the last minute betrays Hollywood's utter failure to grasp the appeal of Lovecraft and their audience.

'The Colour Out of Space' provided the plot for a segment in *Creepshow* (1982), which adopted the look of the notoriously graphic EC Horror comics of the 1950s. The episode aired under the title 'The Lonesome Death of Jordy Verrill' and was played for laughs, though the fact that it starred Stephen King lent it a certain novelty appeal.

It was not, however, until the appearance of Stuart Gordon's camp horror comedy, *Re-Animator* (1985) and its sequels,

Bride of Re-Animator (1990) and *Beyond Re-Animator* (2003), that Lovecraft was billed above the title. Jeffrey Combs' kinetic performance as Herbert West, a witty script and a frenetic pace ensured it became one of the most successful adaptations, while the gore factor and cheesy effects earned it cult status and an eager audience for the sequels.

Dan O'Bannon, who wrote the screenplay for *Alien*, directed a reimagining of 'Charles Dexter Ward', released under the title *The Resurrected* (aka *Shatterbrain*) in 1991. To the minds of all but Lovecraft purists (who'd object to the master being given a modern makeover), it wasn't a bad effort. However, for those who prefer their Lovecraft undiluted, it doesn't raise a black candle to the Corman classic.

Then, along came writer/director/actor Bryan Moore with a decent script, a cast of enthusiastic amateurs and an understanding of what makes for a faithful adaptation. *Cool Air* (1999) was filmed in black and white to replicate the look of an early talkie – perhaps the only sensible way to bring Lovecraft 'shorts' to the screen, unless you have the resources of a major movie studio. Jack Donner nails the part of the obsessive Doctor Muñoz and Moore gives a good account of himself as the young writer who is renamed Randolph Carter for this 45-minute extended version of one of the master's most engaging stories. Moore has a keen ear for dialogue and gave himself a couple of choice lines, most notably his reply to the doctor's enquiry, 'Have you written your great American novel?' To which Carter responds, 'Not unless it's called something like "The Awful Tentacled Thing That Should Not Be."'

One can only hope that one day Moore is given the budget allocated to Stuart Gordon – the director behind a slew of embarrassing flops. He made a fair stab at *Dagon* (2001), a loose adaptation of 'The Shadow Over Innsmouth', but in relocating the story to modern Spain he lost the claustrophobic small-town atmosphere that is so essential to the source material.

Lovecraft made a comeback, so to speak, or at least his loyal fans in the H.P. Lovecraft Historical Society did with their self-produced *The Call of Cthulhu* (2005), a homage to both the spirit of Lovecraft and the silent movie – in which actions and style speak louder than the soundtrack. (The HPLHS production is not to be confused with the similarly titled 2007 film *Cthulhu*, which is a yet another adaption of 'Innsmouth', but this time with an overtly gay central character and absolutely no relation to the source material.) The Historical Society's $50,000 budget didn't stretch to a professional cast or cutting-edge effects, but the limitations work in its favour, producing a film the way Lovecraft himself might have seen it.

Beyond the Wall of Sleep (2006) is another well-intentioned amateur effort. Director Nathan Fisher admitted to some 'poor casting' decisions, but to his credit, he stuck close to the source material and the cinematography has the right noir look – it's just not one to scrutinise too closely. Unless Hollywood is going to finally bestow upon Lovecraft the lavish, big-budget production his work deserves it looks as if such fan-boy productions as these are the future.

Pickman's Muse (2009) has its admirers and picked up the Brown Jenkin Award for Best Adaptation at the HPL Film Festival. Based on 'Haunter of the Dark' and directed by Robert Cappelletto – a cinematographer with an eye for unsettling angles – it benefits from Barret Walz's fine performance as the eponymous artist driven insane by visions of alternate realities. Nevertheless, it never manages to transcend its low-budget origins.

Fortunately, for every dozen duds there's a gem to restore one's faith in film. By the time the HPL Historical Society came to make their second adaptation they had burnished off the rough edges and were brimming with confidence. *The Whisperer in Darkness* (2011) is a considerable improvement on their first effort, with more natural performances, creative camera angles and a glossy Warner Bros look to the lighting in keeping with the '30s setting. As the original story was published in '31 they have made this a talkie which ramps up the uncanny factor significantly.

Regrettably, Guillermo Del Toro's much anticipated multi-million dollar adaptation of 'At the Mountains of Madness' – with Tom Cruise lined up for the lead role – was ditched when Ridley Scott's pretentious *Alien* prequel *Prometheus* (2012) was given the green light. The feeling was that the similarities between the two movies, though superficial, would make Del Toro's redundant.

With its dramatic black and white cinematography and non-professional cast, *Die Farbe* (a 2010 version of 'The Colour Out of Space') would seem to be the German counterpart to the offerings of the HPL Historical Society. Somehow the language barrier only adds to the strangeness (it's subtitled in English) and enforces the impression that this is a dramatized documentary – a must-see for serious Lovecraft fans.

John Carpenter's *The Fog* (1980), *The Thing* (1982) and Del Toro's *Hellboy* (2004) are Lovecraft movies in all but name, while allusions and references to Lovecraft can be found in *The Evil Dead* (1982)and its two sequels, *Dead by Dawn* (1987) and *Army of Darkness* (1991) as well as John Carpenter's *In the Mouth of Madness* (1995) which includes characters reading excerpts from several Lovecraft stories.

Fifteen Reel Horrors

'No new horror can be more terrible than the daily torture of the commonplace.' – H.P. Lovecraft, 'Ex Oblivione'

Lovecraft has been poorly served by filmmakers and the following abominations are certainly best avoided.

The presence of a young Wil Wheaton (*Star Trek: The Next Generation*'s Wesley Crusher) in *The Curse* (1987) didn't encourage Lovecraft fans to have high expectations of this updating of 'The Colour Out of Space' and sadly, they weren't proven wrong. The performances are third rate, the mutant make-up is strictly DIY and the psychotic chickens would fail to put Colonel Sanders off his finger lickin',family bucket. It has the look of a low-budget MTV video and as for the sequels . . . the less said on this subject, the better.

Posters for *The Unnamable* (1988) proclaimed, 'There are things on God's earth that we can't explain and can't describe,' which the producers presumably didn't think would apply to their decision to inflict this farrago of nonsense on an unsuspecting public. To compound the felony they made a sequel imaginatively entitled *The*

Unnamable II (aka *The Unnamable Returns*) in 1992. Neither film made more than a passing nod to the source despite an attempt to deceive unsuspecting punters by subtitling the sequel *The Statement of Randolph Carter*.

The same can be said of *Pulse Pounders* (1988), a fright-free straight-to-video omnibus which includes 'The Evil Clergyman'. Even the presence of David Warner failed to save this production whose entire premise is neatly summed up by a little old lady who reproaches one of the characters with, 'you really have an unhealthy obsession with sex and death'.

Any horror movie which has the gall – or should that be guts – to purloin the name of the dreaded *Necronomicon* (1993) had better endeavour to live up to it. Sadly this anthology leaves a foetid odour more pungent than Asenath Waite's putrefying corpse. Some, however, say that it's so bad its good, so if you don't mind the conspicuous absence of rodents in 'The Rats in the Walls', a lot of sweaty sex in 'Cool Air' and few recognisable elements in 'The Whisperer in Darkness' you may forgive the filmmakers these liberties and have some fun. Jeffrey Combs makes an appearance as Lovecraft – whose true-life counterpart was doubtless spinning in his grave.

Combs returned the following year for yet another modern adaptation, playing a physician in *Lurking Fear* (1994), which suffered from a shoestring budget and some risible makeup, but moved along at a brisk enough pace so as not to outstay its welcome – which is more than can be said for *Castle Freak* (1995), a movie that purports to be based on 'The Outsider'. The result, however, is so incompetently handled by Stuart Gordon that you might prefer to bang your head with a baseball bat. Combs as John Reilly, heir to a twelfth-century castle, is watchable as always, but this is the kind of film that can actually ruin a favourite story.

By the time the serious Lovecraft scholar has viewed 1997's *Bleeders* (aka *Hemoglobin*) starring Rutger Hauer, they must be wondering if their appetite for schlock horror might be satiated.

Writer/director Ivan Zuccon made a fatal mistake with *The Shunned House* (2003) by attempting to intertwine three Lovecraft tales ('The Music of Erich Zann', 'Dreams in the Witch House' and the titular tale) with the history of an old villa and the couple who have acquired it. None of the stories are allowed to play out before he snaps back to the present and the quarrelling couple whose relationship may be of interest to their marriage guidance counsellor, but not to the viewer.

As for director Eric Morgret's *Strange Aeons: The Thing on the Doorstep* (2005), it has all the charm of an advert for the Home Shopping Channel.

Chill (2007) raises the question: 'when does a horror movie contravene the Trade Descriptions Act?' Answer: when it is neither scary nor gory. Perhaps the casting of faces from TV soaps *Melrose Place* and a supporting actress from *Hellraiser* in the lead roles should provide ample warning. A possible cure for insomnia, but of little value to Lovecraft fans who may have guessed from the title that it is 'loosely based' on 'Cool Air'.

Ditto *The Tomb* (2007) which utilises a handheld camera to excess, robbing the film of any tension or sense of atmosphere.

The best that can be said for *The Whisperer in Darkness* (2007) is leave well alone.

And that goes double for *Beyond the Dunwich Horror* (2008) of which the only thing to say is that some abominations should be strangled at birth. And we don't mean Wilbur Whateley's mutant twin brother.

Jeffrey Combs and Dean Stockwell must have regretted signing on for *The Dunwich Horror* in 2009, a limp TV movie which could be easily mistaken for a daytime soap. Cringe-inducing acting, anaemic atmosphere and all the scares of a seaside postcard make for two hours of your life you'll never get back.

And finally, at the very bottom of the barrel, it's not the low budget but the low brain-cell count that sinks *The Last Lovecraft: Relic of Cthulhu* (2009), a comedy horror which is neither funny nor entertaining on any level: a criminal waste of celluloid.

Lovecraft on the Small Screen

Notable adaptations for TV include two stories in Season Two of Rod Serling's *Night Gallery* (1971) – 'Pickman's Model' and 'Cool

Air' – plus a Lovecraft-inspired episode 'Professor Peabody's Last Lecture'; a Canadian TV movie *Out of Mind: The Stories of H.P. Lovecraft* (1998); a modern mash-up of several stories in a modern setting introduced by Christopher Heyerdahl as Lovecraft and Stuart Gordon's segment in the series *Masters of Horror* (2005), 'Dreams in the Witch House'.

Documentaries
The Eldritch Influence: The Life, Vision, and Phenomenon of H.P. Lovecraft (2003)
Lovecraft – The Forgotten Diary (2005)
Lovecraft: Fear of the Unknown (2008)
The Young Man of Providence (2013)

Lovecraft in the Comics
Comics have grown up since the golden, silver and bronze age of spandex-clad superheroes that spanned the thirties to the eighties . . . and their readership has grown along with them. The dualistic DC Universe of good versus evil – personified by Batman and Superman, and their criminal adversaries – was conceived in an age of innocence and unsophistication, when comics were strictly for kids, but in the 1960s comics became cool for high school and college students. Stan Lee and his legion of not-so-super heroes fell to Earth to battle unscrupulous villains and monsters while trying to hold down a job, study for their exams and keep their identities secret from girls they didn't have the courage to converse with without a mask. Stan 'the Man' Lee was at the centre of a monotheistic Marvel universe until the late seventies when DC were roused from their complacency and revamped their fearless champions, giving them all-too human failings and, most importantly of all, emotions – so that comics could handle 'difficult' themes. The proliferation of small independent publishers who appeared in the late seventies were not bound by the restrictions and self-regulatory censorship imposed by the Comics Code Authority in 1954, (precluding the depiction of graphic violence, nudity and police corruption which

the independents chose to ignore) and so were able to address adult topics such as sexuality, politics and drug addiction, initiating a seismic shift in the two-dimensional world of sequential panels and speech balloons. By this time artists and illustrators were straining at the leash to get their teeth into something more adult and so when the graphic novel became the next big thing in the eighties, with many titles outselling traditional comic books, they were ready to do justice to serious fiction. And that's where Lovecraft comes in.

Lovecraft lends himself particularly well to the visual medium of graphic arts and comics where his abominable creations can be fully realised, unfettered by the technical limitations that hamper movie adaptations (especially those made before the development of CGI). The format also improves the pacing by compressing the plot and condensing the amount of exposition. But best of all it is ideal for creating a heightened reality in which credible characters are confronted by incredible beings.

Ten Comic Collector's Essentials

The Worlds of H.P. Lovecraft (Caliber Comics/Tome Press; black and white; 1993). Artists: various. Script: Steven Jones.

Modernised re-imaginings of Lovecraft's tales with some scripts sticking close to the source and others utilising only the basic concept.

H.P. Lovecraft's Cthulhu: The Whisperer in Darkness (Millennium Publications; colour; 1993). Artists: Darryl Banks, Don Heck and others. Script: Mark Ellis, Terry Collins, Paul Davis.

Republication of a three-issue limited series under one cover. Only fifteen pages are directly related to the original story, the rest having more in common with 'The Call of Cthulhu' role-playing game which also features three investigators from the Miskatonic Project, a select unit of paranormal investigators originally created for the comic. One character, the sculptor Henry Wilcox, has no involvement with the events, but appears to have been transported to Vermont in order to shoehorn Cthulhu into the story. The 1920s milieu is well rendered and there is sufficient action to keep one's interest, but there are too many inconsistencies and the original plot is subservient to a larger story inspired by the game.

The Dream-Quest of Unknown Kadath (Mockman Press; black and white; 1997–99). Art and script: Jason Thompson.

Ambitious and remarkably faithful five-issue adaptation of one of Lovecraft's longest and supposedly unintelligible novellas, requiring hundreds of fully rendered panels written, drawn and lettered by the indefatigable Jason Thompson. The descriptive text is taken verbatim from the book and the dialogue extracted almost intact while other elements are incorporated in tiny, but telling details that make it the modern equivalent of an illuminated manuscript with its vivid colours and intricate embellishments. Thompson depicts Carter as a blank-faced cartoon character suggestive of a children's fantasy, yet manages to capture the essence of the hallucinatory dreamscape and the numinous experiences without over-simplifying the book.

Heavy Metal magazine, the Lovecraft issue (HM Communications; black and white, and colour; October 1979).

In the wake of interest generated by Ridley Scott's *Alien* and the press attention given to H.R. Giger, the American adult illustrated fantasy magazine decided to capitalise on the sci-fi and fantasy boom with this one-off special devoted to HPL. A missed opportunity if ever there was one as none of the contributors appear to be familiar with Lovecraft's work with the exception of Alberto Breccia, the Uruguayan comic artist who contributed a severely condensed retelling of 'The Dunwich Horror' and Alain Voss whose 'The Thing' is a reinterpretation of 'The Statement of Randolph Carter'. The latter forgoes the standard narrative panel format in favour of a string of vague recollections in fog-wreathed images that communicate a dream-like quality. An honourable mention though for artist Serge Clerc who captures the spirit of HPL in 'The Man from Black Hole'.

The Haunter of the Dark and Other Grotesque Visions (Oneiros Books; black and white; 2006). Art and script: John Coulthart.

Coulthart's painstaking attention to detail in his depiction of architectural detail makes his adaptations of 'Haunter', 'Cthulhu'

THE CURIOUS CASE OF OF H.P. LOVECRAFT

and 'Dunwich' essential reading for Lovecraft collectors, but for reasons never explained he truncates the latter before Wilbur's monstrous brother can make his appearance.

Graphic Classics Volume 4: H.P. Lovecraft (Eureka Productions; black and white; 2007). Artists: Wan Kok, Michael Manning and others.

Although the cover depicts a garishly inked Cthulhu by Giorgio Comolo, the stark black-and-white artwork between the covers owes more to the quirky and subversive underground comics of the late sixties and so might disappoint those used to the ornate illustrations of the kind produced by Bernie Wrightson.

The same applies to *Graphic Classics Volume 15* which includes 'The Dream-Quest of Unknown Kadath' illustrated by Leong Wan Kok and *Volume 10* which offers 'The Thing on the Doorstep' illustrated by Michael Manning, although both of these are far superior to their newspaper-strip-style companions offered by the other contributors.

H.P. Lovecraft's Haunt of Horror (Marvel; black and white; 2008). Artist and script: Richard Corben.

Corben, whose credits include the magazines *Eerie*, *Creepy* and *Heavy Metal*, as well as the cover of Meat Loaf's album, *Bat Out of Hell*, lent his talents to illustrating some of Lovecraft's 'lesser' pieces: poems and fragments including 'A Memory', 'The Window', 'The Well' and 'The Lamp' as well as titles that have previously been overlooked by comic artists, namely 'Arthur Jermyn' and 'The Music of Erich Zann'.

Includes the complete text for some of the shorter stories.

At The Mountains of Madness (Self Made Hero; colour; 2011). Art and script: I.N.J. Culbard

Lovecraft's magnum opus deserves a serious graphic novel. Sadly this isn't it. Culbard's flat Tintin-style illustrations simply don't suit the subject matter. But its status as the only adaptation of this classic story to date means it merits a single reading at least.

The Lovecraft Anthology: Volumes 1 and 2 (Self Made Hero; colour; 2011). Artists: Warwick Cadwell, Steve Pugh, Bryan Baugh and others.

Unspeakably satisfying collection of Lovecraft's most absorbing stories, superbly rendered in living colour by artists who evidently know and love their Lovecraft. *Volume 1* collects seven tales including 'The Dunwich Horror', 'The Shadow Over Innsmouth' and 'The Call of Cthulhu', whilst *Volume 2* offers nine minor but no less essential tales including 'The Festival', 'The Hound, 'He' and 'The Nameless City'. All told, the diverse styles of the sixteen artists displayed here – from Cadwell's cartoon-esque 'Statement of Randolph Carter' to Pugh's digitally cinematic 'Pickman's Model' to Baugh's *Creepy* magazine-inspired, old-school vision of 'The Hound' – are each as grimly fiendish as you could wish for.

Although superheroes have no place in Lovecraft's universe, his creations and other entities clearly spawned by his abominations have been pitted against Batman, Swamp Thing, Superman, the Justice League of America, the Fantastic Four and the Avengers. And, of course, Batman's forays into Arkham Asylum (in comics, graphic novels, games and Christopher Nolan's movie trilogy) constitute another nod to the master.

In addition, the *Aliens Special* (Dark Horse Comics; black and white; 1997) contains a story that owes a great debt to Lovecraft and ties in with the *Alien* franchise. *Elder Gods* is penned by *Swamp Thing* writer Nancy Collins and drawn by Leif Jones.

This is merely an introduction to Lovecraftian comics – an art form that is multiplying more rapidly than Cthulhu's acolytes. As you read this, you can be sure that somewhere somebody is sharpening their pencil, dipping their pen in pitch-black ink or blending a palette of lurid colours to bring forth the next abomination.

Essential Reading
The following include one or more Lovecraft stories:

Bernie Wrightson: Master of the Macabre Vol. 1, No. 2
(Pacific Comics; August 1983)

The Cosmical Horror of H.P. Lovecraft: A Pictorial Anthology
(Glittering Images; 1991)
Creepy (Warren Publishing; 1979)
Eerie (Warren Publishing; 1975)
H.P. Lovecraft's Call of Cthulhu (Transfuzion Publishing; 2010)
H.P. Lovecraft's Cthulhu (Millennium Publications; 1991–94)
Journey into Mystery Vol. 1, No. 4 (Marvel; 1973)
Lovecraft in Full Color (Adventure Comics; 1991–92)
The Mammoth Book of Best Horror Comics (Running Press; 2008)
Masters of Terror (Marvel; 1975)
Planet Lovecraft (Lightning Strikes Twice; 2008–9)
The Starry Wisdom (Creation Books; 1994)
Strange Aeons (Highland Press; 1997–2010)
The Vault of Horror EC Comics reprint
(Russ Cochran/Dark Horse; 1993–94/2014)
Weird Terror Vol. 1, No. 1 (Comic Media/AHA; 1952)
Weird Worlds Vol. 2, No. 2 (Eerie Publications; 1971)
The Worlds of H.P. Lovecraft (Caliber; 1993–98)
The Worlds of H.P. Lovecraft (Transfuzion Publishing; 2008–09)

I am indebted to Ralph E. Vaughan for allowing me access to his exhaustive research on the subject and specifically the paper he prepared for the 8th Annual Comic Arts Conference in San Diego, July 2000.

For covers and updates visit www.darktreepress.50megs.com and the Periodical Reading Room at Miskatonic University www.yankeeclassic.com

On Record – They Sold their Souls for Rock and Roll

'Well, you've got to pay homage, don't you? Somebody's got to do it. He's not very bloody recognized [in New York], is he? It's disgusting. They come over here and worship bloody Jane Austen and shit like that. Funnily enough, I just re-read "At the Mountains of Madness". It's great, isn't it? I would love to visit Lovecraft's grave.' – Mark E. Smith, The Fall

Had Lovecraft lived to hear the West Coast band who named themselves in his honour, it's likely he would have covered his ears and echoed the final cry of the deranged de la Poer in 'The Rats in the Walls' – 'agus bas dunarch ort!' Lovecraft was partial to music, but amplified rock would likely have assailed his acutely sensitive hearing like fingernails on a blackboard.

Nevertheless, a horde of bands have worshipped at the altar of HPL and the Great Old Ones ever since the occult became a dominant theme of hard rock and heavy metal in the late sixties. From obscure British bands such as Arkham Witch and Slovakian doom-metal merchants Azathoth to monoliths like Black Sabbath and Metallica, rock musicians have seized upon the most evocative images in Lovecraft's mythos to strike a common nerve in the adolescent psyche.

Words of power and iconic images have been central to worship from the earliest times – be they connected to pagan rites, ceremonial magic, the spiritual disciplines of the east or the sacred rituals of organised religion – and when those words are formulated into mantra-like chants and set to music of comparable power the cumulative effect could awaken Cthulhu himself from slumber. Lovecraft disparaged institutionalised religion, the occult and the esoteric, but unwittingly created the basis for a worldwide secular cult by envisioning entities whose names have proven to possess great potency for those who brood upon them intently.

Tibetan monks call these thought-forms tulpa creations and practise projecting their mental energy into living apparitions until they take on real substance and can be seen by others. The trick is to reabsorb them before they take on a life of their own, as the Belgian mystic Alexandra David-Neel discovered during a sojourn in Tibet and as the British occultist Dion Fortune learned to her cost after inadvertently materialising a wolf to avenge herself on a hated rival. The majority of bands who pay homage to Lovecraft's pantheon of gods and elder entities do so as a harmless pop culture reference, but there are some who claim to take it seriously and in doing so could be invoking forces they are unable to contain. To paraphrase the author Dennis Wheatley, it is not necessary to believe in the forces of darkness to summon them from the depths of the subconscious, for it is there that the angels and demons of our nature reside and when those baser instincts are aroused they can cause more damage to the untrained acolyte than Nyarlathotep, the Crawling Chaos. But if that sounds like a load of Yog-Sothothery, by all means programme Cradle of Filth on repeat, dim the lights, light a black candle and visualise the dark god of your choice.

'We wanted to create mood pieces that would emulate the inhuman strangeness that Lovecraft had described so often. As one of the earliest extreme metal bands, we tried to achieve this by incorporating musical elements foreign to the genre . . . So, for example, we included a multi-layered violin . . . played out of tune and rhythm . . . to evoke a chthonian atmosphere.' – Martin Eric Ain, Celtic Frost

'We start using a traditional song structure then pervert and twist it until people become, hopefully, disorientated . . . we have dislocated them from reality . . . this is the effect that Lovecraft's writing has on people too.' – Justin Oborn, Electric Wizard

Essential Listening
H.P. Lovecraft 'The White Ship' (1967)
Black Sabbath 'Behind the Wall of Sleep' (1970)
The Darkest of the Hillside Thickets – anything by this Canadian post-punk band, who are obsessed with H.P. Lovecraft
Celtic Frost *Morbid Tales* (1984)
Cradle of Filth 'Cthulhu Dawn' (2006)
Deicide *Legion* (2000)
Dream Theatre 'The Dark Eternal Night' (2007)
Electric Wizard *Dopethrone* (2006)
Entombed *Clandestine* (2012)
The Fall 'Spectre vs. Rector' (1979)
Manilla Road *Out of the Abyss* (1988)
Mekong Delta *The Music of Erich Zann* (1988)
Mercyful Fate *Time* (2002) and *Into the Unknown* (2007)
Metallica 'The Thing That Should Not Be' (1989)
and 'The Call of Ktulu' (1984)
Morbid Angel *Formulas Fatal to the Flesh* (1998)

Nox Arcana *Necronomicon* (2004)
Rage *Black in Mind* (1995)
Therion *Beyond Sanctorum* (1991)
Various Artists *Dreams in the Witch House – A Lovecraftian Rock Opera* (HPLHS; 2013)
Various Artists *At the Mountains of Madness – International Doom Collection* (Miskatonic Foundation; 1999)
Various Artists *The Challenge From Beyond: A Tribute to HPL* (1999)
Various Artists *The Outsider: An Aural Channelling of HPL* (2002)
Various Artists *Tribute to HPL* (2006)

And for those who just can't get enough Lovecraft, there is the legendary and reputedly unstageable musical spoof *A Shoggoth on the Roof* with new lyrics by He Who Must Not Be Named and music by Jerry Bock. Bock wrote the original numbers for *Fiddler on the Roof* and is apparently not happy about his music being usurped for such blasphemous parodies. However, a group of taste-defying Swedes staged it at the Miskatonicon HPL fan convention in Stockholm in 2005 and a CD is reputedly available under the counter in a plain brown wrapper from selected outlets. For more information visit: cthulhulives.org/musical.

'All I have to do is read some Lovecraft and the strange comes out of me automatically.' – Mark Shelton, Manilla Road

Console Games
Alone in the Dark (Infogames; 1992)
Tired of skulking around Arkham? Looking for somewhere more exotic to explore? Well, what could be more spooky than a Louisiana Mansion inhabited by eldritch horrors and wreathed in bayou fog? Unfortunately, the first 3D survival horror is positively primitive by today's standards, but retro gamers will find a place for it on their fun shelf.

Call of Cthulhu: Dark Corners of the Earth (Headfirst; 2005)
A first-person shooter based on 'The Shadow over Innsmouth' starts with a suicide and gets grimmer from there on in. The lack of any

heads-up display can be frustrating as you have no idea what you need to do or look for in each location. The protagonist can often be heard mumbling something under his breath – which you'll surely miss if you're simultaneously blasting away at something. But after a couple of plays it all comes together and the puzzles become easier to solve as you get to know what to look for. Particularly appealing are the nausea-inducing visual effects that kick in when your character is in shock or has been attacked. When you're at your lowest, the screen goes out of focus . . .

Eternal Darkness: Sanity's Requiem (Silicon Knights; 2002)
Very tenuously linked to Lovecraft, but a genuinely immersive experience.

The Hound of Shadow (Electronic Arts; 1989)
With its 1920s setting, this text-only adventure entices the unwary to 'enter the sinister world of H.P. Lovecraft'; from the same team that created *Daughter of Serpents* (aka *The Scroll*).

Lovecraft Country (Skotos; 2005)
An online, text-based, role-playing game. As a student at Miskatonic University, you interact with other online gamers and characters in the main game, 'Arkham by Night', before setting off on supplementary adventures.

The Lurking Horror (Infocom; 1987)
Although the developers claim it recalls the 'ghastly visions of H.P. Lovecraft and Stephen King', the game makes no direct reference to either. It is, however, steeped in Lovecraftian atmosphere as players confront entities in the tunnels beneath a college campus.

Necronomicon: The Gateway to Beyond (Dreamcatcher; 2001)
Decent graphics, credible characters and the well-rendered rural setting help to pass a couple of hours – just don't expect any serious scares or a jaw-dropping climax.

Prisoner of Ice (I-Motion; 1995)
Good graphics, a strong storyline and a strategy guide presented

as an old newspaper make this game worth playing. Stop the Nazis from releasing Cthulhu!

Quake (id Software; 1996)
First-person shooter featuring Lovecraftian creatures – to be blasted into a gluttonous mess.

Shadow of the Comet (I-Motion; 1993)
From the team that brought you *Alone in the Dark*, another retro classic (or relic depending on your age). Illsmouth, New England, is the setting for the resurgence of the Great Ancients – unless you can stop them.

X-COM: Terror from the Deep (MicroProse; 1996)
The many tentacled god of copyright clearance prevented the developers from using the names of the Old Ones who are intent on awakening you-know-who from deep sleep, but do not doubt that this is a Lovecraft strategy game in all but name.

More Gaming Essentials
Deities & Demigods (TSR; May 1980)
The first edition of this creature 'cyclopedia for Advanced Dungeons & Dragons featured a Cthulhu Mythos chapter which had to be pulled from subsequent editions for copyright reasons.
Call of Cthulhu, (Chaosium; 1981; RPG Board Game)
Cthulhu Live (Fantasy Flight; Live-action version of the above)
The Gateway Bestiary, (Chaosium; June 1980)
'Runequest' supplement includes a chapter of Lovecraft creations.
Arkham Horror (Chaosium; 1987)
Arkham Horror (Fantasy Flight; 2005)
Call of Cthulhu: Collectible Card Game (Fantasy Flight; 2004)
Call of Cthulhu: Card Game (Fantasy Flight; 2008)
Cthulhu Gloom (Atlas Games; 2011)
Elder Sign (Fantasy Flight; 2011)
Munchkin Cthulhu (Steve Jackson Games; 2007)
Mythos (Chaosium; 1996)

When Darkness Comes: The Nameless Mist
(Twilight Creations; 2005)

For details, updates and much more visit boardgamegeek.com

'Who knows the end? What has risen may sink, and what has sunk may rise. Loathsomeness waits and dreams in the deep, and decay spreads over the tottering cities of men.' – H.P. Lovecraft, 'The Call of Cthulhu'

AFTERWORD

'While we may consciously reject [Lovecraft's] cosmology, a part of us finds in it a chilling confirmation of secret fears. At the time Lovecraft created it, the "Cthulhu Mythos" and its threat of Elder Gods rising and returning to rule over earth could be easily dismissed as merely a paranoid fable of the future. Today there is growing suspicion that this future may become our present.'
– Robert Bloch

In 2005, 68 years after Lovecraft's obituary appeared in the *New York Times*, the American press reported that the once obscure pulp writer had finally been acknowledged with a Library of America edition of his most celebrated tales, an honour that set him alongside the likes of Henry James, William Faulkner, and F. Scott Fitzgerald.

Library of America's editor-in-chief Geoffrey O'Brien observed, 'Lovecraft was a genuine original, with a rigorous sense of narrative form at the service of a coherent vision of the universe – a vision that happens to embody the most extreme paranoia and unblinking pessimism. He will, I think, figure as an unavoidable mythologist of the twentieth century.'

Bestselling author Peter Straub, who compiled the LoA edition noted, 'He stands next to Poe as the high-water mark in nineteenth- and twentieth-century American gothic. His influence on other writers, which was immediate, has proved to be unending and fruitful.'

Shortly before his death, Lovecraft had the pleasure of seeing the first printed edition of his work in book form, (discounting anthologies in which his work had appeared alongside others). This was offset, however, by bitter disappointment as the text was peppered with typographical errors which its author insisted on correcting by hand. 'The Shadow over Innsmouth' had been privately published in a limited edition hardback of 200 copies for close friends and a small circle of fans. Double that number had been printed, but the publisher did not have sufficient money to have the rest bound and so they were destroyed, making the surviving copies some of the rarest and most desirable items for Lovecraft collectors, especially those containing the author's own corrections.

Grieving for the loss of his friend and exasperated by the slapdash editing meted out to his texts by amateur publishers and the pulps, August Derleth determined to present Lovecraft's work to a wider audience – and in a form which the author would have approved of. In partnership with Donald Wandrei, Derleth founded Arkham House as the 'official' imprint of Lovecraft's literary estate and announced a trilogy of titles to establish its credentials: 'The Outsider and Others', 'Beyond the Wall of Sleep' and 'The Lurker at the Threshold', the last a posthumous 'collaboration' with Derleth drawing on Lovecraft's notes. These have remained in print ever since. The fortunes of Arkham House (which kick started the careers of several of Lovecraft's contemporaries, namely Ray Bradbury, Fritz Leiber and Ramsey Campbell) have provided a model for other small press publishing houses in the horror field, the majority of whom secured a footing by releasing at least one Lovecraft themed title, while Necronomicon Press and Hippocampus Press continue to publish nothing but Lovecraft-related material. Since its launch in 1976, Necronomicon Press has established an enviable reputation for its journals of literary criticism, whilst Hippocampus boasts many fine volumes of essays and letters as well as reprints of titles that Lovecraft himself considered to be among the finest examples of weird literature.

With the short stories and novellas finally collected under one cover, it became clear that Lovecraft was no more a mere horror writer than Mervyn Peake had been a science-fiction author (his stories had appeared in *Science Fantasy* magazine alongside those of Fritz

Leiber, J.G. Ballard, Kurt Vonnegut, Philip K. Dick, Ray Bradbury and other emerging talents who had been forced by necessity to submit their stories to the only periodicals that would publish them). Peake too was a poet and author whose surreal fantasy, the *Gormenghast* trilogy, is so richly detailed that it needs to be digested leisurely so that its many delights can be fully appreciated, especially its gallery of Dickensian grotesques.

Slowly but surely Lovecraft's reputation grew in the months following his untimely death; first in the amateur publishing world in which he had been so active and among the readers of the pulps, whose editors were prompted to re-evaluate his contributions in response to a deluge of letters from fans. As other writers added to and cited his creations in the ever expanding Cthulhu Mythos, Lovecraft became a point of reference and his work a standard by which every new writer of fantastic fiction would be measured.

But in the wider world, Lovecraft had been all but forgotten. His lowly status as a 'hack' writer of lurid pulp fiction is attested to by his absence from the list of American horror writers named by literary critic Edmund Wilson in *The New Yorker* in spring 1944. Wilson was urged by readers to rectify the omission. But in a subsequent article, 'Tales of the Marvellous and the Ridiculous', he damned Lovecraft for his 'bad taste' and dismissed his poetry as 'second rate'. Unfortunately, Wilson's reputation ensured that his evaluation was accepted as a fair assessment, although he had mistaken Derleth's inferior tale, 'The Lurker at the Threshold' as being solely by Lovecraft and was predisposed to find fault with his work. Indeed, he'd been offended by the writings of Professor Mabbott of Hunter College, a respected Poe scholar who'd dared to express his admiration of Lovecraft and gone so far as to argue that Lovecraft's best work invoked the spirit of Poe – a comparison that was tantamount to blasphemy in Wilson's opinion. Mabbott had authored two influential essays, 'Lovecraft: An Appreciation' (1944) – in which he stated 'Lovecraft is one of the few authors of whom I can honestly say that I have enjoyed every word of his stories' – and 'Lovecraft as a Student of Poe' (1958) making him, by his own admission, the first academic to write about Lovecraft.

Lovecraft was not generally considered worthy of discussion in literary circles until the early sixties when the novelist and self-educated philosopher Colin Wilson published a provocative study of artistic inspiration, *The Strength to Dream*. He concluded that Lovecraft was 'sick' – a 'very bad writer' who had 'rejected reality', a comment he later withdrew, admitting that he had been 'unduly harsh'. His criticism appears to have been born of disregard for anyone who wrote for the pulps.

But within a few years Lovecraft had acquired a cult following and become something of an iconic figure in the underground movement of the late sixties, whose 'tune in, turn on and drop out' generation were hungry for exotic new experiences and seeking ecstatic altered states through mind-expanding music, eastern mysticism, drugs and wyrd tales – the weirder the better. The surreal fairytale visions of Lewis Carroll, J.R.R. Tolkien and Kenneth Grahame (author of *The Wind in the Willows*, from which Pink Floyd borrowed a chapter heading for the title of their debut album, *Piper at the Gates of Dawn*) were required reading by those who were tripping on the sweet scent of incense that wafted through the air during the Summer of Love; swept up in the mood of optimism and childlike wonder that heralded the Age of Aquarius. But not everyone embraced the hippy dream of Love and Peace with such innocent abandon. Those who viewed it all with cynicism, or who had experienced bad trips, communed with dark gurus of the counter culture such as Aleister Crowley and Anton LaVey, founder of the Church of Satan and author of *The Satanic Bible*. In place of mysticism they practiced ceremonial magic and instead of Lewis Carroll they devoured Dennis Wheatley and Lovecraft.

When the hippy dream gave way to disillusionment at the end of the decade and violence erupted on the streets of European capitals in protest at the Vietnam War, it seemed apt that the jangly hippy, trippy soundtrack exemplified by the Beatles should make way for the brooding aggression of the Doors, the Velvet Underground, the Stooges and the Stones, and that the nihilistic philosophy of Lovecraft should hold sway. In 1967 a West Coast American band named themselves H.P. Lovecraft in his honour and recorded 'The White Ship' in a diaphanous languid manner that was very much of the time. They were among the first of many musicians to find inspiration in his dreamscapes and nightmares; his morbid themes and visions of decaying grandeur lending themselves particularly well, but not exclusively, to the dark sombre tones of heavy metal.

The student movement of the late sixties ensured that Lovecraft was introduced into academia through critical essays, theses and dissertations. When these same students entered publishing, film, television and other branches of the media in the '70s, Lovecraft crossed the threshold into the mainstream. The *Alien* film franchise subsequently introduced his name to the MTV generation, bolstered by the endorsement of Stephen King, a bestselling horror author since the '80s.

Soon comics, graphic novels, board games, computer games, movies and even soft toys testified to his pervasive influence – which went viral when his work became public domain (out of copyright) in 2012.

His reappraisal by respected authors such as Joyce Carol Oates – who provided the foreword for a collection published by Ecco Press in 1997 – and the three omnibus editions published by Penguin Classics between 1999 and 2004 all helped to establish Lovecraft's reputation as a major literary figure. Any lingering doubts as to his worthiness must surely have been swept aside with the appearance of *H.P. Lovecraft: Against the World, Against Life*, a study of the philosophical elements in his work by the eminent French cultural critic Michel Houellebecq, which included a brief introduction by Stephen King. In 2008, Barnes & Noble added the author to its *Library of Essential Writers* series, bringing all of his fiction under a single cover for the first time.

Lovecraft is now generally regarded as being as influential and significant a figure as his personal 'god of fiction' Edgar Allan Poe – or even J.R.R. Tolkien – due to the extent to which other writers, game designers, movie makers and graphic novelists have engaged with and contributed to his mythology, philosophy and fictional environment. There is an entire school devoted to aping his archaic style, drawing upon his characters and elaborating upon the books of forbidden lore that he only alluded to. In this way, new writers have secured a foothold on the first rung of the literary ladder, whilst established authors – such as Peter Straub, Brian Lumley, Stephen King, Ramsey Campbell and Neil Gaiman – have repaid their debt to the man who inspired them. So numerous are these alumni that they have spawned a subgenre which began with the Arkham House anthology *Tales of the Cthulhu Mythos* (1969) – the Dark Horse anthology *Lovecraft Unbound* and *Black Wings* from PS Publishing being just two of the most recent additions.

The author himself figures in a series of novels by David Barbour and Richard Raleigh in which he is confronted by his own creations, while Peter Cannon's *The Lovecraft Chronicles* (published by Mythos Books in 2004) speculates what he might have written had he lived.

Lovecraft was not well served by illustrators during his lifetime, but some of the most gifted graphic artists of recent years have envisaged his creations to stunning effect for book covers and graphic novels – so many in fact that they merited a collection of their own. *Artists Inspired by H.P. Lovecraft* (Centipede Press) collected work by Frank Frazetta, Bernie Wrightson, H.R. Giger, Mike Mignola, Richard Corben and John Coulthart. Corben and Coulthart have also illustrated books of their own, *Haunter of the Dark and Other Grotesque Visions* (Creation Oneiros) and *Haunt of Horror: Lovecraft Premiere* (Marvel Comics) respectively. A survey of Lovecraft in film and graphic novels would require a volume of its own (in *The Lurker in the Lobby*, Migliore and Strysik attempt to cover the former; Sanchez's *Lovecraft en los comics* also comes recommended) while books covering specific aspects of his creations would need a shelf to themselves.

Lovecraft died believing himself a failure, but in the intervening years his reputation and popularity have grown substantially, to the point where he is now recognised as being one of the most influential authors of the twentieth century.

For an avowed 'indifferentist' who believed that only oblivion and obscurity awaited him, Lovecraft must surely be relishing this belated recognition. Wherever he may be.

7

RHODE ISLAND PUBLIC HEALTH COMMISSION

Division of Vital Statistics

CERTIFICATE OF DEATH

City or Town No. 808 — 151

1. PLACE OF DEATH
City or Town... Providence, R. I. ... St. and No. Jane Brown Memorial Hospital
(If death occurred in a hospital or institution, give its NAME instead of street and number)

Length of residence in city or town where death occurred 46 yrs. 6 mos. 23 da. How long in U.S. if of foreign birth? ...yrs. ...mos. ...da.

2. FULL NAME Howard Phillips Lovecraft ... War Record None
(Name of War)

(a) Residence:
St. and No. 66 College Street City or Town Providence, R. I.
(If nonresident give city or town and State) (Usual place of abode)

PERSONAL AND STATISTICAL PARTICULARS	MEDICAL CERTIFICATE OF DEATH

3. SEX Male 4. COLOR OR RACE White 5. Single, Married, Widowed, or Divorced (write the word) Single

21. DATE OF DEATH March 15, 1937 19
(month, day, and year)

22. I HEREBY CERTIFY, That I attended deceased from
Mar 5, 19 37 to Mar 15, 19 37
I last saw h.. alive on Mar 14, 19 37 death is said

5a. If married, widowed, or divorced (if wife, FULL MAIDEN name) HUSBAND (or) WIFE

to have occurred on the date stated above at 7: 15 A.M.
The principal cause of death and related causes of importance were as follows: ‡ (See below)

46C

6. DATE OF BIRTH (month, day and year) Aug. 20, 1890

carcinoma of small intestinal 1936

6a. If STILLBORN enter that fact here.

Date of onset

7. AGE Years 46 Months 6 Days 23 IF LESS than 1 day ...hrs. ...min.

8. Trade, profession, or particular kind of work done, as spinner sawyer, bookkeeper, etc. Author

Other contributory causes of importance

chronic nephritis 1936

9. Industry or business in which work was done, as silk mill, saw mill, bank, etc. General Subjects

10. Date deceased last worked at this occupation (month and year) Feb. 1937 11. Total Time (years) spent in this occupation 26 yrs.

Name of operation? None Date of

12. BIRTHPLACE (city or town) Providence
(State or country) Rhode Island.

Was there an autopsy? No What tests confirmed diagnosis? ‡

13. NAME Winfield S. Lovecraft

Blood chemistry, urinalysis

14. BIRTHPLACE (State or country) Mount Vernon New York

23. If death was due to external causes (violence) fill in also the following:

15. MAIDEN NAME (Full name) Sarah S. Phillips

Accident, suicide, or homicide? Date of injury 19

16. BIRTHPLACE (city or town) Foster.
(State or country) Rhode Island.

Where did injury occur? (Specify city or town, county, and State)
Specify whether injury occurred in industry, in home, or in public place.

17. INFORMANT Annie P. Gamwell
(Address) 66 College Street
(Relation to deceased) Aunt

Manner of injury.
Nature of injury.

18. BURIAL CREMATION ☑ REMOVAL ☐ or OTHERWISE ☐
City or Town Providence, R. I.
Name of Cemetery Swan Point Cemetery

24. Was disease or injury in any way related to occupation of deceased? No
If so, specify

19. Signature of Embalmer Harry F. Sanderson # 215
(License No.)

(Degree)

Funeral Director Horace B. Knowles' Sons Co
(License No.)

(Address) 199 Thayer St

20. FILED MAR 16 1937

‡ For more space use other side.

ELF 24433 Dr. William L. Leet, 199 Thayer St.,

BIBLIOGRAPHY

Books

Carter, Lin *A Look Behind the Cthulhu Mythos* (Ballantine Books, 1976)

De Camp, L. Spague *Lovecraft, A Biography* (Ballantine Books, 1976)

Cannon, Peter *Lovecraft Remembered* (Arkham House, 1998)

Haefele, John D. *A Look Behind the Derleth Mythos: The Origins of the Cthulhu Mythos* (2012)

Harms, Daniel *The Cthulhu Mythos Encyclopedia* (Elder Signs Press, 2008)

Hill, Gary *The Strange Sound of Cthulhu* (Lulu.com, 2006)

Houellebecq, Michel *H.P. Lovecraft: Against the World, Against Life* (Gollancz, 2008)

Jones, Stephen *Weird Shadows Over Innsmouth* (Titan, 2013)

Joshi, S.T. *I Am Providence* (Hippocampus Press, 2010)

Lovecraft, H.P. *The Complete Fiction, 2nd Edition* (Barnes and Noble, 2011)

Lovecraft, H.P. edited by Joshi, S.T. *H.P. Lovecraft: Collected Essays Volumes 1-5* (Hippocampus Press, 2004)

Lovecraft, H.P. edited by Joshi, S.T. *The Annotated H.P. Lovecraft* and *More Annotated H.P. Lovecraft* (Bantam, 1998)

Price, Robert *Tales of the Lovecraft Mythos* (Del Rey, 2002)

Roland, Paul *Dark History of the Occult* (Arcturus Books, 2012)

Schultz, David and Joshi, S.T. *An Epicure in the Terrible* (Fairleigh Dickinson University Press, 1991)

Schutlz, David and Joshi, S.T. *Lord of a Visible World: An Autobiography in Letters* (Ohio University Press, 2000)

Tyson, Donald *The Dream World of H.P. Lovecraft: His Life, His Demons, His Universe* (Llewellyn Publications, 2010)

Tyson, Donald *Necronomicon: The Wanderings of Alhazred* (Llewellyn Publications, 2004)

Websites

Aetherial.net, arkhamdrive-in.com, arkhamhouse.com, astrotheme.com, blackgate.com, brainpickings.org, centipedepress.com, chrisperridas. blogspot.co.uk, cocthulhu.proboards. com, chinamieville.com, cthulhulives. org, dagonbytes.com (contains the complete text to all Lovecraft's fiction), depauw.edu, gaslight.mtroyal.ca (the complete text of Supernatural Horror in Literature), grimreviews.blogspot.co.uk, hplovecraft.com, hplfilmfestival.com, lovecraftzine.com, illuminatedlantern. com, Lovecraft.commonplacebooks. com, lovecraft.wikia.com, miskatonicbooks.com, nybooks.com, repository.library.brown.edu, salon. com, slate.com, studilovecraftiani. blogspot.it, stjoshi.org, talesofmystery. blogspot.co.uk, themodernword.com, templeofdagon.com, technet.idnes.cz, tentaclii.wordpress.com, the guardian. com, bbc.co.uk, thequietus.com, weirdtalesmagazine.com, wyrdstuff. com, yog-blogsoth.blogspot.co.uk.

APPENDICES

Appendix 1: 'The History of the Necronomicon' by H.P. Lovecraft (November 1927)

Original title *Al Azif* – azif being the word used by Arabs to designate that nocturnal sound (made by insects) suppos'd to be the howling of daemons.

Composed by Abdul Alhazred, a mad poet of Sanaá, in Yemen, who is said to have flourished during the period of the Ommiade caliphs, circa 700 A.D. He visited the ruins of Babylon and the subterranean secrets of Memphis and spent ten years alone in the great southern desert of Arabia – the Roba el Khaliyeh or 'Empty Space' of the ancients – and 'Dahna' or 'Crimson' desert of the modern Arabs, which is held to be inhabited by protective evil spirits and monsters of death. Of this desert many strange and unbelievable marvels are told by those who pretend to have penetrated it. In his last years Alhazred dwelt in Damascus, where the *Necronomicon* (*Al Azif*) was written, and of his final death or disappearance (738 A.D.) many terrible and conflicting things are told. He is said by Ebn Khallikan (12th cent. biographer) to have been seized by an invisible monster in broad daylight and devoured horribly before a large number of fright-frozen witnesses. Of his madness many things are told. He claimed to have seen fabulous Irem, or City of Pillars, and to have found beneath the ruins of a certain nameless desert town the shocking annals and secrets of a race older than mankind. He was only an indifferent Moslem, worshipping unknown entities whom he called Yog-Sothoth and Cthulhu.

In A.D. 950 the Azif, which had gained a considerable tho' surreptitious circulation amongst the philosophers of the age, was secretly translated into Greek by Theodorus Philetas of Constantinople under the title *Necronomicon*. For a century it impelled certain experimenters to terrible attempts, when it was suppressed and burnt by the patriarch Michael. After this it is only heard of furtively, but (1228) Olaus Wormius made a Latin translation later in the Middle Ages, and the Latin text was printed twice – once in the fifteenth century in black-letter (evidently in Germany) and once in the seventeenth (prob. Spanish) – both editions being without identifying marks, and located as to time and place by internal typographical evidence only. The work both Latin and Greek was banned by Pope Gregory IX in 1232, shortly after its Latin translation, which called attention to it. The Arabic original was lost as early as Wormius' time, as indicated by his prefatory note; and no sight of the Greek copy – which was printed in Italy between 1500 and 1550 – has been reported since the burning of a certain Salem man's library in 1692. An English translation made by Dr. Dee was never printed, and exists only in fragments recovered from the original manuscript. Of the Latin texts now existing one (15th cent.) is known to be in the British Museum under lock and key, while another (17th cent.) is in the Bibliothèque Nationale at Paris. A seventeenth-century edition is in the Widener Library at Harvard, and in the library of Miskatonic University at Arkham. Also in the library of the University of Buenos Ayres. Numerous other copies probably exist in secret, and a fifteenth-century one is persistently rumoured to form part of the collection of a celebrated American millionaire. A still vaguer rumour credits the preservation of a sixteenth-century Greek text in the Salem family of Pickman; but if it was so preserved, it vanished with the artist R.U. Pickman, who disappeared early in 1926. The book is rigidly suppressed by the authorities of most countries, and by all branches of organised ecclesiasticism. Reading leads to terrible consequences. It was from rumours of this book (of which relatively few of the general public know) that R.W. Chambers is said to have derived the idea of his early novel *The King in Yellow*.

Chronology
Al Azif written circa 730 A.D. at Damascus by Abdul Alhazred
Tr. to Greek 950 A.D. as *Necronomicon* by Theodorus Philetas
Burnt by Patriarch Michael 1050 (i.e., Greek text). Arabic text now lost.
Olaus translates Gr. to Latin 1228
1232 Latin ed. (and Gr.) suppr. by Pope Gregory IX
14 . . . Black-letter printed edition (Germany)
15 . . . Gr. text printed in Italy
16 . . . Spanish reprint of Latin text

Appendix 2: 'Notes on Writing Weird Fiction' by H.P. Lovecraft (1933)

My reason for writing stories is to give myself the satisfaction of visualising more clearly and detailedly and stably the vague, elusive, fragmentary impressions of wonder, beauty, and adventurous expectancy which are conveyed to me by certain sights (scenic, architectural, atmospheric, etc.), ideas, occurrences, and images encountered in art and literature. I choose weird stories because they suit my inclination best – one of my strongest and most persistent wishes being to achieve, momentarily, the illusion of some strange suspension or violation of the galling limitations of time, space, and natural law which for ever imprison us and frustrate our curiosity about the infinite cosmic spaces beyond the radius of our sight and analysis. These stories frequently emphasise the element of horror because fear is our deepest and strongest emotion, and the one which best lends itself to the creation of nature-defying illusions. Horror and the unknown or the strange are always closely connected, so that it is hard to create a convincing picture of shattered natural law or cosmic alienage or 'outsideness' without laying stress on the emotion of fear. The reason why time plays a great part in so many of my tales is that this element looms up in my mind as the most profoundly dramatic and grimly terrible thing in the universe. Conflict with time seems to me the most potent and fruitful theme in all human expression.

While my chosen form of story-writing is obviously a special and perhaps a narrow one, it is none the less a persistent and permanent type of expression, as old as literature itself. There will always be a small percentage of persons who feel a burning curiosity about unknown outer space, and a burning desire to escape from the prison-house of the known and the real into those enchanted lands of incredible adventure and infinite possibilities which dreams open up to us, and which things like deep woods, fantastic urban towers, and flaming sunsets momentarily suggest. These persons include great authors as well as insignificant amateurs like myself – Dunsany, Poe, Arthur Machen, M.R. James, Algernon Blackwood, and Walter de la Mare being typical masters in this field.

As to how I write a story – there is no one way. Each one of my tales has a different history. Once or twice I have literally written out a dream; but usually I start with a mood or idea or image which I wish to express, and revolve it in my mind until I can think of a good way of embodying it in some chain of dramatic occurrences capable of being recorded in concrete terms. I tend to run through a mental list of the basic conditions or situations best adapted to such a mood or idea or image, and then begin to speculate on logical and naturally motivated explanations of the given mood or idea or image in terms of the basic condition or situation chosen.

The actual process of writing is, of course, as varied as the choice of theme and initial conception; but if the history of all my tales were analysed, it is just possible that the following set of rules might be deduced from the average procedure:

(1) Prepare a synopsis or scenario of events in the order of their absolute occurrence – not the order of their narration. Describe with enough fullness to cover all vital points and motivate all incidents planned. Details, comments, and estimates of consequences are sometimes desirable in this temporary framework.

(2) Prepare a second synopsis or scenario of events – this one in order of narration (not actual occurrence), with ample fullness and detail, and with notes as to changing perspective, stresses, and climax. Change the original synopsis to fit if such a change will increase the dramatic force or general effectiveness of the story. Interpolate or delete incidents at will – never being bound by the original conception even if the ultimate result be a tale wholly different from that first planned. Let additions and alterations be made whenever suggested by anything in the formulating process.

(3) Write out the story – rapidly, fluently, and not too critically – following the second or narrative-order synopsis. Change incidents and plot whenever the developing process seems to suggest such change, never being bound by any previous design. If the development suddenly reveals new opportunities for dramatic effect or vivid storytelling, add whatever is thought advantageous – going back and reconciling the early parts to the new plan. Insert and delete whole sections if necessary or desirable, trying different beginnings and endings until the best arrangement is found. But be sure that all references throughout the story are thoroughly reconciled with the final design. Remove all possible superfluities – words, sentences, paragraphs, or whole episodes or elements – observing the usual precautions about the reconciling of all references.

(4) Revise the entire text, paying attention to vocabulary, syntax, rhythm of prose, proportioning of parts, niceties of tone, grace and convincingness or transitions (scene to scene, slow and detailed action to rapid and sketchy time-covering action

and vice versa. . . . etc., etc., etc.), effectiveness of beginning, ending, climaxes, etc., dramatic suspense and interest, plausibility and atmosphere, and various other elements.

(5) Prepare a neatly typed copy – not hesitating to add final revisory touches where they seem in order.

The first of these stages is often purely a mental one – a set of conditions and happenings being worked out in my head, and never set down until I am ready to prepare a detailed synopsis of events in order of narration. Then, too, I sometimes begin even the actual writing before I know how I shall develop the idea – this beginning forming a problem to be motivated and exploited.

There are, I think, four distinct types of weird story; one expressing a mood or feeling, another expressing a pictorial conception, a third expressing a general situation, condition, legend, or intellectual conception, and a fourth explaining a definite tableau or specific dramatic situation or climax. In another way, weird tales may be grouped into two rough categories – those in which the marvel or horror concerns some condition or phenomenon, and those in which it concerns some action of persons in connexion with a bizarre condition or phenomenon.

Each weird story – to speak more particularly of the horror type – seems to involve five definite elements: (a) some basic, underlying horror or abnormality – condition, entity, etc – (b) the general effects or bearings of the horror, (c) the mode of manifestation – object embodying the horror and phenomena observed – (d) the types of fear-reaction pertaining to the horror, and (e) the specific effects

of the horror in relation to the given set of conditions.

In writing a weird story I always try very carefully to achieve the right mood and atmosphere, and place the emphasis where it belongs. One cannot, except in immature pulp charlatan–fiction, present an account of impossible, improbable, or inconceivable phenomena as a commonplace narrative of objective acts and conventional emotions. Inconceivable events and conditions have a special handicap to overcome, and this can be accomplished only through the maintenance of a careful realism in every phase of the story except that touching on the one given marvel. This marvel must be treated very impressively and deliberately – with a careful emotional 'build-up' – else it will seem flat and unconvincing. Being the principal thing in the story, its mere existence should overshadow the characters and events. But the characters and events must be consistent and natural except where they touch the single marvel. In relation to the central wonder, the characters should shew the same overwhelming emotion which similar characters would shew toward such a wonder in real life. Never have a wonder taken for granted. Even when the characters are supposed to be accustomed to the wonder, I try to weave an air of awe and impressiveness corresponding to what the reader should feel. A casual style ruins any serious fantasy.

Atmosphere, not action, is the great desideratum of weird fiction. Indeed, all that a wonder story can ever be is a vivid picture of a certain type of human mood. The moment it tries to be anything else it becomes cheap, puerile, and unconvincing. Prime emphasis should be given to subtle suggestion – imperceptible hints and touches of selective associative detail which express shadings of moods and build up a vague illusion of the strange reality of the unreal. Avoid bald catalogues of incredible happenings which can have no substance or meaning apart from a sustaining cloud of colour and symbolism.

These are the rules or standards which I have followed – consciously or unconsciously – ever since I first attempted the serious writing of fantasy. That my results are successful may well be disputed – but I feel at least sure that, had I ignored the considerations mentioned in the last few paragraphs, they would have been much worse than they are.

Appendix 3: 'Howard Phillips Lovecraft as his Wife Remembers Him' by Sonia Davis Foreword by Winfield T. Scott

The most important event in the career of Howard Phillips Lovecraft occurred two years after his death. That was the publication by Arkham House in 1939 of an omnibus of his weird tales, *The Outsider and Others*.

Until the publication of that book, Lovecraft's existence as a writer was precarious and little known. A few anthologists in America and in England had taken note of his ornately terrible tales; there had been a job-printed book of one of his stories, *The Shadow Over Innsmouth*; but for the most part his work lay scattered in pulp magazines and in manuscript.

Born here in Providence in 1890, he lived almost all his 47 years here, but he was as a child so sheltered

and as a man so odd a recluse that hardly a handful of his fellow citizens were aware of his existence. He had a sort of obscure fame in the affairs of nationally organized groups known as Amateur Journalists, and he was celebrated among friends – some of whom never actually met him – as a prodigious correspondent.

Among these were two young writers, August Derleth and Donald Wandrei. They founded Arkham House at Sauk City, Wisconsin, expressly to publish the Lovecraft stories. At first, I think, *The Outsider and Others* gathered attention slowly; but, however slowly, the Lovecraft fame had begun. And in 1943 a second large volume was issued, *Beyond the Wall of Sleep*.

At that time I published in the *Providence Sunday Journal* a lengthy article on Lovecraft and the two books. It was sketchy, yet its results were more significant, for its appearance aroused reminiscence from the people who had known Lovecraft, people in Providence and elsewhere. With their generous help and further research of my own it was at last possible to construct a fairly substantial biographical essay, and this was published in the third Lovecraft book, *Marginalia*, (Arkham House, 1944), as 'His Own Most Fantastic Creation'. That essay and Derleth's *HPL: a Memoir*, (Ben Abramson, 1945), and a considerable number of personal reminiscences of Lovecraft – notably W. Paul Cook's – will provide any interested reader with the basic material of biography and character.

Still a chapter of extraordinary importance in Lovecraftiana was wholly closed or at best dimly known to all of us. And that was the story of his brief marriage to Sonia H. Greene of New York.

By 1943-44, the Lovecraft boom was really on. He was being sought by collectors; his books were fetching high prices; selections and paper-book reprints began to appear; interest in his own life was at least as lively as the bibliophilic pursuit. But (so far as I am aware) none of us knew the whereabouts of the one-time Mrs Lovecraft or even, indeed, if she were still alive.

The whole account of her re-emergence, bearing memoirs of HPL, is more complex than I need tell here. Anyway, in 1947 and altogether unexpectedly, I was put in touch with her by a weird-story writer and Lovecraft friend, Frank Belknap Long of Brooklyn, NY, and so first learned that she was a widow, Sonia H. Davis, living in Los Angeles. We had occasional correspondence and after perhaps a year she sent me the reminiscences which were first published in the August 22, 1948, *Providence Sunday Journal* and which are here with reprinted.

Let me disclose now that these are not all of Mrs Davis' written memoirs of Lovecraft, but rather about half of what she has put down. Newspaper space limitations had to be considered strictly. My eliminations were chiefly of two kinds: biographical facts already in print, and anecdotal material – some of it perfectly good in its own right – which repeated, or was similar to, material others had published. Then with the eliminations made, there were consequent rearrangements and small transitions in Mrs. Davis' manuscript. To all this the author gave most courteous cooperation and approval, and the reader should be assured that in nearly every line the language is the author's and the story is wholly her own.

And it is, as I said at the time of its original publication, *her version* of Lovecraft. Its publication brought forth letters of rebuttal as well as of corroboration. This was to be expected. Lovecraft's was a strange character, and not a kind easily understood or agreed upon. These are, in any case, memoirs by the person who knew Lovecraft most intimately, and they are curiously affecting. No further biographical writing about Lovecraft can be made without reference to them. All the better, then, that here they are reasserted in a more permanent and available form than newsprint.

The Memoirs of Mrs Sonia H. Davis
Howard Phillips Lovecraft and I met in 1921 and we were married at New York in March 1924. What follows here may to all intents and purposes be called the true story of his private life. It differs somewhat from that given by most of his biographers.

For instance, I have recently read the late W. Paul Cook's 'In Memoriam: Howard Phillips Lovecraft'. As far as it goes it is a very interesting and worthy eulogy of a truly great person. But it contains – as do other accounts – several misconceptions about Howard's life, and especially of events in the years 1921-1932 of which no one but myself knows.

Of various early incidents in his life, not generally repeated to others, Howard himself told me. Of other incidents I speak from my own experience while still his wife; some of these are of a very personal nature.

First Meeting
I first met Howard Lovecraft at a Boston convention of the Amateur Journalists. I admired his personality but, frankly, at first not his person.

As he was always trying to find recruits for Amateur Journalism, he offered to send me samples of work – his own and others' – which appeared in the different amateur journals: non-paying little papers and magazines, privately printed and circulated. From then on we kept up quite a steady correspondence, and I felt highly flattered when he told me in some of his letters that mine indicated a freshness not born of immaturity but rather a 're-freshingness' because of the originality and courage of my convictions when I disagreed with him.

I disagreed often, not just to be disagreeable: if possible I wanted to remove some of Howard's intensely fixed ideas.

During many months of correspondence H.P. mentioned the names of several writer-friends, many of whom he knew through letters only. One of these whom he particularly lauded was Samuel Loveman of Cleveland, Ohio. 'Samuelus,' Howard called him – he was always romanizing names of his friends. Howard had a great regard for Loveman and used him in the story called 'Randolph Carter'.

Other Friends

When one of my business trips took me to Cleveland for the first time, I indeed found Samuel Loveman to be all the things H.P. had said about him. And at the end of my day's work there, Loveman surprised me by calling together, at a moment's notice almost, a meeting of all the available Cleveland amateur journalists.

At the end of a very pleasant evening we all signed our names to a Cleveland postcard and sent it to Howard, and when I wrote him later I deplored the fact he too could not have been with us. I said his presence would have made my happiness complete for that evening. His reply, though bountifully mixed with reservations, was quite warm and appreciative – coming from him.

New York Visit

So now I had two correspondents: Lovecraft and Loveman. I decided to invite them both to New York, to meet at last, and to spend Christmas and New Years. I turned my Parkside Avenue apartment over to them. A neighbor gave me sleeping space in hers. And evenings the two men would meet me and we would go to dinner and see a play, or sometimes have a conclave of 'amateur' friends – James F. Morton Jr (who had introduced me to Lovecraft), Frank Belknap Long, Rheinhardt [sic] Kleiner and others.

Never having done such a thing before, I was somewhat amazed at myself – inviting two men at my expense to be my guests. I had one excellent reason having to do with Howard's race prejudices of which I shall speak later on.

I remember one evening we went to a fashionable Italian restaurant. It was the first time Howard had ever been in an Italian restaurant, (he was then in his early thirties), the first time he had ever eaten Minestrone or spaghetti with meat and tomato sauce and Parmesan cheese. He balked at wine. He said he never had tasted any alcohol and didn't wish to begin now.

Soon Loveman returned to Cleveland, but Howard stayed on.

My neighbor who was so kindly making room for me had a beautiful Persian cat. When Howard saw that cat he made love to it. He seemed to have a language that it understood and it

immediately curled up in his lap
and purred.

Half in earnest, half joking, I said
'What a lot of perfectly good affection
to waste on a mere cat – when a woman
might highly appreciate it!'

He said, 'How can any woman love a
face like mine?'

'A mother can,' I replied, 'and some
who are not mothers would not have
to try very hard.' We all laughed and
Howard went on stroking the cat.

Howard's voice was clear and
resonant when he read. It became
thin and high-pitched in conversation,
somewhat falsetto. His singing voice,
though not strong, was very sweet. He
would sing none of the modern songs –
only the more favored old ones.

Howard's mother had hoped her
child would be a girl, and as a baby
he looked like a beautiful little girl. A
photograph shows him with a mass of
flaxen curls which he wore until he was
about six. When at last he protested, his
mother took him to the barber's where
she cried bitterly as he was shorn.
(These curls were kept: Howard once
showed them to me.)

Once when we were looking
at an early photograph of him, he
exclaimed, 'And look at me now!' His
very plain face he attributed, he said,
to two reasons. At fifteen or sixteen
he fell and broke his nose when he
and another boy were racing their
bicycles. The other reason, he said
wrily, was that nightly he would look
up at the stars through his telescope.
Actually, he resembled his mother
very much. Though less pronounced
in the womenfolk, the entire Phillips
family had the prognathous jaw and the
extremely short upper lip. Howard was
fond of making caricatures of himself as
he would appear when he became old.

Well – to return to Howard with
the Persian cat – I felt that if he could
be made to feel more confident of his
genius as a writer and to forget his
'awful looks,' as he put it, he would
become less diffident and more happy.
So whenever an opportunity presented
itself I would not avoid giving
him compliments.

When Howard, still in New York,
went out with 'the boys' for several
evenings I realized how poignantly I
missed him. I suggested that instead of
his going home to Providence, we bring
'Providence' to Parkside Avenue. Each
of us wrote an urgent invitation to the
aunts with whom he lived, Mrs Lillian
Clark and Mrs Annie Gamwell, and Mrs
Gamwell came for a few weeks.

Return to Providence
After their return to Providence I was
not ashamed to write him how very
much I missed him. His appreciation of
this led us both to more serious ground.

I knew Howard was not in a position
to marry. Of his Grandfather Phillips'
estate there was only about $20,000 left,
and that was supposed to last the rest
of the lives of his two aunts and himself.
Had he been less proud to write for
money he need not have starved
himself. He would say 'I write to please
myself only; and if a few of my friends
enjoy my "effusions" I feel well repaid.'

He spent much of his time revising
the atrocious work of others, for which
he was paid a pittance. He would wear
himself out over some of the stupid
trash he was asked to revise, some of
it for authors who later became well
known and prosperous.

Meanwhile his letters indicated his
desire to leave Providence and settle
in New York. Each of us meditated the
possibilities of a life together. Some

of our friends suspected. I admitted to friends that I cared very much for Howard and that if he would have me I would gladly be his wife. But nothing definite was decided.

I came to America when I was nine years old, a White Russian of the old Czarist regime. In 1899, when I was sixteen, I married a fellow countryman who had adopted the name of a Boston friend, Greene. My husband died in 1916. By him I have one daughter who was for several years Paris correspondent for various American newspapers. After my divorce from Howard Lovecraft I married Nathaniel A. Davis, a former professor at the University of California at Berkeley, and we were very happy during the 10 years before his death.

At the time of my meeting Howard Lovecraft I held an executive position with a fashionable women's wear establishment on Fifth Avenue. My salary was close to $10,000 a year.

More Meetings
On my business trips to Boston I would stop off at Providence and the aunts and Howard would dine with me at the Biltmore. They all enjoyed these occasions, but they thought me extravagant. The aunts would not join me in Boston but they condescended to trust Howard alone with me there. I would attend to business during the daytime, while Howard explored museums, graveyards, old houses and whatnot. At least once on each visit we would have our dinner at a Greek restaurant which H.P. favored for its tiled walls depicting scenes from Greek classics. He loved to talk to me of ancient Greece and Rome while I, in turn, considered it a great privilege after a hard day's work to listen to him.

Later he would show me the historical places in Boston and we would walk the old, narrow streets.

Once we visited Magnolia, Mass. As we walked along the esplanade there one evening we heard a peculiar snorting, grunting noise, loud in the distance. The moon made a path on the water. Emergent tops of piles in the water were connected with rope, like a huge spider web.

'Oh, Howard,' I said, 'here you have the setting for a really strange and mysterious story.'

'Go ahead, and write it,' he said.

'Oh, no, I couldn't do it justice.'

'Try it. Tell me what the scene pictures to your imagination.'

After we parted for the night I sat up and wrote the general outline which he later revised and edited. His enthusiasm next day was so genuine that I surprised and shocked him right then and there by kissing him.

He was so flustered that he blushed and then he turned pale. When I chaffed him about it he said he had not been kissed since he was a very small child. (I know he had loved his mother and he loved his aunts in a positive way, but he was not demonstrative in his affections.) He said he would probably never be kissed again. But I fooled him.

Decision to Marry
It was after that vacation in Magnolia that our more intimate correspondence began which led to our marriage. H.P. wrote me of everything he did, everywhere he went: sometimes filling 30, 40, even 50 pages with his fine writing. There were two years of almost daily correspondence. Then he decided to break away from Providence.

Early in March 1924, Howard came to New York. I had asked him to tell his aunts he was going to marry me, but he said he preferred to surprise them. In the matter of details – securing the license, buying the ring, etc. – he seemed to be jovial. He said one would think he was being married for the 'nth time, he went about it in such a methodical way.

The man at the marriage bureau thought I was the younger. I was seven years Howard's senior, and he said nothing could please him better: that Sarah Helen Whitman was older than Poe, and that Poe might have met with better fortune had he married her.

I thought a civil marriage would be sufficient, but Howard insisted that we be married by a Christian minister and that the marriage take place in St Paul's Church – 'where Washington and Lord Howe and many other great men had worshiped!' In this, as later in so many other things, I let him have his way. In nearly everything he was the 'victor' and I the 'vanquished'. I would gainsay him nothing if I thought it would eradicate his complexes.

Houdini Manuscript

The night before our marriage Howard absent-mindedly left in the Providence station the Houdini manuscript – that is, an article which he had ghost-written for the famed magician. It was not, as someone has said, 'a public stenographer' who copied the handwritten notes which H.P. still had. I alone was able to read those crossed out notes.

I read them slowly to him while he pounded at a typewriter borrowed from the hotel in Philadelphia where we were spending our first day and night. So we spent them, and when the manuscript was finished we were too tired and exhausted for honeymooning

or anything else. But I wouldn't let Howard down, and the manuscript reached the publisher in time.

The only money Howard ever spent on me which he had earned was what he had received for that article. When I insisted only half the amount be used for a wedding-ring, he insisted the future Mrs Howard Phillips Lovecraft must have the finest, with diamonds all around it, even if it took all the proceeds of that first well-paid story.

I called him a dear, generous spendthrift. He said there would be more where that came from – which, alas, did not materialize except in stipends when he sold a story (not too often) to *Weird Tales* magazine.

When we were married he was gaunt and hungry-looking, too much so even for my taste. I used to cook a well-balanced meal every evening, make a substantial breakfast (he loved cheese souffle for breakfast!), and I'd leave a few (almost Dagwoodian) sandwiches, cake and fruit for his lunch.

Sometimes he would meet me after my day's work; we would dine out and go to a theater. He had no conception of time. Even in bitter wintry weather I often had to wait in some lobby or at some street corner from three-quarters of an hour to an hour and a half. He was always late for an appointment, whether it was with me or anyone else.

H.P. L. and Mummies

Here I must record an extraordinary story about this master of weird stories. Howard was allergic to the spices of the mummified corpses at the Metropolitan Museum. Near them, his hands and wrists became swollen. Sometime after we had left the museum the swelling went down and we thought no more of it. But about a week later we returned to see and study as much as we could of Tut-ahn-ka-men's tomb, and again Howard's wrists and hands began to swell. I urged him to consult a doctor, but Howard laughed it off and refused. He never wanted to have a doctor, no matter how ill he was.

But, anyway, during our life at Parkside Avenue he became quite stout, and he looked and felt marvelous. He really became a more interesting human being. I think he half-starved himself before he knew me, and probably starved once more after we separated permanently.

I criticized his ten-year-old overcoat and insisted on buying him a new coat, suit, hat, gloves, and even a billfold; (I didn't like the tiny, old-fashioned pocketbook he would unsnap to take out change). Looking at himself in the mirror he protested: 'But, my dear, this is entirely too stylish for "Grandpa Theobald," it doesn't look like me. I look like some fashionable fop!' And I really think he was glad when the new suit and coat were later stolen; he had the old ones to resume.

And Money

Before our marriage I tried to contribute to his ease and comfort by sending him the stamps for his voluminous correspondence, and by gifts of money at birthday and holiday times. If at any time he lacked money I did not know it, and while he was my husband I saw to it that he was supplied out of my earnings. His aunts, out of his own share of the Phillips estate, were supposed to send him $15 a week; but while I provided for him they sent only $5 and that not always regularly.

I told Howard they need not send him anything if they found it difficult, that some day he would earn more

than I. In jest I used to say, 'You'll pay it all back with interest, I'm sure.' And we'd both laugh about it. Often he would spend much of the money on books, for me or for some of his friends; and he sometimes gave them money. Two of the amateur brotherhood wrote him the letters of gentle grafters and he would go without things himself in order to aid them. No one knew of this save myself and his beneficiaries.

I effaced my own interests and deferred to him upon all matters and domestic problems regardless of what they were. Even to the spending of money I not only consulted him but tried to make him feel that he was the head of the house.

In Brooklyn Alone

I soon found it necessary to accept an exceedingly well-paid job out of town. I wanted Howard to make his home with me there, but he said he would hate to live in a midwestern city, he would prefer to remain in New York where at least he had some friends. I suggested he have one of them come to live with him in our apartment, but his aunts thought it wiser for me to store and sell my furniture and find a studio room large enough for Howard to have the old (and several dilapidated) pieces he had brought from Providence. It was then the Clinton Street, Brooklyn, address was decided upon.

I could be in New York only a few days at a time, every three or four weeks. I gave him money each time I came to town and I sent him weekly checks.

Racial Prejudices

He admired the quaintness of that part of Brooklyn, and at first he seemed to love his Clinton Street setup. But the crowds in the subway, streets and parks he hated, and he suffered through that hate. He referred chiefly to Semitic peoples: 'beady-eyed, rat-faced Asiatics,' he called them. In general, all foreigners were 'mongrels'.

Long before we were married, Howard wrote me in a letter praising Samuel Loveman that the only 'discrepancy' he could find in Loveman was that he was a Jew. I replied in amazement at such discrimination and reminded him – as I did constantly – that I, too, come of Hebrew people. It was his prejudice against minorities, especially Jews, which prompted me to that simultaneous invitation of Howard and Loveman to New York of which I have spoken.

Later H.P. assured me he was quite 'cured'. But unfortunately, (and here I must speak of something I never intended to have publicly known), whenever we found ourselves in the racially-mixed crowds which characterize New York, Howard would become livid with rage. He seemed almost to lose his mind. And if the truth must be known, it was this attitude toward minorities and his desire to escape them that eventually prompted him back to Providence.

Soon after our marriage he told me that whenever we had company he would appreciate it if 'Aryans' were in the majority. As a matter of fact, I think he hated humanity in the abstract. He once said: 'It is more important to know what to hate than it is to know what to love.' And he believed it was better to be dead than alive, best of all not to be born. It was good, he thought, to be in that state of oblivion before birth.

'Henry Ryecroft'

A better understanding of Lovecraft may be gained in reading Gissing's *Private Papers of Henry Ryecroft*, a book Howard gave me early in the life of our romance. Throughout it elucidates much of Howard's own personality, his attitude toward the masses and toward life in general. Non-religious and anti-democratic, Howard's code was to let his fellowmen alone and mind his own business. As for me, whenever I protested I was one of the 'alien hordes,' he would say: 'You are now Mrs H.P. Lovecraft of 598 Angell Street, Providence, Rhode Island.'

Mr Cook quotes the line: 'I . . . still refrained from going home to my people lest I seem to crawl back ignobly in defeat.' This is only part of the truth. He wanted more than anything else to go back to Providence but he also wanted me to come along. This I could not do because there was no situation in Providence fitting my abilities and needs. And since he was reluctant to return without me, he remained at Clinton Street, whence the foregoing cry.

I believe he loved me as much as it was possible for a temperament like his to love. He'd never mention the word, 'love.' He would say, 'My dear, you don't know how much I appreciate you.' I tried to understand him and was grateful for any crumbs from his lips that fell my way.

Our family nicknames of 'Socrates' and 'Xantippe' were originated by me. I saw in Howard a Socratic wisdom and genius. I had hoped in time to humanize him further, to lift him out of his abysmal depths of loneliness and psychic complexes by a true, wedded love. I am afraid my optimism and excessive self-assurance misled us both.

(His love of the weird and mysterious, I believe was born of sheer loneliness.)

I had hoped, in other words, that my embrace would make of him not only a great genius but also a lover and husband. While the genius developed and broke through the chrysalis, the lover and husband receded into the background until they were apparitions that finally vanished.

It has been said – quoting letters of Howard's – that our separation was mainly caused by his lack of money. That is not true. The real reasons my own story makes evident. Marvelous person though he was, it was probably to 'save face' that Howard, having to give a reason, offered one that might be most easily believed.

When Howard felt he could no longer tolerate Brooklyn, it was I suggested he return to Providence. He'd say, 'If I could . . . live in Providence, the blessed city where I was born and reared. I am sure, there, I could be happy.' I agreed. I said, 'I'd love nothing better than to live in Providence if I could do my work there.'

Providence Again

Well, he returned, and I followed him much later. Again: it is not true that his aunts 'dispatched a truck which brought Howard back to Providence lock, stock and barrel.' I made a special trip from out of town to help him pack his things, to see to it all was well before he left, and to pay – his railroad fare and all – out of my own funds.

Eventually we held a conference with the aunts. I suggested I take a large house in Providence, hire a maid, pay the expenses, and we all live together; our family to use one side of the house, I to use the other for a business venture of my own. The aunts gently but firmly

informed me that neither they nor Howard could afford to have Howard's wife work for a living in Providence. That was that. I knew then where we all stood.

To be not too far from Providence where I could spend some weekends, I took a new and less well paying job in New York. (The time was now 1927.) But there was a Chicago job too good to refuse, and I knew I could have Howard meet me in New York every few weeks on my buying trips. I hated Chicago, though, and after six months – at Christmas – I decided to try Providence for a short vacation while waiting for something to happen, I didn't know what.

Visits and Letters

I spent several weeks there. But I soon needed money, so I returned to New York, rented an apartment, retrieved from storage what was left of my furniture and set up housekeeping by myself. I opened a small millinery shop in the neighborhood.

Our marital life for the next few months was spent on reams of paper in rivers of ink. That spring I invited Howard to visit me and he gladly accepted, as a visitor only. To me, even his nearness was better than nothing. The visit lasted throughout the summer but I saw him only during the early morning hours when he would return from jaunts with Morton, Loveman, Long, Kleiner, some or all of them. Then he visited Vrest Orton at Yonkers and returned to Providence in the early fall.

Then we lived in letters again.

Howard was perfectly willing and even satisfied to live this way, but not I. I began urging divorce. He tried every method he could devise to persuade me how much he appreciated me: divorce would cause him great unhappiness; a gentleman does not divorce his wife unless he has cause, and he had none.

I told him I had done everything I could think of to make our marriage a success, but that no marriage could be such in letter-writing only.

Howard said he knew of a very happy couple whose marriage was kept intact by letters: the wife living with her parents, and the husband because of his illness living elsewhere.

I replied that neither of us was really sick and I did not wish to be a 'long-distance' wife. I told him it was all impossible, that he ought to divorce me and find and marry a young woman of his own background and culture, live in Providence and try to live a happy, normal life.

'No, my dear,' he would say, 'if you leave me I shall never marry again. You do not realize how much I appreciate you.'

'But your way of demonstrating,' I would reply, 'is so unheard of!'

Divorce

The divorce came in 1929. On a friendly but impersonal basis we occasionally corresponded.

In 1932 I went to Europe. I was almost tempted to invite him along, but I knew he would not accept. However, I wrote him from England, Germany and France, sent him books and pictures of every conceivable thing I thought might interest him. And I sent him a travelogue which he revised for me.

Final Meeting

After my return to the United States I was quite ill. On recuperating, I went to Farmington, Conn. I was so enchanted by the eighteenth-century beauty of it

that I wrote Howard at once to join me there, which he did. We explored the town and also Wethersfield.

I believe I still loved Howard very much, more than I cared to admit even to myself. Although in my travels I had met many eligible men and some offering proposals of marriage, for eight years I met none who did not seem inadequate in intellect compared to Howard. When we parted for the night I said, 'Howard, won't you kiss me goodnight?' He said, 'No, it is better not to.'

The next day we explored Hartford, and when we parted that night I no longer asked for a kiss. I had learned my lesson well.

I never saw Howard again.

H.P. L.'s Death

Off and on we still corresponded, after I moved to California. Here I soon met and married Dr Davis. It was here, too, I met Mr Wheeler Dryden who told me of Howard Lovecraft's death.

I do not believe it an exaggeration to say that Howard had the mind, taste and personality of a much greater artist and genius than that with which he was accredited in his lifetime. He will be I am quite sure a legendary, mysterious figure. The irony is that he died before the rewards and celebrity of his labors occurred. I like to believe that time mellowed him, that he found other men of all sorts to be normal, kindly folk. And even though I am not his widow, I mourn in sorrow and reverence his untimely passing.